RUTH GORDON
AN OPEN BOOK

RUTH GORDON AN OPEN BOOK

By Ruth Gordon

DOUBLEDAY & COMPANY, INC.
GARDEN CITY, NEW YORK
1980

BG664 o

ISBN: 0-385-13480-0
Library of Congress Catalog Card Number 78–68335
Copyright © 1980 by Ruth Gordon

For
JACK GWYNNE EMMET HARRIS

CONTENTS

RUTH GORDON
AN OPEN BOOK

VISCERAL MYTHS

I wanted this book printed on different colored pages, pink, blue, yellow, apricot, green, lavender, but how many books get into the bookstores the way you want them to? Don't tell me, I hate facts, but as you read remember the pages are different; this one is lavender like lilacs when they bloom for Decoration Day. Turn the page.

If you want to be modern, Memorial Day. Or is it the other way around? Modern or dated, this page is *still* lilac.

This page is the color of Pauline Holmes' pale green muslin dress trimmed with narrow black Valenciennes lace. I was six years old when I saw it and wanted one, then got it but it didn't touch Pauline's.

Still like Pauline's dress.

Pink to match the roses back of our white picket fence at Edgartown, on Martha's Vineyard. They stab you with their red thorns. "Look out!" I used to hear Isabel Wilder warn Thornton when he was getting out of his "best little car in the world," his Thunderbird.

Still pink, no thorns.

Think of the first daffodil in spring. Can you tell the difference between a daffodil and a jonquil?

Laurence Olivier's little boy was named Tarquin. I asked him, "Do you have any trouble with your name?"

"No," said Tarquin, "except one boy at school couldn't remember it and called me Jonquil."

Still yellow.

The color of a June sky.

A June sky in Edgartown, Massachusetts, the best colored
skies.

Choose a color, you're on your own, don't be helpless.

"The dreaming soul of the human race," said Thornton Wilder, "believes life will come out right."

It has, more often than it hasn't.

For a long time now the pages are pink.

I love to write and some people don't trust anyone who loves to write. Said the great Fanny Brice, she didn't trust anyone who didn't say "shit."

I say shit and I love to write, because nobody tells me how to.

"You're just like my wife," shouted theatre impresario William A. Brady, "you can't tell her a damn thing."

That's not only writing, but acting. I don't like to be told how to act either. When I'm left alone thoughts come.

"Don't *try* to think," said our New England philosopher, Emerson, "leave yourself open to thought."

If you find out stuff for yourself, you get to know what you believe; what you like, how to live, how to have a good time. It's important to have a good time.

I have a good time standing on the stage with rows of people out front, eight hundred, a thousand, fifteen hundred, and where I have the *best* time is standing on a stage in New York between West Thirty-eighth Street and West Forty-ninth Street left and right of Broadway, those blocks are paved with hopes and prayers I would get a job and when I got one, paved with hopes and prayers, I'd learn how to act my part. I learned, but it was out in the faraway places, where the thermometer in Indianapolis and Nebraska reads 110 in the shade in July. In Burlington, Iowa, in December it's zero, in Yakima, Sioux Falls the windows nailed down, 40 below. Hot in Boise in June, hot in Vancouver, in Cheyenne a thunderstorm knocked out the lights and instead of footlights we held a candle to light us. Somewhere between changes in the temperature I learned to act.

I could have learned faster on West Forty-third Street, if the dazzling Henry Miller, who built his beautiful Henry Miller Theatre, had engaged me to be in any of his productions; he could teach anyone to act. Top director, important star, elegance itself, charm to kill and as abundant as his charm and elegance, that short was his temper.

People were fascinated by him and scared, even his son Gilbert, *going* to be a producer, but not son Jack, going to be a ne'er-do-well. He drank, smoked, wouldn't go to school, wouldn't work, got into scrapes, scrounged money from everyone.

Before the matinee, Mr. Miller in the star dressing room, was smoothing greasepaint onto his handsome face.

A knock at the door.

"Who is it?"

"It's Gilbert, Father."

"Come in."

In came Gilbert looking shaken. "Father, I have bad news. It's about Jack."

Mr. Miller dipped a powder puff in the powder, shook some out, powdered over the greasepaint. "What's he done now?" He took a small narrow brush and brushed the powder out of his eyebrows.

"They're putting him in jail, Father. He was peddling dope."

Mr. Miller turned and glared at his son. "Dam it, Gilbert, don't you know your brother Jack would never do anything useful?"

It would have been useful if Mr. Miller had taught me to act.

And up Broadway two blocks on Forty-fifth Street, it would have been useful in 1918 if I'd learned that the sure way *not* to get in the movies is to let them make a test. I was living at Martin's Theatrical boardinghouse, 227 West Forty-fifth Street, where the Piccadilly Hotel is now. Across the street at the Booth Theatre I was playing the Babytalk Lady in Booth Tarkington's play *Seventeen*. The phone rang, it was my friend Mrs. Wheaton. "Anna wants you to ride up to Riverdale with her, she's going to make a movie test, she wants someone to talk to on the way." Click.

Anna was Mrs. Wheaton's daughter, star of the big hit musical comedy *Oh Boy*, down Broadway on West Thirty-ninth Street at the Princess Theatre, lyrics by P. G. Wodehouse, music by Jerome Kern. Applause, encores every time Anna did a number.

Her claret color limousine drove through the gates of the Triangle Studio as a black limousine was ready to pull out. The window rolled down and out looked beautiful, golden-haired Mae Murray, by night star of the *Ziegfeld Follies* at the handsome New Amsterdam Theatre down Broadway on West Forty-second Street, by day star of Triangle pictures up the Hudson. Did she think Anna was competition? "What are you doing?"

"I'm making a test for Allan Dwan."

She must have figured no worry here. "If they sign you, make them put in the contract any costume got lace on it, it has to be *real* lace." The window rolled up and she drove away.

Allan Dwan welcomed Anna into the studio, showed her the set, three walls, a door, two chairs, table, on the table a letter and a revolver.

"Think of what you want to do, Anna. When you're ready, tell me."

"I'm ready," said Anna.

Talk about confidence! Why not? Encores every night in *Oh Boy*. She wasn't beautiful, but vivacious, dark hair, sparkly eyes, figure like the line drawings that used to be in *Vogue,* navy blue wool dress from Harry Collins, than *which!*

"Make your entrance through the door," said Allan Dwan, and told the electricians to light up, the cameraman to roll.

"Ready," he said to Anna.

She came through the door, looked at the room, noticed the letter on the table *and* the revolver, opened the letter. Read it. Read it. Read it. Turned it over, read it, read it, read it.

Was it good? Was it bad? You couldn't tell from Anna.

Read it. Read it. Read it. Opened it the long way, read it, read it.

She's taking a lot of time, I thought, but how did *I* know? She was Anna Wheaton, star of *Oh Boy,* I was just playing a part and hadn't gotten very good notices.

She read it, read it, came to the finish, thought about it, reached for the revolver and shot the letter.

That was the best movie test I ever saw and they didn't sign her to a contract. Why didn't I learn the lesson?

Time went by and someone asked me to make a movie test.

Word came back, "She acts all right, you can't photograph her."

Time went by, someone wanted me to test for a *big* part. A serious part in *Little Man, What Now?*, best-selling novel.

I spent a whole day at the studio, they set my hair, did it, made me up, put a dress on me, you couldn't tell *who* I was.

"Acts fine, can't photograph her."

Time went by, the great Mr. Robert E. Sherwood made a movie script out of his play *Abe Lincoln in Illinois,* he wanted me to play Mrs. Lincoln.

"Great!"

"The salary is two thousand a week."

Two thousand dollars! In 1939! How many thousands was I in debt to my friends?

"A four-week guarantee."

Two thousand dollars for *four weeks!*

"We'll give you a drawing room on New York Central's Twentieth Century, and Santa Fe's Chief. Could you test on Friday?"

A long pause. Had I learned? Had I? "I don't test."

"Well, this is just going through the motions. Mr. Sherwood *wants* you for Mrs. Lincoln."

"I don't test." Was I right? *Was* I? Eight thousand dollars!

"Tell you what we'll do for you. Drawing room on the New York Central, Santa Fe Chief, we'll pay your expenses there. Eastern tests are no good, we'll give you our great makeup man who will work on the picture, same electricians and cameraman we are going to use."

Four weeks, eight thousand dollars. Maybe . . . "I don't test."

I got the two thousand a week and they found out how to photograph me.

If I'd learned that lesson after Anna's test would I have become a movie star twenty-one years before I did?

"The dreaming soul of the human race," said Thornton

Wilder. He was talking about what he called "the visceral myths," Red Ridinghood, Cinderella, Goldilocks, and the Three Bears, stories that have gone on and on and on, full of fear and trouble, endless worry to begin with, then came out right.

Am *I* a visceral myth? I've gone on and on and on. Not as long as Little Red Ridinghood, but 1896? A dark October morning old Dr. John Alexander Gordon pulled up his horse and buggy in front of 41 Winthrop Avenue, stepped out, reached under the seat for the round block of granite, fastened to a worn black leather strap, dropped the block on the ground, hitched the strap to his horse.

At our open front door stood neighbor Mrs. Charlie Brigham in a flannel wrapper. Upstairs Mama was having a hard time.

"I'll try and save the mother," said Dr. Gordon, and tossed me off somewhere.

Is that how to get to be an actress? Is that how to get to be a visceral myth? From somewhere came a feeble wail. Dr. Gordon gave me some slaps and they said they could hear me across the street at the Congregational Church. Important for an actress to be heard.

Of course, all this is hearsay. I don't remember a thing until I was four. What *isn't* hearsay is my birth certificate, locked up in Quincy City Hall across the street from the big granite Unitarian Church under the broad steps of which are buried the second President of the United States, President John Adams, and son President John Quincy Adams. We're the only city in the country where two presidents were born and lived and are buried.

Two years ago, this present generation of Adamses, represented by Charles Francis Adams, gave Quincy the fields and meadows and salt marshes that President and Mrs. Abigail Adams had owned and added to. The land stretches from the handsome Adams mansion to the Quincy shore. On my eightieth birthday Quincy honored me with a ball and at the ball it was announced they were building a Ruth Gordon Theatre on part of the Adams land, to be finished by this next October.

City Hall
Quincy, Mass.
October 30, 1896
Ruth Gordon Jones
Born to Clinton
and
Annie Jones

At first they thought of calling me Ethel.

Ethel Jones?

Is that a name for a visceral myth? Ethel Barrymore, *yes*. Ethel Jones, no.

Then Papa decided to call me after the President's daughter, little Ruthie Cleveland. And of course my middle name had to be for Dr. Gordon, who had brought me into the world.

On my bureau is the silver cup I drank Mellin's Food out of, gift of Dr. Gordon, on it engraved, "Ruth Gordon Jones."

Hearsay except for my cup and birth certificate. I didn't get organized until I was four. Then along the way to civilization I learned something.

"Ruth, did you know that today is 1899?"

"Yes, Mama."

"And tomorrow is going to be 1900?"

"Yes, Mama."

"Ruth, did you know yesterday was 1899?"

"Yes, Aunt Emma."

"And today is 1900?"

"Yes, Aunt Emma."

"Ruth, did you know—"

What I learned was to let my mind wander. Nod my head, say, "Yes, Mama," "Yes, Aunt Emma," until they said something interesting. Useful in private life, *never* do it on the stage.

I didn't have to let my mind wander a lot, good things happened in 1900. Celebrations. Philadelphia sent its Liberty Bell to visit cities.

"Ruth, would you like to put on your new white dress with

Aunt Fanny May Jackson's famous drawnwork she sent you
from Asheville, North Carolina, with black velvet ribbons run
through?"

"Yes, Mama."

Mama put on her new gray striped voile, pink velvet edging
the collar and sleeves, Papa put on his white duck pants and we
went down to the Old Colony Railroad station where all Quincy
was spread out.

"How do."

"How do."

"How do."

"How do."

"How do."

"How do."

In Quincy everybody knew everybody and if they didn't they
said, "How do" anyway. If they were in Quincy they must be
lovely people.

"How do."

"How do."

From way down under the Adams Street bridge came a small
puff of white smoke. "There it *is!*"

"There it *is!*"

"Can you see it, Ruth?"

"Yes, Mama." It looked like what you see every day, then
slowly, slowly, on an open freight car, came Philadelphia's Liberty Bell.

"Here it comes!"

"Here it comes!"

"Here it comes!"

"Are you looking, Ruth?"

"Yes, Mama."

It was going to go right past our station platform where Papa
took the train to go to work every morning. Under our Beale
Street bridge it rolled slowly right in front of us.

"Are you looking, Ruth?"

"Yes, Mama."

Talk about excitement!

"I see the crack! Do you see the crack?"

"I see the crack."

"I see it."

Slowly, slowly.

"Ruth, can you see the crack?"

"Yes, Mama." I couldn't but I didn't want to make her feel bad. And what did I want to see a crack for? I was looking at the bell.

Four years old, knew what was going on and what was going on around *me* was trouble. Money trouble. Everything went up but Papa's pay. Once I called it "salary," but he said a foreman of a factory doesn't get salary, he gets pay.

At 41 Winthrop Avenue, our landlord, Mr. N. G. Nickerson, raised our rent. "The N.G. stands for No Good," said Papa, and we moved around the corner to 41 Marion Street, a cheaper two-family house.

Mr. Sparrow and his boy carried down Mama's bed I was born in, loaded it onto his wagon, piled in our furniture and hauled it around the corner. Mama carried her Limoges plate, gift of Mr. Edward Atkins, whose secretary she was when she worked in his wholesale china store on Atlantic Avenue in Boston. Papa carried his spyglass he'd brought back from a voyage to Hamburg, Germany, in his seafaring days, I carried our heavy black cat given us by Captain Humphrey, the last sea captain Papa sailed with on whose chair down in Hingham was carved "Captain Barnacle."

Some Sundays we'd take the trolley car for Sunday dinner with Captain and Mrs. Humphrey and daughter, Mabel. Papa loved to relive the days Mrs. Humphrey and little Mabel sailed on the voyage. "Becalmed in the Indian Ocean, sails drooping and Mrs. Humphrey would say, 'Frank, bring my sewing machine up on deck.' My name was Clinton, but my papers said Frank. Clinton was no name for a seaman. I'd put her Singer sewing machine in the shade and she'd shake out some pink cal-

ico she'd taken on in Calcutta and measure it on little Mabel. It
was a pretty sight to see her stitch away on deck."

We turned the corner onto Marion Street. What I saw I saw
before and pretended I didn't. 41 Marion Street was no good.
41 Marion Street was no place for a visceral myth. Mama
moved in, Papa moved in, our cat moved in, I *looked* as though
I moved in, but I took off for the Never-Never Land where everything is going to be great, everything is going to come out
right, nothing ever happens to you that happens to the people
next door!

How right I was. Last summer after I played a matinee of a
play I wrote and Garson Kanin directed we drove to our favorite restaurant down on the shore. As our car stopped, a car
pulled up just behind us, out jumped a lady and two little boys,
one held up his autograph book and a pencil, shouted at Garson
and me, "Which one of you is Ruth Gordon?"

Could that happen to the people next door?

Next door lived Mrs. Percy Moorehouse, she gave me my first
piano lessons. Mama went a day a week and sewed to pay for
them. Mrs. Moorehouse's daughter was fifteen years old and a
cello soloist. Mama made her a pink dress, a white dress, a pale
blue dress with skirts that had room for Marion and her cello.

When I had learned my first piece Mrs. Moorehouse invited
me to play it at her afternoon musicale. Mama made me a
cream-colored challis with rosebuds, the bertha, star-shaped,
edged with moss-green velvet baby ribbon and ecru lace. "Our
musicale will open with 'The Pixies' Drill' played by Ruth
Jones," announced Mrs. Moorehouse, standing beside her grand
piano. I sat down on her piano bench, new patent leather
slippers from Thayer-McNeil not reaching the pedals, but I
played and didn't hit one wrong note.

If Horowitz or Rubinstein had opened their concert with
"The Pixies' Drill," could they have done more? Artur Rubinstein would probably have hit a wrong note.

"He's so great!" raved a music critic.

"But he hits so many wrong notes," carped one of the public.

"Yes he does, but *what* wrong notes!"

After Artur's eightieth birthday, he and Garson and I were having dinner in San Francisco's Trader Vic's. A glass of Dom Perignon in his hand, "Do you know," said Artur, "I am playing my best. Do you know *why?* I'm eighty years old and I don't give a *damn* if I play a wrong note, I just *play.*"

At Mrs. Moorehouse's I didn't know enough to hit a wrong note. The ladies applauded and I knew I would hear that all my life.

At 41 Marion Street what I heard was more trouble. Everything went up some more. Mr. Sparrow's wagon hauled our furniture down the hill to a cheaper two-family house on the plains, 14 Elmwood Avenue.

In Quincy if you live up on the hill you're all right. If you live down on the plains you *might* be, but down on the plains there happened the second most important thing in my life. The most important is being born, the second most important is knowing what you want to be. While I was living at 14 Elmwood Avenue my voices told me, but until they spoke, trouble, worry, fear, what was I going to do? I had to earn my living, but I didn't want to be a nurse, I didn't want to be a nun, I didn't want to be a teacher, I didn't want to be a secretary.

At Quincy High I took the college course with the other girls. They were going to Radcliffe, Wellesley, Smith, Holyoke, where Papa didn't have money to send me and where I didn't want to go. I wanted to go where they taught how to make a lot of money, how to astonish people, how to be a somebody, how to be popular. Would you believe I found out where? Boston's beautiful Colonial Theatre!

Home from boarding school in Kansas City for Christmas, my friend Anna Witham invited me to a matinee. She could have invited Joyce Buchanan, she could have invited Katherine Follett, but she invited me. "It's a musical comedy called *The Pink Lady.* In Kansas City they say it's pretty raw."

"Oh, that's all right."

The plays Papa had taken Mama and me to were *Shore Acres, Way Down East, As Ye Sow, Woodland, Roseland.* From the first balcony of the Colonial, two rows from the back and pretty far left, I looked down at nothing like I'd ever seen before. The most *adorable* girls, in the most adorable pink chiffon dresses with beads and tassels, nothing warm underneath and it was January, were dancing with adorable fellows in top hats, white ties, tails, singing and behaving the way Mama would think was promiscuous, but *I* thought looked popular.

Then the violins struck up "To You Beautiful Lady," and on came the most beautiful lady ever seen, Hazel Dawn, The Pink Lady. Soft gold hair, a smile like a valentine, pink chiffon dress, pink hat with pink ostrich feathers that curled around, curled around.

" 'Dream, dream, dream and forget,' " sang Hazel Dawn. " 'Care, pain, useless regret.' "

And from back of me in the balcony my voices spoke, "Go on the stage. Be an actress. Be an actress. Go on the stage."

Back at 14 Elmwood I knew what I was going to be. I was going to be an actress, nothing would stop me. Now I had to find out how to get from Elmwood Avenue to Broadway. I wasn't pretty, I was five feet tall, I didn't know anyone on the stage, I didn't know anyone in New York, I didn't have any talent, I didn't have any money. How would I pay for a railroad ticket from our Old Colony Railroad station, where the Liberty Bell rolled past, to Grand Central station, New York?

I told only Mama. She burst into tears. "Ruth, why do you always have to be so different?"

Should I have said, "Because I'm going to be a visceral myth, Mama?" It wouldn't have made her feel any better.

"Why couldn't you marry some good man?"

I did, Mama, but not for a while.

"Be a Physical Culture instructress, snuggy." Papa wiped his whiskers and leaned back in his chair at our dining room table.

"I'll stake you to a year at Sargent's School of Physical Education."

"Papa, I don't *want* to be a physical culture instructress."

"Why the hell not?"

Could I tell him I hated serge bloomers, Indian clubs, dumbbells? "I just don't, Papa."

"Well, what *do* you want to be?"

"I don't know."

"Yes, you do, Ruth, *tell* Papa." Mama, who had always stood *by* me? Who had always shielded me from Papa? *"Tell* Papa, Ruth, he wants to know."

Would he hit me? The night I came home from looking in the window at Gertrude Waterhouse getting married Papa yelled, "Where have you been?"

"Up watching Gertrude Waterhouse get married."

"You old *goat,*" he shouted, "you old *goat,*" and grabbed my head and kept banging it down on the dining room table where now we were just finishing supper. He felt badly because in the old days Mr. and Mrs. Waterhouse and Mama and he played whist, but today they had to say no to the invitation and sent a cut-glass water pitcher because Papa didn't have a dress suit. A few years ago when Kitty Carlisle was playing a performance in Wichita, a lady came up and asked if she knew Ruth Gordon. She did. "Please tell her that her mother and father gave my grandmother and grandfather a cut-glass water pitcher when they got married and it is our most treasured possession."

If I told him I wanted to be an actress, would Papa hit me like after the Waterhouses?

"Come on, spit it out!"

Would he hit me? Be ready, but don't let it change anything. "I want to go on the stage." It was almost a whisper.

He didn't say anything . . . He didn't say anything . . . I couldn't move. I didn't dare look up. He didn't say anything. He didn't say anything and then, "What makes you think you got the stuff it takes?"

And it all poured out. "Papa, I have to start right *now*."

"Not finish your schoolin'?"

"Papa, every minute counts, what's important to get on the stage is be young!"

"You finish your schoolin', you'll need it every day of your life. You graduate from high school and I'll see you get your chance. I was going to stake you to one year at Sargent's Physical Culture School, I'll stake you to a year to go where they teach you how to act. When you get up in meeting you got to deliver the goods."

And one hot June night, I came down our stairs in my beautiful graduation dress Mama made out of fine white net, a single ruffle for the sleeves, a roll-over collar hand-embroidered with polka dots that ended in a V. The skirt had loosely gathered ruffles, one after the other down to my ankles. June 22 in my diary I wrote, "I am going to graduate. I am the happiest thing. I look like an actress."

Papa looked at the neckline. "You look like a concubine."

At Quincy High School, "Miss Ruth Jones."

I walked across the platform of the auditorium to receive my diploma from Mr. Frank E. Parlin, Superintendent of all the Quincy schools and author of the *Frank E. Parlin First Grade Spelling Primer*. From the table beside him, Superintendent Parlin handed me a white scroll wound round with orange satin ribbon, our class color, tied in a bow.

"Thank you," I said to him, to myself I said, "You're Superintendent of all the Quincy schools, you're the author of the Frank E. Parlin Primer for Spelling, but you are *never* going to be a visceral myth, I am the only visceral myth in this auditorium."

On the trolley going home I gave Mama my diploma and never saw it again, but Papa was right. In Room 24 at Quincy High School I learned the most useful lesson of my life. Room 24, presided over by beautiful Miss Elizabeth Irene O'Neill, brown pompadour, sherry-wine-colored eyes, brown velvet voice, dresses out of *Bon Ton Magazine,* her subject was Latin, but she *taught* inspiration. Every girl had a crush on her, every boy was in love. Roy Larkin, captain of our football team, stated publicly he would like to date her.

She towed us through Caesar and his Gallic Wars. "*'Gallia est omnis divisa in partes tres,'* not *'Omnis Gallia est divisa in partes tres,'* but *'Gallia est omnis divisa in partes tres.'* " I've forgotten things, but I remember *that.* Why? Because Miss O'Neill taught it to me.

"*Quousque tandem arbutere, Catilina?*" demanded Cicero. Miss O'Neill demanded we reach for the heights! "*'Ad astra!'* Don't just live to support yourself, *be* somebody!"

"*Arma virumque cano,*" sang Virgil. "*Troiae qui primus ab oris.*"

Miss O'Neill had taught me to read it *and,* the most useful lesson of my life, to learn how to learn.

Mr. Sparrow hauled away the trunk full of clothes Mama had made me to be an actress. Papa and I took the Fall River Line boat for New York. I wore my going-away suit, olive-green broadcloth. Olive-green because I read in a biography of the French tragedienne Rachel that she had an olive-green dress, with buttons of solid gold olives. My buttons were made of fur Mama had cut from Mrs. Charlie Brigham's muff passed on to Mama when Mr. Brigham gave his wife a new one for Christmas.

In Carnegie Hall at the New York office of the president of the American Academy of Dramatic Arts I recited two recitations from a booklet the Academy sent me to memorize for the entrance examination.

One, describing a racing scene, was comedy, a serious one was from "Ingomar the Barbarian." Shall we draw the veil?

"Do you know any other?" asked the president of the Academy, a melancholy man.

"No, sir."

He looked off to nowhere, over the roofs of West Fifty-seventh Street.

"Do you do imitations of your friends?"

"No, sir."

He seemed relieved. "You'll do."

I burst into tears. Papa had a hard time, but managed. "I'm short of words, but Mrs. Jones will write you a letter." He got out a roll of dirty bills, counted out four hundred dollars for a year's tuition. It had been collected from borrowing against Mama's life insurance and closing out Papa's Shawmut Savings account.

That was October. In May I stood where I had done the recitations.

"You've tried, hard," said the president, "but we don't think you're suited to the stage. Don't come back."

Twenty-one years later I stood on the stage of England's National Theatre, London's Old Vic, the audience applauding, we were in a line, holding hands to take the opening night calls for *The Country Wife*. The curtain went up, we bowed. I let go of Michael Redgrave's hand, let go of Edith Evans', stepped forward, bowed, stepped back, took Michael's hand, took Edith's hand, the audience shouted:

> "Ruth Gordon!
> Ruth Gordon!
> Ruth Gordon . . ."

"You'll have to make a speech, ducky," whispered Edith.

"I can't, I'm too scared."

She kept hold of my hand, held up her other to the audience.

"I know you want to hear from our American visitor, but I should like to say a few words." Then she talked until my hand stopped shaking, turned toward me. "Our American visitor, Miss Ruth Gordon."

Well.

Next morning the New York *Times* ran the cabled report, "Last night Ruth Gordon took London by storm."

The visceral myth, it all came out right. Edith Wharton's *Ethan Frome*, Thornton Wilder's great adaptation of Ibsen's *A*

Doll's House. Everything going right, hard times over, everything smooth from now on!

That's in the visceral myth. In show business it doesn't work. You're on top, then you open in *The Birds Stop Singing*. Bomb! It opened in Princeton, then played Philadelphia. I begged our producer to close.

"For this relief much thanks," said co-star Walter Abel. He bowed from the waist and kissed my hand.

I accepted *Portrait of a Lady*. Bang-bang! Close in Boston.

Maybe try something more literary, not such a big part? Paul Vincent Carroll's, *The Strings, My Lord, Are False*. Co-star with Walter Hampden, directed by wonderful actor Elia Kazan, who had just directed his first play, *Café Crown*, a hit.

After our preview we were overjoyed. Elia came back in my dressing room. "It'll be tremendous. A few places not right, but I know exactly what to do." He stepped out of my room, the management said to him, "You're replaced."

We opened and a few days later closed on Saturday night, but! Then came *The Three Sisters*, starring

Katharine Cornell
Judith Anderson
Edmund Gwenn
Dennis King
Me

The play was a hit, I was a hit, and, Mama, I married the good man. Mama, I married the best man in the world. We've just celebrated our thirty-seventh wedding anniversary.

It takes courage. It takes believing in it. It takes rising above it. It takes work. It takes you liking me and me liking you. It takes the dreaming soul of the human race that *wants* it to go right. Whatever you do, never stop dreaming.

Think it over.

ACTING
LESSONS
I

———————————————

"For creative people it is important to save room for life," said Edith Evans, finest actress of her day and maybe of anybody's.

On the twenty-first of August, 1977, a Sunday, at 6:40 A.M., I looked for an answer and got it: "At eighty-one years old," I asked myself, "do I have to do it? I mean any and every old thing that arises?"

"Do it if you like to," came the answer.

How far would I go with that?

First, to make it work, I braced up my intentions. I intend to make it work. Intention has been going for me for a long time, I got it started in 1912, but what counts is what you decide on *today*. Decide to have intention. I'm a believer in *today*.

Do you believe you get there on American Airlines or do you believe you get there on intention? American Airlines is good, so is TWA, so are the friendly skies of United, so is a Lincoln Continental, so is a Chevy, so is walking, but for getting there, count on intention.

Intend it.

Notify your built-in confidence.

Work on it.

Do *not* face the facts.

Keep your bowels moving.

Walk, think.

Where are you? Maybe you're there.

I hope this page is pink.

Do you think out what you're doing? Or think *after?*

Traveling on the Golden Arrow from Victoria Station to Dover, Garson and I were shepherding a huge packing case, kept it in our cabin on the Channel boat, saw it get on the Flêche d'Or, Calais-to-Paris express. Along with it were our fourteen pieces of luggage.

Garson took his eyes off the beautiful country sliding by our compartment window and stared at the packing case.

"Would you say René Clair is a mean man?" asked Garson.

"Of course not."

"Is he stingy with his wife?"

"You know he's not, her clothes come from Dior, even her furs. She has beautiful diamonds. What kind of a question is René stingy with Bronia?"

"Would he give her ten dollars?"

"Garson, are you all right?"

"Would he?"

"Of course."

"Then why the hell are we dragging this case of forty-eight full-size boxes of Kleenex to Bronia, because it's ten dollars cheaper in London?"

Once I said, "My ambition is to have a lot of good meals and keep out of everybody's way." In my private life I meant. For an actress to keep out of everybody's way would mean empty seats, nobody backstage to say, "I love you."

"Green room perjury," Thornton Wilder called that. I call it necessary. Who wants people backstage to say it's no good? Critics get paid to tell us and who needs that?

Do you do everything right?

Do you try to?

Isn't that a bore!

Or is it?

Do you follow your convictions?

Spencer Tracy said, "I'm not young, I'm not sexy, I'm not handsome, all I have are my instincts."

He was talking to movie director George Cukor.

Instincts take you a long way.

On the Quincy High School bulletin board was a notice.

ROOM 24

THIS AFTERNOON 1:30.   EVERYBODY WELCOME
                    DRAMA SOCIETY

                                MISS BROWN
                                MISS O'NEILL.

"I'm not going," I told Katherine Follett.

"You're the one wild to be an actress, why wouldn't you be wild to act?"

"I don't know how."

"Miss O'Neill and Molly Brown will show us."

"Do *they* know?"

"Well, it's only high school."

"If I get discouraged, I might give up."

"Not you."

My instinct told me not to, why was I in Room 24?

"First we'll choose a name," said Molly Brown, pretty and going to be married in the summer. When she acted in the Quincy Women's Club production of *Galatea,* Mama said she was as good as a professional actress.

"The Drama Society," suggested Horton Page.

Molly flashed a blond smile in his direction. "'A rose by any other name would be as sweet.' Let's hear some others."

"Theatre Club?" Margaret Magee, brown hair, violet eyes, prettiest girl in the senior class and most popular.

"Your class motto is 'Summa Summarum,' " suggested Miss O'Neill. "Shall we reach for the heights?"

The big turnout was for her.

"I'd like to choose a name in Latin." Blond curly-haired Willard Crocker was second to none in his love.

"How da y'say Theatre Club in Latin?" asked Roy Larkin.

"At Radcliffe our club was 'The Comedia Society.' " Molly's voice was like clear water.

Miss O'Neill thought about it, " 'Comedia' was attractive at Radcliffe, but our members were girls. Larkin and Page, suggest deeper qualities."

Larkin was the most raffish guy in the class.

The brown velvet voice came through the laughter. "Would you think of calling it 'The Thalia Club'?"

"Touchdown!" shouted Page.

Larkin was on his feet. "I move we call our drama society The Thalia Club."

"Second the motion," shouted the room, then laughed, then shouted, "Yea!"

"So ordered. Molly, take over."

I *knew* I shouldn't join, why did I?

Willard Crocker played the bachelor in *A Bachelor's Banquet*. I played Constance. My failure was bitter.

After the performance, riding home in the trolley, Mama said, "How can you be an actress, Ruth, you couldn't even be heard?"

Mama, who loved and believed.

In my lap were six carnations Katherine sent. Can you hate flowers? Flowers are for success.

The trolley bumped along Newport Avenue.

"Silly play! Willard Crocker in a tea apron! What did he come out and say?"

"I don't remember."

"Why, how can you be an actress if you don't remember?"

" 'Half past five and not a canapé ready yet.' "

Where was my courage?

In trouble I quaked, just when I needed confidence.

Mama and I walked up Elmwood single file, up the front steps, Mama unlocked the front door, I walked past to the kitchen, lifted the stove lid and threw in Katherine's flowers.

"Ruth, how can you be so selfish?"

"I'll be unselfish when I'm a success."

It was my only amateur appearance in a play. That was 1914 and over forty years later Gar and I went into the Walter Baker Play Company on Summer Street in Boston. "Have you a copy of *A Bachelor's Banquet*," I asked an elderly Dickensian clerk in charge of this elderly Dickensian business.

He disappeared in the shadows, our wait stretched on.

"What do you want it for?" asked Gar.

"I don't know, but I do."

Some soft steps, then clerk came up to us. He held a buff-colored thin play. "It's the only one in the world so take care of it."

He refused money.

Don't give up is part of life, part of acting. That buff-colored playlet was a healer. *A Bachelor's Banquet* was a play printed for amateurs and only an amateur would attempt it. Nobody could act *A Bachelor's Banquet*. Thank you, Walter Baker, for picking up the blame.

When I was growing up I wrote letters to friends or anyone I could think of. I liked to get answers and to use sealing wax. When you haven't got many chances to choose it's a pleasure to pick out what color. If I ran out of names I wrote to a department store for samples of yellow messaline, pink Swiss muslin, yellow rosebud dimity, light blue Dorothy Dainty ribbon wide enough for a sash. In winter, a sample of brown wide-wale silk corduroy, orange crepe de chine, tango color Henrietta cloth, Nile green nun's veiling, pale pink panne velvet.

When I got the money I'd know what to buy. I got enough to buy the yellow rosebud dimity, Mama made a long dressing gown, sleeves and front edged in yellow batiste.

Saving up and with help from Mama, in the autumn I got the brown wide-wale silk corduroy. Mama made a dress with a Norfolk jacket, amber glass buttons. In spring we squeezed out enough to buy black and white check for a cutaway effect suit, the jacket outlined in black silk braid, orange crepe de chine lining, beautiful and actressy, I hoped people would say I looked striking.

The tango-colored Henrietta cloth Mama made into a dress for my first visit to meet an actress in her dressing room, Miss Doris Olssen's, leading lady of the Castle Square Stock Company. The skirt was draped with a small slit in front, like a photograph in *Theatre Magazine* of a costume by Paul Poiret for Gaby Deslys. Reveres folding back from a gathered white net yoke, each revere embroidered with a sparrow, my own idea. A narrow strip of brown fur at the neck and wrists, a wide belt of Henrietta cloth that buttoned with a big flat nickel button. In Miss Doris Olssen's dressing room I looked more actressy than she did.

Mama had balked at the birds and the slit in the skirt, but in the end it was less trouble to just do it.

To be an actress have ideas and make them work. That was how I got to see Miss Doris Olssen, I wrote her and wrote her and wrote her. How did she find the time to reply? At the Castle

Square Stock Company she played a new play every week. Between learning the part of the leading lady for the next week's play and being leading lady for this week's, she found time to write to some Ruth Jones who wanted to be an actress and had to see her.

Is that what *I* do when I get letters like that?

The first letter I ever wrote was to Aunt Alice Morgan, no relation, but a friend of Mama's, like Aunt Josie Babcock, Aunt Fan Hoyt, Aunt Editha Keefe, Aunt Fanny May.

I thanked Aunt Alice for the Christmas book she sent. I was six. When I'd been four Mama and I went to stay at her house in Windsor Locks, Connecticut. Everything away from home was different. At breakfast their big black cook dropped scraps of dough into deep fat and served it like doughnuts. One she dropped on her bare foot and put it back on the plate, someone ate it, was it me?

In the fields behind the house they grew tobacco. In Quincy, nobody grew tobacco. Away from home is a surprise.

One night Aunt Alice drove us in her carriage to Hartford's Elizabeth Park, full of bright lights and music and noise. My first time out at night.

Before we left Windsor Locks, Mama took a snapshot of me climbing an apple tree, it came out blue. It wasn't a color photo, but instead of gray, I and tree were blue.

I was glad to get home where our snapshots came out gray or yellowish and Mr. Brooks our drugstore man couldn't make some come out at all, but none ever came out blue. And tobacco was in Papa's box of Dill's Cut Plug and Mama never cooked breakfast barefoot and dropped things on her toe.

Did your St. Tropez guidebook mention that early in the morning you hear oxen go by? Clop, clop, the wagon creaks, the yoke creaks, a bell goes dingle, the oxen driver lets out oxen language noises.

Away from home is different. Once at breakfast in the garden there I heard a nightingale. "Have you?" I asked bird lover Brooks Atkinson. "Not me."

Is anybody thinking when they say, "Have a good day"?

Where I live, when day starts to get light looking over Central Park, sometimes the sun comes up behind the Hotel Carlyle, then days pass and the sun comes up further down Fifth Avenue over Temple Emanu-El.

"Memorable events transpire in the morning," wrote Henry David Thoreau.

Pronounced writer Chamfort, "Eating a live toad is only a little worse than what may befall you today."

Anybody really thinking when they say, "Have a nice day"?

Do you engage people to trim your Christmas tree? I'm not asking about nonsense like blue, pink, or white artificial ones, I mean a green balsam or spruce with ornaments for it that have decorated more than this year's tree and last year's. Some of mine have been on my tree since 1929. Some get broken, but still go on. Some are additions, new tinsel to add to the old, new popcorn strings, old tarleton bags with new candy and always new peppermint canes. Up on top is the star of, just below hangs Père Noël, with a spun glass skirt from the Galeries Lafayette in Paris, year of 1929. He crossed the Atlantic Ocean and holds up fine at fifty years old! Is he a visceral myth?

When I was little everybody had wax candles on their tree. Hard to light, also had to be watched so as not to burn up the house, but pretty. In their memory I don't put electric lights on my tree. Ever notice a tree with its ornaments has its own light?

Some things say twice, like Gertrude Stein. Who forgets "A rose is a rose is a rose"? That's three times, so don't write and tell me. I'm also three times something, an actress, writer, speaker. I picked up speaking and writing; acting I had to learn. No one is born talented, to be talented you have to want to be, aim high and when doubts come don't accept them, know you're going to make it, know you're going to. What else is there? You have to!

"Pride goeth before a fall," warned Mama. Just a harmless saying she admired. I don't know what she thought it meant. Nothing. Who makes it being humble? Even poor Jesus, meek and mild, with all the good he did, got done in. Do *not* be humble, aim high, teach yourself or find somebody to teach you. Nobody is too old to learn, if you'll forget facts; facts prove you cannot do anything. Anything you aim for you can do and when you *do* it, don't feel humble. Know the *doing* is the thing. Prizes are for the general public, *doing* is the prize. Think what time goes into receiving an honorary college degree! Some hot June day a walk in a line across campus, wearing a thick black down-to-the-ground, a flat thing on your head that doesn't keep the sun off, its tassel just the length to hit your nose. And before you get this, God knows what has gone on!

What I value is what I give myself. In a play, in a movie, on the Johnny Carson show, an evening at Town Hall and when it's over I bestow or hold back my own medal or prize or pat on the head or back or wherever.

Say people, "You're not the best judge of when you're good."

People say anything. Give the prize when you do what you aim for. Anticipation and realization are hard to bring together.

If you want to be talented, worship talent. Horowitz plays and I take off from the world like a souped-up faint, when I come back it's frightening.

I saw Liv Ullmann in *A Doll's House*. After it was over I wept. Not because Nora left home, but because of Liv Ullmann's great gift.

Confidence feeble? Forgive and encourage it. Isn't that how life thrives?

Today's mail had an offer of Doctorate of Fine Arts. I must be only human. "Yes, thank you," I wrote.

My day ends with a prayer. It's more cheerful than when I was down on my knees at four.

> "Now I lay me down to sleep
> I pray the Lord my soul to keep,
> If I should die before I wake
> I pray the Lord my soul to take."

Why teach kids that? Why talk of dying at four?

Tonight my prayer is more optimistic. "Thank you God for your loving care. God bless So-and-So and So-and-So and So-and-So, and So-and-So and So-and-So and So-and-So and So-and-So and So-and-So and thank you for your loving care.

Papa, who was an atheist, took time off to admire Robert Herrick's prayer which began:

> Here a little child I stand
> Heaving up my either hand . . .

People used to die at home, now it's at the hospital. And who is born in their mother's bed?

I was, and Mama was and died in a nursing home. Money troubles sunk us, the South Quincy secondhand man came and Papa sold him Mama's Limoges plate from Mr. and Mrs. Edward Atkins, the bed I was born in. The secondhand man hauled off to South Quincy eight rooms of our life. All that was left was Mama's flat silver saved for me at Aunt Ada's, where Mama was brought for the funeral. Her last time with Papa and me and her flat silver. I had to go on the stage and when you have to, Limoges plates and a birch double bed go up to South Quincy or someplace that gets them out of the way to act Nibs in *Peter Pan*.

The best thimbleberries grew a block away from 14 Elmwood
Avenue in the Fayette Street dump. Do plants like peaceful rub-
bish in tangled weeds? Nobody loosening earth around them, no
manure to take away the green smell of spring? Beside the good
thimbleberries grew a hollyhock, pink blossoms with a claret-
colored frill. One night Papa took our coal shovel and he and
Mama and I went while he dug it up.

"Are we stealing?" I asked Mama.

"Ruth, think of something more appropriate than is your father a thief."

But were we? Was after dark just a coincidence?

Only a year away from 14 Elmwood Avenue where I slept in the same bed except for two weeks in the summer at French's Boarding House in Christmas Cove and now a different bed every night.

"Are you a member of the show troupe?" asked the hotel clerk.

"Not me. I'm traveling for Onyx Hosiery."

Commercial travelers were thought not to steal towels, actors were thought to. In our company Bessie "Bundle" Brown, touring with the Robert Mantell Shakespearian Company, boasted a towel from every state in the union except Vermont. Vermont had all its towels because it didn't have a theatre.

A bellboy or just someone showed me the room and left my suitcase. Room good, bad, better, horrible, accept it and walk over to the theatre to see how the stage manager had assigned the dressing rooms. Wouldn't one dressing room be as good as another in Baraboo, Wisconsin? In Vermillion, South Dakota? In Albert Lea, Minnesota? There's rank at any level. Upstairs, down cellar, near the toilet, near the stage. Those things count.

After dressing rooms, pick up mail in the letter box, after mail, over to department store to see beautiful winter hats with a willow plume, kid boots, handsome fur-trimmed suits, white kid gloves, silver mesh bags, signet rings, a fur muff like Mrs. Charlie Brigham's. In a one-night-stand company nobody has money to buy anything, but we have time to look.

"Can I help you?"

"We're just looking."

Last stop was the remnant counter. "Oh, my!" I picked up a piece of pale green washable satin.

"What could you do with it?" asked Grace Hayle. "It's not big enough for anything."

"Don't throw your money away," advised Bessie.

"Any idea what you'd make?" asked practical Gretchen.

I held it up and studied it. "I think I could get a pair of drawers."

Consternation!

"Ruth, you are not going to wear *green underwear!*" stated a shocked Grace.

In 1916 underwear was white and nobody saw it unless you got married or got run over. How did I get talked out of it? 1979 and I *still* wish I had those green pants.

One afternoon I was speaking in Dayton's department store, Minneapolis, told them how full of treasures department stores are. How important to people are remnant counters and how I'd missed the best remnant I ever saw. "But I am a believer, and one day before I close out I bet I *will* have some green satin drawers."

My talk went on for another forty minutes, then cheers, a thousand ladies and gentlemen stood, applauding, when down the aisle rushed a man waving a pair of green satin drawers, he'd been to Dayton's lingerie counter, bought and presented them to me.

It seemed as though it was taking place in Minneapolis, but of course it was the Never-Never Land where things happen that *never* could happen to the people next door. Did anyone give Mrs. Percy Moorehouse green satin drawers in front of a thousand people in a department store?

Think it over.

Sometimes what you want you don't get until you don't want it anymore. It's happened to me, but not that afternoon at Dayton's Department store with the thousand in the audience seeing that darling fellow making a wish come true. Not only believe, but believe in believing. That's what makes green pants come out of nowhere, makes the taxi driver find my Vuitton pocketbook on his cab's back seat, makes the New York *Times* critic say, "You were ever so gay as Nibs," makes life come out right on several occasions and helps you hang on until the next.

And speaking of green, no peas ever taste like peas from Aunt Ela Simpson's East Milton garden. I haven't had them for seventy-two years, but I'd recognize their flavor. And also the flavor of the dark red cherries on Uncle Dan Weymouth's cherry tree back of his Mather Street house in Dorchester.

Once touring *The Matchmaker* in the English provinces we drove over to see a different Dorchester, the one near Bournemouth where we were playing. That Dorchester didn't look anything like Uncle Dan's, but it was the original one, our Dorchester was just a copy.

Uncle Dan was Papa's brother-in-law from Papa's first marriage. He went to lodge meetings and marched in the G.A.R. parade and Papa didn't like him. Papa didn't like anybody but Mr. Carroll and Mr. Gourley, Mr. and Mrs. Walker, Captain and Mrs. Humphrey, Mr. Fred Gee. Then Mama died and he quit being foreman at the Mellin's Food factory, settled in Honolulu where the climate is temperate and Papa liked everybody, especially Captain Chester Nimitz, who married Ikey Freeman, who lived on Grand View Avenue in Quincy. In Pearl Harbor where Chet Nimitz was in charge, he let Papa go on trial submarine runs.

"Ikey married a good man," wrote Papa, "and if she didn't have so many freckles you'd say she got better looking."

Truman Capote was wearing a brown suit somewhere sometime and Halston remarked, "You have a lot of courage to wear
brown."

It's not my definition of courage, but why do I never wear
brown?

Think twice before you find out who you are. I was looking for my roots and should have looked first to see if I needed them. My father had a horrible father. My father's mother killed herself. Her grim sisters at Orleans on Cape Cod brought Papa up and were horrible to him.

My mother's mother, Ada Gordon Byron Beale from East Milton, Mass., married Jacob Zeigler, they lived in Bainbridge, Georgia. When my great-great-grandfather died, his heirs had his estate summed up. Nothing like facts to lower your spirits, I wish I had never heard of my roots. I have enough awful stuff *I* did, why look back for somebody else's?

ADMINISTRATION BOND—ESTATE OF MICHAEL ZEIGLER

SOUTH CAROLINA   )
BARNWELL DISTRICT)   By Orsamus D. Allen, Esquire,
                              Ordinary

Whereas Conrad Zeigler and Jacob Ridgedill made suit to me to grant them letters of Administration of the Estate and effects of Michael Zeigler deceased. These are therefore to Cite and admonish all and Singular the Kindred and Creditors of said Michael Zeigler deceased that they have appeared before me, in the Court of Ordinary, to be held at my office in Barnwell, on Friday next after publication hereof to show cause if any they have, why the said Administration should not be granted. Give under my hand and Seal, this tenth day of April, in the year of our Lord 1809, and in the Thirty third year of American Independence.

/s/ Orsamus D. Allen LS

Published at Felders Meeting House the fifteenth day of April 1809.

By, ───────────── /s/ Benjamin Tarrant

In 1809 lawyers seem just as dull, this is of no interest, skip it.

ORDER TO APPRAISE THE ESTATE OF MICHAEL ZEIGLER.

SOUTH CAROLINA)   BY ORSAMUS D. ALLEN,
                          ORDINARY

Barnwell District   )   These are to authorize and empower you
or any three of four of you, whose names are hereunder written to
repair to all such parts and places within this State, as you shall be
directed unto by Conrad Zeigler and Jacob Ridgedill Administrators of Michael Zeigler late of the District & State aforesaid deceased, where so ever any of the goods & Chattels of the said deceased and or do remain within the said parts and places and which
shall be shown unto you by the said Conrad Zeigler and Jacob
Ridgedill, and their view and appraise all and every the said Goods
and Chattels being first sworn on the Holy Evangelist of Almighty
God to make a true and perfect Inventory and appraisement
thereof and to cause the same to be returned under your hands, or
any three or four of you to the said Conrad Zeigler and Jacob
Ridgedill on or before the 21st day of May now next ensuing.
Dated the 21st of April 1809, and in the Thirty Third year of
American Independence.

To Mrss's: Peter Felder, David Felder, /s/ Orsamus D. Allen,
Ordinary   Ordinary, Benjamin Tarrant, Gasper
             Trotte, Elijah Ford

MEMORANDUM: This 11th day May 1809 personally appeared
before me Gasper Trotte, Esquire one of the Justices assigned to
keep the peace in Barnwell District, Peter Felder being two of the
appraisers appointed to appraise the Goods and Chattels of Michael
Zeigler deceased who being duly sworn made oath, that they would
make a just and true appraisement of all and Singular the Goods
and Chattels (Ready Money only Accepted) of Michael and Jacob
Ridgedill Administrators of Michael Zeigler deceased and that they
would return the same certified under their hands unto the said
Conrad Zeigler and Jacob Ridgedill within the time prescribed by
Law.

Sworned before me,   /s/ Peter Felder, Senior
/s/ Gasper Trotte   /s/ David Felder

Just get the drift, don't read every word.

South Carolina)
Barnwell District)   We do hereby petition the Ordinary of the
aforesaid District to Grant us an Order for Sale of the Personal Estate of Michael Zeigler deceased, for the payment of Debts and to
prevent the loss of perishable Articles. And Oblige Yr. Petitioners.

May the 19th 1809   /s/ Conrad Zeigler Adm'or
                                     /s/ Jacob Ridgedill Adm'or

Coming up is what I wish I didn't know. Also remember Barnwell.

Recorded Book A page 8, (April 21 1809)

South Carolina)
Barnwell District)

                    Conrad Zeigler)   Administrative
                    Jacob Ridgedill)   Bond
                    John Holman   )
                    Jacob Zeigler   )   [My grandfather]

   "Ten Thousand Dollars ($10,000.00)"

   Now read:

"May 8, 1809

Michael Zeigler, Deceased: Inventory
Recorded in Book A, Page 10

   An Inventory and Appraisement of the Goods and Chattels of
Michael Zeigler deceased made by the subscribers appointed Ap-
praisers of the same as have been shown by Conrad Zeigler and
Jacob Ridgedill Administrators of the said Estate.

12	Head Sheep	$	19.00
37	Large Hogs, 59 Shotes	$	133.00
5	Cows & Calfs, 1 Heffer, 1 Bull, 1 Calf	$	64.00
1	Timber Cart 2 Log Chains	$	18.00
1	Waggon 2 Jo'r Hand Gears Tresses & Wagon Cloth	$	15.00
1	Chain 8 Harness	$	40.00
1	Grind Stone	$	5.00
1	Hand Mill & Spindle	$	12.00
1	Vice Anvil, set of Blacksmith Tools	$	35.00
	Bar Iron & Steel	$	4.00
	A Lot of Old Iron	$	8.00
2	Cross cut saws 1 Whip Saw	$	5.00
	A lot of plantation & Carpenter Tools	$	19.50
3	Bee Hives	$	3.00
5⅓	Bales Cotton	$	180.00
	Seeded Cotton	$	30.00
1	Saw Gin	$	10.00
1	Lot of Pease	$	10.00
1	Lot of Fodder	$	12.00
	A lot of Corn	$	175.00
5	Barrels, 2 Collars, 2 Pr Tresses & Flems, 2 Saddles, 4 Plough Bridles, 1 Horse Ball & Leather	$	10.00
	A Bay Horse	$	70.00
	A Sorrel Horse	$	25.00
		$	902.50
	Bro'wt Fwd.	$	902.50
	A Bright Bay Horse	$	25.00
	A Bright Bay Horse	$	60.00
20	Geese & Turkeys	$	12.00
12	Bols	$	
	A Roap	$	10.00
	A Lot of Tobacco	$	2.00
3	pr Sthlyards 1 pr Scales & Weights	$	4.00
34	Paper Boxes, 3 Potts, 3 Mugs	$	2.00

	A stock lock, shoe tacks, 6 ladys stirrups, a lot of thread	$	2.00
	A lot of Black Pepper	$	1.00
7	Barrels & 7 Half Barrels Flower	$	10.50
	A lot of sugar	$	6.00
	Course rye & oats	$	1.25
50	pieces Bacon	$	35.00
	A Table, 4 Jugs, 1 jar	$	4.00
22	Flower Barrells, 6 Kegs, 4 Hogsheads	$	5.50
4	Iron Potts, 1 Dutch Oven, 1 Kettle 1 Frying Pan, 2 Pott Hooks, 2 Hangers, 2 pr Tongues, 1 Shovel	$	11.00
3	Tubs, (3 parts 2 kollers) a lot of Copper Wire	$	3.00
2	Dishes, 2 Basons, 10 Plats of Peioter, 6 Small Plates & 1 wire seive, 2 coffee mills, 1 saucer, 1 tray, 1 Callender	$	2.00
1	pine table	$	3.50
2	Looking Glasses	$	20.00
3	Coffee Potts, 1 Candleborn, 2 Candle Sticks, 1 Tin Pan, 1 Pint Measure	$	2.00
1	Table, 1 Mahogany Table	$	1.00
12	Knives & forks, 8 spoons	$	1.00
16	A lot of Crockery Ware	$	4.00
2	Decanters, 2 Glasses, 2 Tumblers, 5 tin churns, tin milk Potts, 8 Tea Spoons & pewter paper box	$	1.25
20	chairs	$	8.00
1	Chest of Draws	$	20.00
2	Spinning Wheels & pr Cards	$	3.00
6	Reaping Hooks	$	.50
1	Bedstead, 1 Trunk	$	3.00
2	Beds & Furniture for 1 Bed	$	33.00
1	Bed Head Cord & Hyde	$	2.00
1	Bed & Furniture & a Commode Chair	$	24.00
1	Bedstead Cord & Hyde	$	2.00
1	Bedstead, Bed & Furniture	$	19.00
1	Chest, 1 Trunk	$	4.00

10	Bottles, 2 Cloth Brushes	$	.75
3	Blankets, 1 Quilt	$	7.00
15	Yards Cotton Baggin	$	9.00
1	Bedstead, Bed & Furniture	$	18.00
	A lot of wool & A lot of Feathers	$	4.00
	About Eleven thousand feet ranging Timber	$	165.00
1	Waggon Wheel & wet stone & oil stone	$	1.00
	A Canoe	$	3.50
	A negro Man *Bob,* and his wife *Katty* and three they'r Sons, *George, Salomon,* and *Bob*	$	1250.00
	A Negro Man *London*	$	350.00
	A Negro Woman *Sally,* her boy *Sam,* & her Daughter *Fanny*	$	500.00
	A Negro Boy *Ben*	$	300.00
	A Negro Man *Harry*	$	400.00
	A Negro Man *Sambo*	$	250.00
	A Negro Man *Thom*	$	275.00
	A Negro Woman *Rose*	$	275.00

and deliver up the said Letter of Administration. Then this Obligation to be void or else remain in full force.

Signed Sealed and
delivered in the
presence of

/s/ Daniel Tobin

/s/ Conrad Ziegler   LS
/s/ Jacob Ridgedill   LS
/s/ John Holman   LS
/s/ Jacob Zeigler   LS

I don't need roots, I need my father's courage, my mother's rising above fear. Fearing burglars, every night she packed the flat silver in a wooden box Papa had a carpenter at the Mellin's Food factory make her, carried it upstairs, put it under the bed. Why tempt a robber upstairs to scare us to death?

Old actor Hal Russell placed a chair in front of his boardinghouse door on the inside and on it he put his watch and chain, stickpin, wallet, so a robber wouldn't wake him up.

When the robbers came to Garson's and my house they came over the roof, found nothing on the fifth floor, nothing on the fourth, slashed dress bags hoping for furs. If they couldn't find the light they lit matches and dropped them anywhere.

On the third floor, they found the jewelry. Took the valuable, left the semi. They heard our chauffeur open the front door and left over the roof. For the next three months a Pinkerton man came at sundown, sat in our front hall, gun in hand, sleeping until 8 A.M. They'd taken all the jewelry, why did I fear? Why couldn't I rise above it? Was it my roots? Sixty-five years before, Mama had gotten robbed when she and sister were going to visit their Aunt Molly. From the Wellesley railroad station they took the narrow path across the fields, walked single file, Mama behind sister Emma. "Out of the bushes stepped a man wearing sneakers." I got scared every time she told it.

"He pointed a long knife, cut the strings of my bag where I carried your grandmother's amethysts and disappeared in the bushes. Emma didn't hear him, the men haying didn't, and up ahead Aunt Molly in her white duck shirt was coming out of the house. The bag was found in the bushes, everything gone. On the train he must have seen me show Mama's earrings to Emma."

That all took place way back in 1891, but doesn't get lost. Fear and rising above it are part of show business. After my darling first husband, Gregory Kelly, and I lost all our money in our stock company, we had to take the first offer, a road tour that

opened in Perth Amboy, New Jersey. Rise above it! Not much
to fear but plenty of rising above it. Our money was gone, a
friend we were counting on had disappointed us. "I'm writing a
play for you and your wife," said Frank Craven to Gregory and
me. He was the star of a musical show, *Going Up*. Gregory was
featured in *Clarence* and all three of us were playing Chicago. A
non-pro says playing *in* Chicago.

Frank Craven's wife was a non-pro, but playwrights asked her
to read their plays, producers urged her to come to dress rehearsal. If Maisie Craven said a show would do, it did.

"I'm writing a play for you and your wife," said Frank, and
invited us home to supper.

For actors, home is anyplace they rent. He and Maisie had
rented an apartment down Michigan Avenue opposite the old
Michigan Central station.

"Your part is great." Was Maisie looking at *me?* It was the
first time anybody ever wrote a part for me.

Frank outlined the plot. "It's about a young couple getting
engaged, getting married, busting up, getting together again."

"It's great." Maisie Craven had a voice that sounded like she
had a throatful of gravel. "Your part's as good as his is." She
sounded great!

Clarence closed its Chicago season, our Indianapolis stock
company used up our money, no word from Frank, so Gregory
went back to *Dulcy,* he'd played it in Chicago. No part for me.

Ever get a jolt from the New York *Times?* "John Golden to
produce Frank Craven's new comedy, 'The First Year.' It will
open at the Little Theatre, starring Frank Craven and Roberta
Arnold. It deals with a young couple getting engaged, getting
married, busting up, getting together. The opening date . . ."

Draw the veil!

Opened and was a hit.

"It's your play," said Frank, "but the one I wrote for me
didn't pan out. Will you play the Chicago company?"

That didn't pan out either, we signed to play all the towns
Frank didn't want to. When you need money you open in Perth

Amboy, play New Brunswick, play a night in Newburgh, Onteora, Amsterdam, Rome, Albany, Utica, Syracuse, Buffalo,
Rochester, Dover, Trenton, Easton, Frederick, Hagerstown,
Lynchburg, Roanoke, two nights in Richmond where the
Abrams sisters ran a great cake shop and the hotel had a tank in
the lobby with an alligator and a sign "Please do not poke the
alligator."

We had bought us each a Taylor trunk and I engaged Gertie,
my theatre maid from Chicago. Why did she stay?

"Because you need me," said Gertie.

After Virginia, then South Carolina where the tough, rough
Southern voice spoke to our English stage manager, Mr. Bramhall, "You take off your hat to that nigger and we'll take you
out on a rail."

Michael Zeigler's great-great-granddaughter was going to act
The First Year in Barnwell, South Carolina, where his slaves
had been and his will was filed and a stagehand threatened our
Mr. Bramhall about our Gertie.

Up in our room at the hotel, bedbugs were walking on somebody's last night's sheets. Horrible, but not in comparison to in-
sults to our Gertie! Our Mr. Bramhall!

Across the hall the bed was made up. "We'd like the room
across the hall," said Gregory at the hotel desk.

"It's taken."

"The one you gave us has bedbugs."

"No, it don't."

Darling lady Mrs. John W. Ransome, wife of an actor in the
play asked where the Catholic church was. She went each day
and prayed.

"We have a Methodist church, a Baptist church, and the Klu-
Klux Klan," said the hotel clerk.

Nobody had the room across the hall so we took it. It had
bedbugs, too. We took another, down the hall, and were charged
for three rooms, but the third had no bedbugs.

Today, the mail brings me more roots from my adorable
Cousin Sally Thomas.

"Cousin Ruth dear, I hope it wasn't Barnwell, South Carolina you hated so, because the record shows Nathaniel Zeigler settled in Barnwell, South Carolina, did well in business, established a family, married a Georgia beauty, member of the rich Bruton family and at their plantation in Barnwell bore a son Nathaniel, then Michael, Jacob, your great-grandfather, Joseph, a daughter Elizabeth . . ."

"Why do you stay?" I asked Gertie.

"You need me," said Gertie.

Gertie, I wish you were my roots.

Before we took off on that unraveling *First Year* tour we went through such disappointment only the money earned and saved could make it up to us. From Perth Amboy to Nashville we just existed, we didn't enjoy, we just got through it until we could give our six weeks' notice with the money banked to match our partner's, Bob McLaughlin, and produce Booth Tarkington's and Harry Leon Wilson's play, written for us, called *Tweedles.*

We gave our six weeks' notice in Nashville. In all that tour I never got good in the part. Counting on *The First Year,* who could predict the agony it gave us? Frank, our friend, turned into a horror. A horror who had been so dear a friend, who had thought up the whole play for us.

Oh God! What you go through. Oh God Oh God Oh God! We said if we can't play Chicago and have to play all those one-nighters we want to play it for two weeks in New York here at the Little Theatre when Frank and Roberta Arnold take their vacation. We signed a contract with producer John Golden for seven hundred and fifty dollars a week which we needed after our losses. Frank said he would direct us. At rehearsals he said I talked like the Babytalk Lady. Every other word he stopped me.

"I don't hear it," defended Gregory. After two days, Gregory said he would not put me through it, took our contract and went over to the Lambs Club where Frank had lunch.

Frank was willing to cancel the contract, but said we had to

ask producer John Golden. He and Gregory went over to Mr.
Golden's office. Gregory explained how I cried and he thought
rightly.

John Golden just glared. A heavy-set, dark-haired, dark-eyed
man, he had a great glare. "I'm damned if I'll have any actor
quit me because they're unhappy! I won't do it. You let me
come to a rehearsal and I'll see if I want her or not," said John
Golden.

No way Gregory could move him further. "We'll be in the
lounge of the Little Theatre, nobody but Mr. Golden and Frank.
I said we'd do the fight scene." Gregory put his arms around
me. He hated to have to tell me.

Big John Golden sat glaring, Frank looked displeased as
Gregory and I tore into our marital spat that developed into a
rouser. When I finished and walked off, discouraged with myself
and hating everything in the world I heard John Golden say,
"Jeez!" I turned and glared at him. But he snapped back,
"Jeez, what an actress! You play this part *great*. You play it at
the Little and for the road tour I'll give you Winchell Smith to
direct it."

Winchell Smith was his partner, the firm was Smith and
Golden. Smith was a wonderful playwright and a director who
was kind and could teach anybody to act. We would have
worked for him free; but that wouldn't be till autumn.

For our two weeks, Frank scared me so I never was any good
in the part. One moment I had to use a breakaway prop. It was
a vase that looked like heavy pottery, but was made out of a
preparation like sealing wax and when I threw it at Gregory in
our fight it looked as if I'd killed him but the stuff broke at
touch. I knew it wasn't pottery, but nobody told me I must *look*
as though I was seizing it and must actually just hold it by the
tips of my fingers.

We never were given it to use until dress rehearsal on the day
of our opening. I snatched it up, it broke in a thousand pieces

in my hands! Gregory just smiled, out front Frank sneered, "I wish you'd use as much force for your performance as you do to pick up the vase. I suppose we'll have to use another one."

Later Gregory told me the property man made about seventy at a time, the cost was maybe three cents.

Well!

It's the worst when you start to be good, have glimpses of what's to come, *then* have it destroyed. It takes time to be *really* confident. If we're sensitive enough to act, then that sensitiveness is easy to graze. I don't know where courage mends itself, but it does and has to.

Live long enough and the circle comes around. Fourteen years after *The First Year,* Frank Craven came backstage at *The Country Wife,* full of praise. He sent me three antique volumes bound in red morocco, *Les Théâtres de Paris.* On the first page of volume one, he wrote:

> Ruth Gordon, a
> great lure of the theatre
> from
> Frank Craven

Live past the moment. Get past it, don't give up, hang on till the valuable books show up and the Oscar and doctorates and people's love pour in.

To be born in 1896 means you hook in with a lot of past. In Quincy the Elizabethan language kept going as late as 1900.

"Where be ye?" called Dotty Miller's grandmother.

We laughed at her talking old-fashioned.

"Don't *do* so," she scolded Dotty. She could have been born around 1834. *Her* grandmother could have been born around 1767.

"Where be ye?" in 1900 still hadn't got lost.

Quincy is drenched with history. I saw Brooks Adams, very old, riding out from the stableyard of the President's house, where he lived on Adams Street. His great-grandfather President John Adams lived there, and his grandfather President John Quincy Adams, whose Ma had taken him out on the salt marshes to see the firelit sky from the battle going on on Bunker Hill. Now the city of Quincy is building a theatre there called the Ruth Gordon Theatre.

Along the way to civilization, don't sit it out and if you were born the right place, use it. At the hard-to-get-into Fontainebleau Hotel, Miami, I asked Garson, "Couldn't we stay another week?" Ridiculous question? Ridiculous question. February, Miami Beach, the trains, planes to and fro are booked solid, so is every hotel. Blizzards in New York, Chicago, Washington, but in Florida that's what we're paying for. All *we* worried about are man-of-war jellyfish that love that warm Florida water where they can nip Northerners.

"Sure we can stay, but who's going to ask? Not me," spoke Gar, a guy who knows what's going on.

"I will," spoke Chicken Little. "Who'll I talk to?"

"The top, Duke Stewart, the manager."

"Operator, please connect me with Duke Stewart. This is Ruth Gordon in suite 1001, 2, and 3."

Pause.

"Duke Stewart?"

. . . .

"Oh, my *God!* You darling, I can't believe it! How could you have been born and lived in Quincy with a name like Duke?"

. . . .

"Well, *my* real name is Jones. My middle name is Gordon after Dr. Gordon. Remember him on Hancock Street?" An aside to Garson, "He's from *Quincy!* He's not Duke, he's *John* Stewart, we can stay a week." Back to Duke. "In these rooms, Duke?" To Garson, "These rooms and *longer,* all we have to do is tell him."

Along the way to civilization be born in the right place and have money. A usable combination right down through history, even older than Dotty's grandma asking, "Where be ye?"

Good acting becomes great acting if you've got the great part.

A night I feel my performance is off I ask myself, Why? Am I making too many pauses? Am I doing great acting?

Pauses are easy to get rid of, it's hard to get rid of great acting. And don't ever get distinguished. That doesn't just apply to acting. Getting distinguished can apply to anyone. Getting distinguished is another term for someone who has retired without acknowledging it. Stay human.

Think it over.

DON'T
FACE
FACTS

How punctual are you? Sort of, or on the dot? Some people think everyone will wait for them, not Alexander Woollcott. He sat at his table in Mr. Mueller's Voisin Restaurant, his guests were due at seven. Woollcott's watch said seven five, seven ten, seven—then Helen and Charles MacArthur walked in.

"You're late, find a table."

"The traffic," reminded Charlie.

"Don't bore me. Waiter, I'm ready to order."

Woollcott waited for no one. Neither did the White Star liner *Majestic*. Herbert Bayard Swope, editor of the New York *World*, was taking his family to Europe, sailing at midnight. At midnight the gangplank rolled off the ship onto the pier, the ropes were tossed off, the whistle gave that hair-raising blast, two tugboats shunted her out into the Hudson River, helped turn her and push her toward Sandy Hook where they would reel in their ropes and the big liner steam away.

At the White Star liner pier, two limousines drove up. In them were Swope, his wife Pearl, his daughter Jane, son Ottie,

Pearl's mother Mimi, Pearl's brother Bruce and his wife Edna, and the Swopes' great maid May, all passengers on the *Majestic*.

"Where the goddam hell is she?" demanded Swope.

"Sailed. It's ten after midnight."

"Call the *World*." He told the ship desk to arrange for a tug. At Sandy Hook, Pearl, Mimi, Jane, May, Edna, Bruce, Ottie, and Swope went up the rope ladder that had been let down for the harbor pilot to leave the ship. Full steam ahead went the *Majestic* to her pier at Southhampton with all aboard.

Great if you're the editor of the New York *World*, not so good if you own *The New Yorker*. Owners Ruth and Raoul Fleischmann drove up to the French Line pier.

"Sailed half an hour ago."

"But my children are on board," howled Ruth.

"They'll be looked after, do they know anyone?"

"Only their governess."

Raoul Fleischmann called up *The New Yorker* but they didn't have a Ship Desk.

Little Gardner and Steven and governess made the trip on the *Paris*, Raoul and Ruth with no luggage sailed next morning.

I'm punctual, but got left once. The Twentieth Century pulled out of Albany, I had stepped off to walk up and down. Early that morning Garson had gone back into the Army, I was on the way out to California to act in *Edge of Darkness* with Errol Flynn.

Where was my mind? The train rolled slowly by and I asked, "Will that train come back on another track?"

"Not till tomorrow."

Draw the veil.

Where was Garson and now where was I?

On an open trolley the place to sit was the end seat. Smell the hot grease, hear the snap of daisies and Queen Anne's lace as the trolley rattled past?

If Mr. Craig was the conductor he didn't collect Mama's nickel, because he lived in East Milton where she and her three orphaned sisters had lived with their Aunt Molly Dewing.

I asked Mr. Craig what happened to the front half of his thumb that was missing.

"It's home playing the piano."

I looked at Mama.

"Mr. Craig is joking."

When he was back on the rear platform, Mama said, "Mr. Craig is a nice man, but don't notice his conversation."

Are you consistent? Run your life by set rules?

"Let's have order, but not too *much* order," said Professor Alfred North Whitehead to Professor Felix Frankfurter, who was leaving Harvard Law School to take his place on the United States Supreme Court.

I wonder if that's the right idea? Maybe not for show business, as practiced at the Women's Club, New Rochelle.

A lean period, no plays offered, better have some money coming in.

"If you're an actress, act," said Thornton. "No matter where, step on any stage and bring it up to your own great level."

On the hall table was a message, "New Rochelle would like you to do 'Saturday's Children' for a week at the New Rochelle Women's Club."

Did Thornton mean step on the platform of the New Rochelle Women's Club?

"If you're an actress, act," he urged. "The great Edith Evans went across the Thames and acted on the Waterloo Road and all London flocked to the Old Vic. Step on any stage . . ." and so forth.

I called up Ruth Hammond, who had acted with me in *Saturday's Children* when we did it in New York. Some parts can be played by a lot of people, but only Ruth could play Florrie. She said she would. "Sign Ruth Hammond," I told New Rochelle, "then me."

Rehearsals were at the Women's Club, Ruth and I went back and forth on the train. Walking to the New Rochelle station, I said, "I have to buy a button for my Act Two apron."

"We'll find one."

"Find one where?"

"Walking along. The world's full of buttons. Here's one."

"Why Ruth!"

"But it isn't like your apron one." She threw it away.

"How about this?" I picked up a brown one.

"You need white."

"It won't really show."

"We'll find one."

On the maple-lined sidewalk, our eyes on the uneven tar pavement, there lay the white china mate to one on my blue checked apron! Did the great Edith find a button on her way to the Old Vic? The New Rochelle button came up to my apron's level, would the Women's Club stage come up to mine?

Opening night going all right, Act I over, in Act II, my husband Rims and I have a quarrel, he goes, my father comes on. The quarrel has discouraged me, I need advice. "Dad, do you think I ought to have a baby?"

In the script, it says her father looks at her, surprised, and that's the way we rehearsed the scene. Tonight the actor playing my father kept *on* looking surprised. Why didn't he say, "What?"

In the play I'm supposed to repeat my question, then he'd say, "How old are you, girlie?" but he didn't say it. This was getting to be too long a pause. If every look took that long, Ruth and I would miss the train. He was *still* looking, maybe speed things up? "I guess you wonder how old I am, Dad?"

Now he looked *really* surprised, because I was paraphrasing his line he was supposed to say to me.

I waited, wondered, went on. "Oh, I know it sounds foolish to ask you," I paraphrased.

He just looked surprised.

Try again? "I guess you're wondering why anybody wants to have a baby. Why anybody should ever want to get married?" I paraphrased his lines, then said my own. Pretty soon Ruth Hammond had the kindness to come on way ahead of her cue. *Finally,* the curtain came down, Dad had not said one line!

The stage manager grabbed my hand. "Oh, my God, oh, my *God!*"

"What *was* it?" I couldn't unclench. "What do you think it *was?*"

"I don't *know!* Oh, my *God,* I give you my word I never in my *life!*" He clattered down the cellar stairs beside me to my dressing room.

Was the stage raising? "But, my God, is he *drunk?*"

"No, I'm *sure* not. I'm sure not. My *God!*"

"But what about Act Three?"

"Should I go on and read the part?" he offered.

"My God!" I went into my dressing room.

A knock at the door.

"Yes?"

"May I speak to you?" It was Speechless.

I held my dressing gown around me and opened the door.

"Can you ever forgive me?"

"My God, what happened?"

"I don't *know* what happened."

"But what *did?*"

"Miss Gordon, I just don't *know*. I don't drink, I never before had trouble with my lines. You *know* in rehearsal I never once had to be prompted. Could you bear to give me a chance to go on this act?"

"Of course." Raise the stage level!

"Oh, thank you." He took my hand. "I'll never forget you for this."

"Don't think about it."

"Thank you, thank you."

"Well, fine. I just have to change now."

Act III opened with the boardinghouse lady snooping around, then my father came on. *Not one word*. I didn't wait, I rushed onstage, flung my arms around my father as I was supposed to do. "Oh, Dad, I'm so glad you came. Do you like my place?" I hugged him hard again, to show I wasn't cross.

Silence.

I reworded his lines. "I bet you think it looks familiar. I bet you think it looks like places *you* lived in before you married."

Silence.

"It must be different, though." That was *my* line and his cue.

Silence.

I reworded his line. "I guess there's nothing new about these places except the boys and girls that live in them." I glanced around the shabby room and reworded his next one. "I guess you're not crazy about this."

That steady stare.

"Well, I'm not either. But they won't take girls in many places and I like their scale of prices here."

Silence.

Could I remember all his lines? "Do you ever walk by our little house? I guess it must look pretty lonely. I guess it makes *you* feel lonely, it's been three weeks. Is that what decided you to come over and ask about it?"

"Well, Dad, I wanted to be alone and I have been."

Silence.

What was his line? "I guess you're going to say I could have my old room back—at home?"

"Dad, I'll *never* go home. It would be like going round in a circle, I'd be right back where I started."

Wesley Addy, who played Rims, my husband, mercifully came on, then the boardinghouse lady and the short third act ended, Rims nailed the bolt on the door.

Curtain!

The stage manager following me down the cellar could only gasp, "My God!"

Ruth Hammond put her arm around me. "I'm as speechless as he was. You were magnificent, darling." Loyal Ruth!

"Well, don't worry, I'll get Thomas W. Ross, who played it with you in Ogunquit," promised distracted stage manager. "I'll rehearse him all day. Don't worry."

Even on the train I was in a kind of nightmare.

Early morning the phone rang. Distracted stage manager, more distracted. "Tommy Ross is on the Coast. I asked our guy what he thought. He says he'll be fine."

"Let him," I said.

"Any stage you step on, pull it up to your own great level."

Second night.

"Dad, do you think I ought to have a baby?"

"What?"

"Do you think I ought to have a baby?"

"How old are you, girlie?"

"Please don't be foolish."

"Yes. I suppose you *are* old enough. That was the wrong thing to say, but looking back at my beautiful wasted youth— why anybody should want to have a baby—why anybody should ever want to get *married* . . ." He was playing the scene beautifully. That night, the next night, all week.

Did I raise the Women's Club stage level?

Do you think if you can handle trouble you get it and if you can't take it it bypasses you?

Professor Alfred North Whitehead, dear, wherever you are, in summer stock you cannot have too much order.

Everybody has *some* courage, it takes courage to get up in the morning. And to go to bed. More people die in bed than anywhere and dying needs courage.

I cross against the red light but that isn't courage, that's New York: If you wait for a green light you must be a Californian or feeble or shouldn't live in New York. If you can make it on a red light you can make it, New York traffic and you are tough.

In *Rosemary's Baby,* the final take was of Fifth Avenue and Fifty-seventh Street, peak afternoon shopping traffic, Mia Farrow was supposed to be eight months pregnant, Roman Polanski directed her to run from one side of Fifth Avenue right through the traffic.

"They'll run over me," quavered Mia, who had done everything so demanded, even eating a raw chicken liver as part of the witch spell.

"They won't run over a pregnant woman, they slow down when they see you," said Roman.

The New York traffic came tearing at Mia stuffed out with four pillows, but that was *her* business. New York traffic swerves, but halts for no one.

Where did I meet her? Facts get lost, thank God, because what does it matter? I met Dumpy Oelrichs and we liked each other. Elegant, blonde, pretty like strong china. No frail teacup, Dumpy.

Every Christmas Eve she and her husband, Herman, gave their party at the Oelrichs' Fifth Avenue apartment.

"This is Herman," said Dumpy.

Good-looking, dark, he stood there, *I* stood there, *he* didn't say anything, *I* couldn't think of anything, he stood there.

Say something, I urged myself.

He stood there, I stood there, maybe twenty people around us talking, *he* didn't, *I* didn't. Out of desperation, I pointed to a sofa-to-ceiling mirror in a heavy gold frame. "That's beautiful."

"Take it!" He jumped on the sofa, started to rip it down off the wall.

"What are you doing, Herman?" asked serene Dumpy.

"Miss Gordon likes the mirror, I'm giving it to her."

"Oh, good."

At dinner I sat next to him. A friend we shared was critic George Jean Nathan. "Do you know his new girl?" asked Herman.

"Some."

"She's a bit of the true cross."

He reported that George Nathan had come for a weekend at Newport. Dumpy asked if he'd like to play tennis. He came down in a heavy once-white turtleneck sweater with a faded blue C left over from his Cornell days. "He was the only tennis player I ever saw," reported Dumpy, "to serve and miss the ball."

When Justice Frankfurter sent me his eulogy of Justice Cardozo, I knew the "Mr. Justice for valiance and truth" was a quote, but I didn't know from what. I asked a lot of people who also didn't know.

At the Oelrichs' for lunch I asked Herman, voted most brilliant in his class at Columbia University.

"From *Pilgrim's Progress*."

Too bad his millions couldn't halt his fierce illness. He bequested a lot to find out how to cure us others.

Christmas at the Oelrichs' was nice and nothing like Christmas in Quincy. Mama's friend Aunt Josie Barnes gave me *How a Little Girl Can Learn to Do Things*. Chapter I, "How to Dust the Stairs. Do not overlook the bannisters and railing and the spaces between the railings."

Might Chapter II brighten up? "To make a duster cut the cheesecloth, baste a narrow hem, featherstich it if it is a present, if for home, hem it."

In New England, if you get a present you use it, eat it, read it. Chapter III, "Make a plate of papier mache, color it pink or green with cake coloring. Select a picture from The Saturday Evening Post, cut it out and place it face down on another plate, pour on the papier mache. When hard, remove with a spatula to loose the edges, it will make an ornamental plaque to hang on your wall or give as a nice present."

On!

Chapter IV, a dessert to surprise. "Freeze lemon sherbert, cut up oranges and bananas in finger bowls, sweeten to taste, cover with sherbert and serve."

Our finger bowls were put away and our oatmeal bowls took a lot of sherbert to cover. By the time I got one bowl covered, anticipation wasn't worth the realization.

Aunt Josie Barnes's book was tiresome, but in summer she made up for it, she grew good strawberries. Back of her house on Highland Avenue there were rows of beauties, also varicolored sweet peas. The house is still there and where grew strawberries and sweet peas are dead grass and parts of a discarded washing machine. The house was full of age with none of its charm, but the back garden had it and to spare. Once Aunt Josie had a strawberry festival. Little dishes of strawberries and cream and powdered sugar and spongecake right where the rusty washing machine lies useless.

Show business got started a long time ago and probably those early actors learned how to do it the same as we. In Rome, their favorite, Roscius, stood beside the grave of his friend, tears welled up. Wrote Roscius, "I took note of the effect, but the fact that I noted the tears made them none the less genuine."

Acting is the use of human experience with talent added, plus living and feeling and thinking. Roscius grieving for his friend could still think how to portray *real* grief and be nonetheless grieved.

There is a difference between real grief and grief acted. In *The Good Soup,* Diane Cilento played me in my youth. One scene only we came together—when we must part, youth says goodbye to middle age. With grief I saw youth move away, no more part of my life.

The Good Soup played Washington, packing the National Theatre, notices fine, but it was an evil play and at the matinee would the ladies rebel? When I walked down the long narrow alley from the stage door to my limo the usual number of ladies were waiting. Would they upbraid me? As a path opened for me to walk through, they broke into applause such as after *The Matchmaker, The Three Sisters.*

In New York, Walter Winchell printed false rumors, wrote that our author had been a German sympathizer, had sided with the Nazis. In Paris, *The Good Soup* was the rage and ran for three years, the author was a Belgian whose French citizen papers were signed by General de Gaulle, Nazi-hater second to none.

Winchell printed, "On opening night a bomb will go off at the Plymouth Theatre." It didn't, but the air was poisoned. Charities which had bought out performances canceled, we closed.

For the last time on that closing night the goodbye to my youth moved me to tears, I controlled mine, but the audience didn't. Diane Cilento moved off, never to be part of my life again. As she went out of sight of the audience, she turned and waved her *own* goodbye to me.

My throat strangled, tears shot out of my eyes. Ordinarily, I acted as if the words wouldn't come, tonight they wouldn't. It was real and totally ineffective.

When Roscius reproduced his tears, they would be *stage*-real, not the tears he shed beside his friend's grave.

Down through the ages we *think* we act it real, but real acting is different from real living.

Humidity, humility, two words that don't appeal.

When did Thoreau find out what he wanted to become? What told him to go to Harvard College? Did Harvard teach him how to write his journals? Did Harvard help him build a life at Walden? Did Harvard show him how to make fine pencils? Where did he learn he didn't want to? Why did he become a surveyor? Was it the search to earn his living and also be out in fields and marshes and woods?

While searching, think what you'd *like* to do and can you live off it. Do you want to make a name for yourself? Be learned? Be a scientist? Be a banker? Be a member of the country club?

Matthew Arnold's "Scholar-Gypsy" roamed the fields and scarce ever came in contact with his fellow man. Was he like Thoreau? In his *Journal* Thoreau doesn't like most of *his* fellow men.

He took his exam and got into Harvard, but I think he knew what would be his life and found the job to go with it.

Bernard Berenson admired paintings and made it earn his keep.

Trollope, a post office worker, liked to write novels and wrote so many hardly anyone knows the number except Nancy Hamilton, who owns and has *read* them all!

Rousseau painted his pictures after he did his hours in the Paris Customs Bureau, then escaped to the jungle in his head. Critics spurned his paintings, made fun of them, he thought they didn't understand and next exhibition wrote a description to go with the paintings. They slammed painting *and* explanation.

Anyone know who those critics were? We know the paintings.

Hard to find your way. At Laurenceville, Thornton Wilder taught French and one pupil couldn't stop looking out the window. Marks for looking out the window were below passing.

Years later, Thornton Wilder noticed a reference to a great ornithologist, the leading authority on bird life. At Laurenceville his interest had been out the window, not on subjunctives.

Outside or inside the classroom or inside your head, keep your eye on what speaks to you, then how to get it to support you.

"Nothing more dignified than earning your living," advised Thornton Wilder.

But be dignified *your* way! You have to not only find yourself, but keep on finding. Directing Robert E. Sherwood's play *The Rugged Path,* Garson asked did he want criticism or should Gar keep mum.

"I'll accept criticism," said Sherwood, "so long as it's not *constructive.*"

Who thought up criticism? Does anybody really know about things?

A career only keeps going with "starts." "Same olds" don't nourish a career.

The Country Wife was over. Now what? Thornton and I talked.

"Another classic," said Thornton. *"Mistress of the Inn, Hedda Gabler, A Doll's House."*

"A Doll's House, would be easier to get produced. One set, four great parts."

"It has to be a new adaptation. Professor and Mrs. Pegaway's won't do for today. You must have a new adaptation."

"Would *you?"*

"I wouldn't want to work over the Master."

I asked Sam Behrman, Lillian Hellman, Noel Coward.

I asked Jed Harris, top producer, if he'd produce it. "Not the old version."

I asked Eddie Dowling, he'd produced a play or two. Odd to choose the husband of the great Rae Dooley of vaudeville and *Ziegfeld Follies.* Eddie sat in his office in the now-torn-down 44th Street Theatre, feet on his desk, hat on like a cartoon of a manager. I asked if he would produce *A Doll's House.*

"Get me a copy." He pulled out a roll of bills and tossed two dollars across the desk. I took them and went home, the production was ahead two dollars.

"I can't get it on," I told Thornton. "Jed will do it if there's a good adaptation, but Lillian and Sam Behrman and Noel all say what do I want to do it for?" We were on the phone, long distance New York to New Haven. A pause. "I guess you wouldn't."

A pause. "I will."

He was writing a play and stopped midway, took pen in hand, studied the German version that Agnes Sorma triumphed in, studied his thoughts and made the best adaption of a foreign play.

Jed would produce and direct it. He'd get a great cast and Martha Graham to teach me a great tarantella.

Rehearse the start of next season.

The Country Wife had closed in New York. It hadn't lost anything, but Gilbert Miller told his partner Helen Hayes if we went another week it would.

"Why don't we see?" asked Helen.

"That's not the way you do it. It will lose, because there's no advance sale. We'll close."

Helen didn't think that was the way to do it, but he was a producer and she wasn't.

That left a long stretch till rehearsals of *A Doll's House*. Ursula Jeans said, "Why not come back to London with me? You don't want to miss the Coronation."

⁄ Ursula and I had become friends in London between that first night of *The Country Wife* at the Vic when she'd looked up from her needlework after my first speech, "Where are the best woods and fields to walk in in London, sister?" and could see only the whites of my eyes. Now it was April in New York and a lot had happened. In New York to play Mr. Horner, Michael Redgrave played in London, was Roger Livesey, Ursula's feller. Soon after we opened at the Henry Miller, adorable Roger seemed to be leaving the theatre a good many evenings with beautiful Edith Atwater.

"Before you go tonight, come in a minute," I said to him. Redheaded, sexy, sandy-voiced, wonderful actor, we liked each other. "Roger, how serious is it with you and Edith?"

Roger, a solid fellow, not one to show surprise, waited before he spoke, then, without irritation, "What is that to *you?*"

"Ursula is my friend, is it serious with Edith?"

"Ah! I don't believe I know."

"I'm going to write Ursula. I didn't want to without telling you." They had been together, was it two years? More?

"Ah, yes," he said.

I wrote Ursula about our conversation, about Edith, an adorable girl. I wrote that if our cases were reversed I would want to know and *I* would come over.

She came steerage on the *Europa*. A momentous struggle on her part, the sight of a wave made her seasick and she loved luxury. For beautiful, slim, blonde, elegant Ursula Jeans to come over steerage won not only Roger's heart but respect. The night after she arrived, they came in my dressing room and asked if I would stand up with them, they were going to be married next day.

At The Little Church Around the Corner, Ursula put her wedding ring from her first marriage in the poor box, and walked down the aisle with Roger to the Reverend Randolph Ray, me beside them.

Roger and Ursula and I celebrated with lunch at the Rainbow Grill, then parted to think it over, they at the Algonquin, I at my small brick house, 60 West Twelfth Street.

When *The Country Wife* closed Roger was engaged for the Theatre Guild's production of *Storm over Patsy,* which he'd made a big hit in in London and which the Guild would produce immediately, retitled *Storm in a Teacup.* Ursula would go back to London to get her flat ready for him to move in. Nobody figured what would happen if *Storm* was a hit. It opened and there was no danger. Roger and Ursula had dinner at 60 West Twelfth, he left for the theatre and Ursula urged me to sail with her, the *Queen Mary,* second class, day after tomorrow.

How could I get ready?

The doorbell rang. "Maybe that's Jed?"

Outside, I heard that inimitable voice saying, "Be patient, Moonbeam."

There was only one dog in the world named Moonbeam, there was only one voice like Mrs. Pat's. Could I believe my ears? Mrs. Patrick Campbell, the original Eliza Doolittle, was paying a call?

Some things no one can believe, but they happen. Mrs. Pat took a seat, Moonbeam was made comfortable and Mrs. Pat handed me a gift she'd brought. A large red velvet coat hanger with a two-foot length black satin sachet hanging from it. In the years to come the sachet wore out, dropped off, got lost, but I still have the outsized red velvet coat hanger, gift of the first Second Mrs. Tanqueray.

Mrs. Pat thought I should go with Ursula. When Jed came he said I should. "I'll probably be over later."

That settled it. Mr. Fleischman, our part-time handyman, lifted the big Vuitton trunk downstairs, no trouble about getting passage, I'd share Ursula's cabin. What excitement to pack and arrange and say goodbye. My son Jones would leave for Camp Rip Van Winkle up the Hudson at Catskill in June. Miss Ryan, his governess; Suzanne, our cook; Katherine Waldron, our maid all thought it was exciting for me to go. Only the previous September I'd sailed on the *Queen Mary* to make my way on the London stage. I'd made it and now was sailing back to loving friends.

Roger waved us goodbye, but it wasn't a sad one. He'd be sailing in a few weeks. Ursula was happy to be going to get everything ready for him. I was excited to go back to the scene of triumph. Roger smiled from Pier 92, Ursula's hand with the wedding ring waved. I was just excited.

Do you laugh more in second class than in first? We laughed all the way to Southampton Water. It started with Ursula pointing to a framed notice on the wall of our cabin:

Your Steward

is

Fred Snooks

Shall we say, "Bring our tea, Snooks"? "I'm feeling the motion of the ship, Snooks"? "What's the weather, Snooks?"? and would he reply, "A clear day, Toots"?

Nobody we ever heard of in first or second class, the ocean stayed flat, I even persuaded Ursula into the pool for a swim, and into the cinema.

"I'll write Podge, he'll never believe it, he thinks I'm seasick if I *look* at a wave."

Southampton Water and in the back of my mind was *A Doll's House*. The back of my mind was a good place for it, look at the Isle of Wight on a fine April day and not think how close I was to playing Nora.

Waterloo Station with shared reminiscences of the Old Vic further along the Waterloo Road. Into a grand shiny black London taxi and Ursula gave her address, College Court, College Crescent, College Green, Swiss Cottage. Through Regent's Park onto Avenue Road and before you reach Hampstead Heath, turn sharp left. We covered a lot of ground, saw a lot of things to point out. Regent's Park was abloom, Avenue Road with stylish houses.

"That one is Maria Tempest's. All English show business referred to her as Mar-eye-a. That one is Cedric and Picsie's." Sir Cedric and Lady Hardwicke. Picsie was short for Helena Pickard, who had played in the New York *The Country Wife*.

"That one John Gielgud used to live in."

College Court, College Crescent, College Green, Swiss Cottage looked the way it sounds. Nothing of an entrance, walk up a flight and into Ursula's pretty apartment. Twin beds in the bedroom, one for her, one for me. *First* shopping trip would be to Peter Jones, Sloan Square, to select a good *double* bed for when Podge arrived. Pretty drawing room with pretty drapes and upholstered couch and chairs. We just looked *in*. All morning in bed, tea and Hovis toast and marmalade. Orange juice for me.

"You'll kill yourself drinking orange juice and tea," predicted Ursula. "Oh, my dear, the tannic acid, oh, my dear!"

We sat up in bed, drank tea, phoned and answered the phone. She was popular, I was.

"Ruth's staying with me."

My turn. "I'm staying with Ursula."

Invites, plans, arrangements, everybody here for the Coronation, everybody with ideas what to do and when. Tony Guthrie, our great director at the Old Vic, was in Ireland.

"I'll ask George Chamberlain for his address." Ursula called a number. George was stage manager for the Vic. "George, Ruth is with me. She wants to write to Tony. . . . Yes, I know, but where shall she send a letter? . . . What? . . . Oh, my God! . . . Wait, I'm writing it. . . . Spell that! . . . Oh, no! . . . Wouldn't Tony have an address like that! Let me read it back to you, George. 'Tyrone Guthrie, Anna-Ma-Kerrig, Doohac Newbliss, County Monaghan, Eire.' "

(to be continued on another blue page)

Edith Evans invited me to go to Coronation with her. The Court had acknowledged actors for the first time in a Coronation ceremony and a few actors were given seats in the stand just outside Buckingham Palace. Edith chose me to go with her.

Up at five in the morning, walk through the trafficless street to meet Edith at her Halkin Street flat. Walk to the stand. "What will we do?" I asked. "We'll be sitting for hours."

"You'll see."

I did.

We watched the first signs of the palace wake up. We watched the gold coach being driven in. We watched—we never stopped watching until all the troops, the carriages, the old Queen and the princesses, the King and Queen passed by. Then while they were at Westminster Abbey, the ceremony taking place, my friend Lady Juliet Duff had arranged for some of us to walk through the Green Park to a private room at the Ritz for lunch and listen to what was going on at the Abbey.

And in and out of all this came terrors about would I be good as Nora in *A Doll's House*?

Asking for the opening engagement was the Festival at Central City, eight thousand feet up in the air in Colorado. What a long way from sitting beside Noel Coward and eating cold salmon at the Ritz while down yonder King was getting his crown on.

Still blue pages

And up in Central City's hotel, lined up with some of last

night's audience at the door marked WOMEN, I thought what a long way from when the Court honored actors for the first time at Coronation and I stood with those people when the gold coach came by.

A Doll's House was going to be all right. So was my tarantella taught me by Martha Graham. So was Dennis King, who played Torwald Helmer and relinquished Dr. Rank to do so. "Anyone can score as Dr. Rank, but Helmer's hard to do and without a Helmer it won't matter when Nora leaves home."

Generous Dennis. He thought of the play, Paul Lucas scored as Dr. Rank, Sam Jaffe played Krogstadt and Dennis King was Torwald. "The best Torwald Helmer ever seen," said Gilbert Miller.

People had said it was too old-fashioned, but it broke the record for *A Doll's House* and beloved Thornton's play that got interrupted midway for Thornton to help set me up in *A Doll's House* is *Our Town*.

Thornton!

"By the time you know how to act, you're too old to do it," said Laurence Olivier.

He says I said it.

"I wish I *had*, but *you* said it, Larry."

"My darling, I quote it often and always credit you," said the theatre's only Lord and greatest actor.

It's October but in Edgartown the pink rosebush is in bloom. The weather-shingled house it leans against is closed till summer, only a trespasser to look at its four pink roses.

"No trespassing by Order of the Edgartown Police Dept." reads the sign. I'm doing what I'm not supposed to, but four pink roses *are*. They bloom even when their owner has left for the winter and nobody on the place to look at them.

That's in the back of the house. In the front, early spring low pussy willows border the cliff that drops down to Edgartown Harbor. I trespass and look at them. Scattered over the lawn are wild strawberry plants, the design of their leaves is on the Queen of England's crown that all Westminster Abbey admires. On Mr. Slater's lawn only one trespasser, with maybe the Edgartown police checking up.

A lady-slipper blossoms among the dead leaves and will fade before summer when Mr. Slater will drive in. If you're fond of a lady-slipper, police, it's two yards on the left side of the driveway, don't break the law and pick it.

Pussy willows, wild strawberry plants, a lady-slipper, pink roses do what they're supposed to with or without anyone looking. Do I? Do you?

Opening nights are awful and unpredictable. Actors' hearts must be different from the rest of the race.

Fanny Brice advised, "Take an Anacin, take two, take 'em till y'settle down." She carried a bottle in her handbag, in her coat pocket. Fanny had a heart attack. At Cedars of Lebanon Hospital nobody was allowed to see her, but nobody didn't include her beloved Spencer Tracy. Fanny's face was white as the pillows that propped her up. Spence gently held her hand. "What is it, Fanny?"

Fanny's eyes were two black coals, her voice a whisper, "Too many first nights."

Spencer nodded. He knew.

Fanny motioned him to lean down. His face went close to hers. "And that fuckin' Anacin didn't help either."

Don't try any short cuts to a first night.

"What does a man do with his despair?" asked Thornton Wilder. In the weeks before he died he was writing down what he thought.

On the stage we use it to improve. Until I was an actress I never had despair. Worry, fury, jealousy, everything else that's a name for trouble. But I knew I'd get things going, I knew I'd be fine, I knew I'd be a star. In my 1914 Quincy diary I wrote, "I am willing to wait five years." When I got in plays I knew it took more than writing it in my diary. When I got in plays and couldn't act I knew despair.

The critic wrote, "Gregory Kelly was perfect as Willie Baxter, but as the Babytalk Lady Ruth Gordon was no good."

I cried.

"It's only Utica, little feller."

Gregory and I had been married four months. He was the star of Booth Tarkington's *Seventeen*. He got wonderful notices everywhere, I couldn't get by in Utica.

"What the hell kind of a critic is he? Utica only gets two shows a year."

I cried. Maybe the critic was not good, but neither was I. Not only no good, but bowlegged.

The end of that season, Gregory and I went to Chicago, convinced the renowned Dr. Ryerson that all I thought of was my legs. He broke them, set them straight so that until I got to be a good actress I at least had good legs.

Despair is your friend in show business. I don't believe you can act if happiness is your lot. It's the ups that keep you living and the downs that mete out talent.

"It's no more than what we deserve," said Spencer Tracy when he and I and Garson were floating in the blue water of our yacht basin at Les Rochers, the villa that Paris Singer built for Isadora Duncan in St. Jean-Cap Ferrat and Garson and I had rented the summer of 1953.

"It's no more than what we deserve."

Anchored offshore was the white steam yacht that belonged to

Sir Bernard Docker, manufacturer of British Daimlers. Was that no more than what he deserved?

"It's no more than what we deserve." When it comes out right, enjoy it for itself and also enjoy it for the wind and the rain on Forty-fifth Street that was a part of deserving it.

Long days of job hunting trying to get to be an actress through August, September, October, now it was cold November 1915 the wind blowing the rain. A long walk to get back to the Three Arts Club, Times Square to Eighty-fifth Street. Try one more place, maybe get a job, maybe get warm. I turned off Broadway and went in a crumpled building. Up three flights was the door marked Billy Shine's Movie Extra Agency. The room was jammed. Did that mean he was casting? Everybody shifted from one foot to the other, the room seemed to bob like a boat.

"Big call?" I asked.

"Big! Day after tomorrow."

Let my coat swing open, tilt my white velvet hat at a more come-hither slant, arrange the streamer with the bunch of cherries over my shoulder where it could be noticed whenever the door marked

BILLY SHINE

PRIVATE

opened.

An extra who looked like Teddy Roosevelt bared his teeth and smiled. "It's Murray's Hanging Gardens, white tie and tails, ball gown!"

In 1915 if you had a ball gown and worked as an extra, it paid five dollars!

The door opened.

The room stopped rocking, everybody turned into a statue.

"Hello, Mr. Shine."

"Remember me, Mr. Shine?"

"I don't remember anybody." Even with his jacket off he was a snappy dresser. "You," he pointed. "You." He did a sharp expert point.

A woman in a purple coat pointed to herself.

"*Not* you." He pointed past her. "You."

Purple coat smiled a quick smile. "Oh, come on, let me."

"Naw."

The smile stayed, the backing went out.

"You. You. You." He pointed to Teddy Roosevelt.

"That's bully!" Teddy Roosevelt could count on five dollars.

"You. You. Murray's Hanging Gardens day after tomorrow, ball gown, full dress, makeup, ready seven A.M. wait till I pass out slips, the rest of ya don't hang around." The door closed.

For a ballroom scene he couldn't have chosen everybody. Tomorrow put on lip rouge, get hired.

The lip rouge looked actressy, Billy Shine would point at me. "You," he'd say.

More people today. "You. You. Not you." He passed me. "You."

Don't give up, go to Murray's Hanging Gardens at seven and bring ball gown, wouldn't somebody oversleep?

At six-thirty the Three Arts Club dining room opened. Only grand ladies on the board of directors would think six-thirty was when breakfast for actresses should begin. Rain beat against the window, some of Murray's Hanging Gardens' chosen wouldn't show up. My white net graduation dress was in my suitcase, embroidered collar cut off, neck cut low to look like a ball gown. Did I really look like a concubine?

Either you have luck or you don't, the stage doorman didn't ask for my slip! "Come *in*," he said, "get warm."

Inside bright lights, warmth, a sea of tables, actors in white tie and tails talked to actresses in anything that could pass as a ball gown.

"Two hundred people!" exclaimed Teddy Roosevelt. "Bully you got hired, sit down."

I put my suitcase under the table. "I'm here if anybody doesn't show up."

He nodded. "A rainy day, people with colds stay home."

The hanging gardens went round like a carousel, on each table a steaming pot of coffee, Teddy Roosevelt poured. How delicious! Five dollars and not get your good clothes wet looking for a job!

"What's in the suitcase?"

"My ball gown, Mr. Shine." He needed someone, I was there, I stood up.

"Did I engage you?"

"No, but I thought somebody wouldn't show up."

He pointed to the door. "That way."

"Where I change?" I picked up my suitcase.

"Where it says EXIT! Where it says, O.U.T. *Out!* Get the hell *out!* I *told* ya *no,* I'm telling ya *again!* Get the hell outa here and get the hell out *quick,* I'm personally gonna see you never work *again!*" His voice clanged all over the ballroom.

Could I move? Could I ever move again?

"Get that suitcase outa here!"

I started to walk around the edge of the room.

"Not *that* way, ya could *hide* on me. *There!*" He pointed across the Klieg-lit dance floor. Two hundred pairs of eyes watched me carry my suitcase across the dance floor.

"And don't ever come back to anywheres near where I am! Ya hear me? I'm talking to *you* with the suitcase!"

"Yes, sir." I didn't stop I was afraid I'd pee, I stepped on somebody's foot. "Excuse me." I didn't stop. *Could* he keep me from working?

The white Klieg lights were behind me.

"Wait," said the doorman, "it's coming down."

My voice stuck. I shook my head. I was out on dripping Forty-first Street.

"*Out!*"

Would I ever work again?

"*Out!*"

Things had to get better, they *had* to! Even on that horrible morning I *believed* it and I was right. I did work. In *Peter Pan,* in *Fair and Warmer*, in *Seventeen*, *Piccadilly Jim*, *The First Year*, *Tweedles*, *Mrs. Partridge Presents*, *The Fall of Eve*, *The Phantom Ship*, *Holding Helen*, *Collision*, *Saturday's Children*.

Intend it to work and when it does, give Billy Shine hell, it's no more than what we deserve.

John Quincy Adams read two chapters of the Bible every start of his day. I tried, "The sabbath was made for man, not man for the sabbath," Chapter 2 St. Mark.

John Quincy Adams read his two chapters before 4:30 A.M., I read mine after I knelt at my kitchen door, thanked God for his loving care, said my prayer and looked for stars, but there were raindrops falling.

A way to feel good is go to a hospital without a suitcase. Feel sympathetic when someone goes with one, but be glad you aren't carrying yours.

"Never let a man see you with a hole in your stocking," said Mama. "I once knew a lovely man engaged to a girl and as she walked ahead of him he saw the hole. Some days after, he broke the engagement."

"One lucky girl," spake Zarathustra.

Good taste *was* a cup of tea with your little finger sticking out. *Now* who thinks so?

Spoon the soup away *from,* never *toward?* Why was or is that good taste?

Soak bread in the gravy if there's no company, if there is, forget it.

Spit at me like you do when there's no company, sneered Mabelle Webb at son Clifton.

Not good taste. And not good taste when Winsor French and chum Leonard Hanna had an audience with the Pope and Winsor started writhing around on the floor. Len looked horrified.

Screamed Winsor, "Can I help it if I have fits?"

Not what the Pope got every day, but did he remember Jesus forgave a lot of bad taste?

Good taste to drink out of your saucer? Mama thought only Mrs. Carlsen, our washerwoman, did. In Las Vegas the owner of the antique shop she ran in her parlor thought to drink out of your saucer was the thing to do, resting your cup on your cup plate. She pointed one out to me.

"I thought that was a butter dish."

"It's a cup plate."

"Oh, saucer."

"*Not* a saucer, it's to put your cup on. When you drink out of your saucer you don't want to put your cup on your nice damask cloth, do you?"

Mama lay down her own rules.

"Ruth, please don't go to stay with Mrs. Cody, Mr. Cody runs a saloon."

What did Mama know about anything? I went. Dinner was in the kitchen, Mr. Cody spit on the floor.

Next day I went home. I didn't care if Mr. Cody kept a bar-room, but spit on the floor didn't suit my rules.

If I write a play about a guy that sleeps with his mother, then put out his eyes, would people say I showed poor taste? When Euripides wrote it, did they say that. Then *later*, "It's a classic"?

Was it bad taste in Providence, Rhode Island, at Colonel Felix Wendleshaefer's awful old hotel that I let the phone ring at one o'clock, knowing it would be Mr. Henry Sharpe calling to take me to lunch? A handsome, charming man, a friend of Papa's from the Holly Inn at Christmas Cove. Why let the phone ring, why couldn't I answer it? Mr. Sharpe didn't give a damn about me, he was being courteous, he liked *Papa*.

I thought how awful I was, but maybe Mr. Sharpe thought, "Thank God, I'm off the hook!"

Could being generous with yourself also with your friends be good taste?

Ever waste anything? Try it. Don't give your chinchilla coat to the Salvation Army, but I hope I can hypnotize myself to throw away unused stamps stuck to envelopes, old tissue paper, bras that don't bra, string, shoes that got out of shape, hairbrush missing bristles, old sour balls I got free on TWA, what's left in the wine bottle, boxes, wire mesh that came in a dish of flowers, writing paper that ran out of envelopes. I'm working on it.

"Waste not, want not." One has nothing to do with the other. I've wasted, I've wanted. After twenty years count up. What's the difference?

First loves were thimbleberries; presents; a letter; lunch at the New England House, a heavy-looking building with a few rooms to stay overnight. The dining room clear of decoration, one long table for twenty, the diners were market men from Faneuil Hall Market and the Quincy Market, lunch was corned beef with dumplings or boiled fowl. Nobody could finish what was piled on his plate and nobody winced at the price. Choice of pie for dessert, pay your bill near the door to the big-bosomed cashier who knew the diners. Her parrot seated on her shoulder had a nod or something to say to each customer.

It's gone. Durgin Park, Faneuil Hall Market, Quincy Market you can find, but goodbye Polly and the New England House, Edward O'Connor loved you. Ed, he's gone, too.

Madame de Gresac served perfect fruit. Perfect every time she served it. No hit or miss. Every peach, every pear, a cantaloupe exactly ready to eat.

She lived just off West End Avenue in the upper Sixties, one room in a brownstone walk-up. In that cluttered one room the table she set was the best in town. Before she broiled her steak she sprinkled it with whiskey, for dessert the nonpareil fruit.

"Where do you buy it?" I asked her.

"It doesn't matter where," said the goddaughter of France's Sardou. "I put it in a brown paper bag, tie it up and leave it in the back of my closet." She opened her closet. A few dresses, a coat, two pair of shoes and in the corner four brown paper bags. "Sometimes a week, sometimes longer. When they're ready you know."

Sardou knew plays, Madame de Gresac knew fruit.

"Like looking for a needle in a haystack," say they.

Who are "they" and did they find it?

Today is the day I start looking. Curtain going up! It's a good-sized needle, I'll find it. Now I have to find the haystack.

There's a rule where to put a comma, a rule for what needs a semicolon, a law says use a colon, start a paragraph, a rule for don't put your elbows on the table, a rule for a man to take off his hat to a lady, a rule to let an old person get out of the elevator first.

Mama loved rules. "Don't stare, it isn't polite." "Don't talk with your mouth full, it isn't pretty." "Use your fork to eat the peas."

Papa thought out stuff for himself. "I don't give a damn if Claflin has window curtains, he may like things to collect dust."

"Muslin curtains aren't dusty, Clinton."

"If there's muslin over the window how are you going to look out?"

There are no curtains between me and Central Park, I want to look at the sunrise. Some seasons it comes up behind the Carlyle Hotel. Right now it's moved down Fifth Avenue to behind the General Motors Building. The sunset is over the Empire Savings Bank; the storms over everywhere, the moon begins over the Americana Hotel that's now become the Sheraton Something and finishes over Fifth Avenue. The clouds are over falling leaves, the snow, the willows turning yellow just before it's spring.

"Have a good day," they say to me. Do they know what they're doing? Does anybody? Even the President of the United States is like the rest of us flounderers. He acts confident and a lot of times acting as though you know what you're doing *works*.

Before acting as though you knew what you're doing, kick stuff under the rug, don't face facts, unless the fact is you won the million dollar lottery, the Nobel Prize. Short of that, don't face it. It may disappear, but if it *doesn't,* act as though you could handle it, do like they tell you, "Have a good day." My address is P. O. Box 585, Edgartown, Mass. 02539, but in the Never-Never Land we learn life is *doing* it, not worrying it or about it.

A day to look forward to when Mama finally told me I could wear my new tan sandals.

What a feeling when you lose something and find it! Or somebody finds it for you.

"Prepare for a rainy day," say the preparers.

How I prepare is get a good pair of gum boots, rubber boots, rubbers. In England they call rubbers "Wellingtons." Get a raincoat you *like*. A summer one, one for winter, maybe two, have four umbrellas that cost enough not to blow away if you know how to hold on. If it's a good one you find out how: they cost a lot. In Paris the great Vedrenne made them to order at his shop on the Rue Something off the Rue St. Honoré down near the Palais Royal. I had three beauties, a violet taffeta with a carved ivory handle at a price that wouldn't *dare* blow wrong side out.

Ever notice the number of wrong side umbrellas in or on top of trash cans? Did you ever see a violet taffeta with a carved ivory handle?

"Prepare for a rainy day," say the preparers, meaning hard times. I never had an umbrella blow wrong side, but the *times* blew wrong side out plenty. At four I fell and hit my head on the granite foundation in East-*ham,* Mass., a splinter of granite got in my temple. When we got home to Quincy, Dr. Gordon operated on me on our kitchen table, his nephew, young Dr. Burke gave me the ether. Ever smell any?

Dr. Gordon cut my forehead open, took out the piece of grit and sewed me up. Teeth wear out, hair thins, skin dries, scars last. I have my granite scar, my scar from vaccination that made me sick for three days, my leg turned yellow and black like a John and David Anderson gingham. It doesn't look good for a leg, but think how you'd look if you got smallpox.

Both legs have two scars got at the Presbyterian Hospital, Chicago. When Dr. Ryerson made a cut two inches above my anklebone, then broke the bone with a hammer, made a long cut over my shinbone, the same distance from my ankle, sawed the bone in two and the same with the other leg. Pale scars that even a summer of lying on South Beach in Edgartown never sunburn or tan.

My oldest scar is the scar on my right thumb when the toilet seat at 41 Winthrop Avenue fell down and Mama said my thumb hung by whatever a thumb hangs by at two years old.

What identifying marks? asks the passport. They should allow more space.

Never mind preparing for a rainy day, prepare to feel good, then get ready for trouble, nuisance, irritation which are due almost any old time and hope they come one by one and never on opening night. Shakespeare wrote a sonnet to say if things are going to come at you, let them all come at once.

Not me. And not close together.

"Where can I go to learn acting?" people ask.

New York streets, Chappaquiddick Island, Crescent Drive in Beverly Hills, the plane. Learning acting is learning not just to look, but to see.

Edith Evans said to learn Shakespeare read aloud the hard passages that lay down the plot. If you can make the plot passages understandable that's the test, you can speak Shakespeare.

While learning acting don't slight the technical side. Twenty-four hours every day do things the way you have to in a play. If you open a door, playing a scene, open it, don't fumble, don't grope for the doorknob, don't miss it, and have to reach for it again. Don't drop things. In a scene I do *not* drop my hairbrush, I do *not* break a tumbler, I do *not* stumble over a curbstone, I do not turn my ankle because if I did I'd want to kill myself and even worse it would kill the scene. Every day use your hairbrush, your tumbler as props to practice on for when you use them in front of the audience.

You begin acting with getting the right things to use, the right things to wear. When they asked Horowitz what he does before his concert he said he makes sure his shoestrings are right.

When they asked Grandma Moses how she started a painting she said she looked for a good frame.

Then, forget some things you're advised. "Any profession that didn't offer me a berth in six weeks," wrote my father, "I would deem it wise to seek another profession."

One August I left home to go on the stage and didn't get in a play till December thirteenth. Not yet in show business, I'd learned its first lesson: never listen to good advice. I didn't listen to Papa's. I didn't listen to Mama's "Never speak to strangers," or I wouldn't have picked up Thornton Wilder and forfeited a friendship from the spring of 1930 to December 7, 1975, which brought his loss. His love and friendship and guidance answer my questions, offer me wisdom though no longer is he in his Edgartown chair.

In the summer, twice a week Thornton and Gar and I met

for dinner. Each had his regular chair. Thornton took his, Gar his, I mine and when Isabel joined us she knew hers and sat in it.

"Thus spake Zarathustra," I said to Thornton. "Tell me about that, I'm using it in my book."

"Nietzsche said it. Nietzsche was rich. He was a full professor in his mid-teens. Full of optimism. Zarathustra was a combination of the Greek Zoroaster and others. How are you using it in your book, dear?"

"I won't tell you." That sounded ungracious. "I'll tell you, but I don't want criticism, I hate criticism."

"I don't like criticism either."

"In my book when I say something I may not want to have sound as though *I'm* saying it, I say: 'A cat has nine lives. Who doesn't? Thus spake Zarathustra.'"

"Yes." He turned toward Gar, then turned to me again. "That's not a bad idea."

We put some lamps on, in Edgartown we don't draw the curtains.

"Thornton, how did novels get started? How did Samuel Richardson think to write one?"

"He wrote letters for a living. 'He says.' 'She says.' 'He says.' 'She says.' Day after day after day and it gave him the idea to write a story via 'He says,' 'she says,' and that turned into the novel."

Maybe refresh his Bourbon and branch on the small table next to him. Gar also helped himself.

"Not ready," I said. "Thorny, what's a philosopher?"

"One who seeks to find the meaning of life. Philo means study of. Soph: wisdom."

"Is Thoreau a philosopher?"

"Yes. No. To me he's too enclosed."

"Emerson?" asked Gar.

"Well."

"Dewey," said Gar.

Silence.

From me, "Tell me about Aesop's Fables. Who was Aesop?"

Thornton consulted his watch. "Hot or cold I go out of here at nine-thirty." A line he spoke on all our evenings. Thornton loved the old Savoy and Brennan vaudeville joke. Bert Savoy telling about a corpse laid out in the parlor.

"He looks so *natural*," moaned a friend, "he looks like he's going to talk."

Camped Bert "Marge" Savoy, "Well, hot or cold he goes outa here Tuesday!"

Reassured that it was nowhere near nine-thirty, Thornton went on. "Aesop was a slave who told stories, his master freed him. All the stories had a moral. The city mouse, the country mouse goes to the city, forsakes evil, returns home."

. On the evening after Nixon has resigned, Thornton talked of Shakespeare. "Remember the great Cardinal Wolsey scene?" He recited a lot of it. "Doesn't it remind you?"

More talk of Shakespeare. "Why did he retire?"

"Well, it's hard work, writing all those plays. He wanted to sit under his mulberry trees. His father had been made a squire, he had the coat of arms.

"Ben Jonson came to see him. 'What's doing up in London?' 'Some of us are getting together a new version of the Bible.'"

"Thornton, in *The Merchant of Venice*, they talk of rings: Bassanio's ring given Portia, the ring given Nerissa, the last line about her ring." "Sens. obs." said the note.

"I'm surprised you don't have the twelve volumes of the Oxford. Remember when Alec Woollcott made a list of presents he expected for his birthday? By prearrangement, Charlie Lederer and Charlie MacArthur and Harpo each sent him the first volume, written in so he couldn't return it."

"What's in it?"

"Oh, answers to questions. All the things people dig out. How the word 'arrangement' got into the language."

"You mean we didn't always say 'arrangement'?"

"No, it's from the French."

"Where does Poe strike you?"

"At home, they said he was a 'magazinist.' In France he was the idol of three poets. Mallarmé, Verlaine, Baudelaire. And later Valéry. They not only revered his poetry, but his essays on how to construct a poem. The French mind loves order and pattern. To have a poet set down the mathematics of poetry appealed to their French soul. Was it Mallarmé who wrote the inscription for his tomb? 'Poë,' they called him. Poe, said as we say it, sounds badly to the French ear. The same with Sue. Pronounced Soo-ay. *Sué* in French is the past participle of 'sweat.'"

"Do you really like *Love's Labour's Lost*?"

"Oh, yes indeed."

"Can you say why?"

"It's a lovely play, it was written for the young students at the Temple. It's very young. All the archery talk is sex symbols. Shakespeare was young. It's a lovely play."

What was the question we asked? And Thornton answered, "The dreaming soul of the human race, we live by the visceral myths, they always turn out right."

Too soon it got to be nine-thirty. He didn't go to bed early, but we do. He would drive his "best little car in the world," a Thunderbird down to the harbor, walk up a flight of stairs at the Shanty and sit down at the big table he called his *"Stammtisch."* The waitresses who in the autumn became students at college, the waiters would gather around, order a Coke or a beer while Wilder would dispense lore and answer anybody's questions. Nobody was a stranger.

Mama, there are strangers and strangers.

DON'T
BE
HELPLESS

No curtains on my back windows that look out on the rear of the Osborne apartment house. Some lights are Leo Lerman's, some Lynn Redgrave's and John Clark's, some Michael Redgrave's grandchildren, Kelly and Benjy Clark. I see the roof of the Art Students League, a patch of Broadway, the stage door of Dick Clark's Pyramid show where used to be Dick Cavett, where used to play Sidney Howard's play *The Silver Cord* at what was first called the John Golden Theatre. A glimpse of the fire engine in the fire station just below our dining room window, the siren, its lights warn "our boys" will pull out. Up above, the MONY sign, Mutual of New York, flashes the time and the temperature unless it goes off which it had done for a month and flashed back by overwhelming request. Things go right, things go wrong, handle a day with care.

On the new high rise left of MONY we used to see men in hard hats riding on an open elevator to start the iron framework for the seventeenth floor, a few days later the eighteenth, later the thirty-first where now a pink lamp lights up, another floor some soft yellow lights and so on and so on at the Carnegie Mews apartment house where nobody wears hard hats.

If you're thinking of becoming a critic, why not make other plans?

Wrote Alexander Woollcott, "The first time I ever went to the theatre was a matinee at the Coates Opera House." Later he became critic on the New York *Times*, New York *World*, et cetera.

"The show was *Sinbad the Sailor*, an extravaganza employing the talent of Eddie Foy. Although I would never see six again, I had not yet become fastidious. When later I would write on such matters I would deplore as heavy-handed such antic moments as when Sinbad, with what struck me at the time as great presence of mind, threw a cake of soap to a man overboard so he could wash himself ashore. In 1903, it had me in stitches.

"On the way home in the trolley car, I demanded how long this sort of thing had been going on.

"When I became a critic, I'd lost that sense of enjoyment."

He *never* lost it, but he was rare, so be rare before you put yourself in a spot where you might really deteriorate.

If you're thinking of becoming an actress, learn to keep going. Keep going till you get a part, keep going in a scene, keep going in a quick change. On the set of *Ethan Frome*, the crew was hauling off furniture, bringing on other pieces and unmindful of all that, Pauline Lord who played Zeena Frome, I who played Mattie Silver, were stripping off our costumes, the dresser handing us those for the next scene when Pauline's breast came out of her chemise. A stagehand carrying the geranium in an old tin can looked at Pauline, made a slurping sound meaning delicious and kept going with the geranium. Pauline, who could get sore at almost anything, laughed and kept going.

Do they teach this in dramatic school? Does a director tell you practical stuff like that? The first night Alfred Lunt and Lynn Fontanne played *Amphitryon 38*, Alfred began making odd gestures, sort of pointing to Lynn above the waist. The curtain came down, Lynn turned on him in a fury. "You played that scene different, Alfred, you never rehearsed it that way."

"Darling, your breast was out."

"Don't tell me things like that before I know my lines!"

Does anybody teach anybody that?

Books I think I'll read over again:
Louis Bromfield's *House of Women*.
Edith Wharton's *The House of Mirth*.
Booth Tarkington's *Gentle Julia*.
Samuel Merwin's *Hashimura Togo*.
George Cable's or George Barr McCutcheon's *Brewster's Millions*.
Willa Cather's *My Ántonia*.
Edna Ferber's *So Big*.
Any C. N. and A. M. Williamson novel.
Kate Douglas Wiggin's *The Birds' Christmas Carol*.
H. G. Wells's *The History of Mr. Polly*.
Thoreau's *The Wellfleet Oysterman*.
Henry James's *What Maisie Knew*.
Alexander Woollcott's *While Rome Burns*.
Schnitzler's *Bertha Garlan*.
Anything by William James.

When you don't know what to do with yourself, read William James's letters, lectures, philosophy, anything, then read it again. Read it till it speaks to you. Begin in the middle or anywhere, some books have slow beginnings.

"When we tour, read *War and Peace*," urged Katharine Cornell.

We were in *The Three Sisters*. The sign out front of the theatre read, "Katharine Cornell Presents."

I didn't read it in Boston, Buffalo, Pittsburgh, Cleveland, now we'd settled for six weeks in Chicago at the Erlanger Theatre.

"Aren't you going to read it?"

"Has it got an easy beginning?"

Said the Queen of the American stage, " 'Natasha came down the stairs wearing white satin and diamonds.' "

Don't write me that's not how *War and Peace* starts, Katharine Cornell, *telling* me it did, started me.

"Why was the world created?" asked Martin in *Candide*.

"To drive us all crazy," spake Voltaire.

Was he thinking of specifics? Was he talking about music everywhere? Gertrude Stein said music should be played only if listened to. Today it's used to sell shoes, wash dishes, take a
shower. Outdoors music drowns out the rustle of autumn leaves
raked with a wood rake and memory of a lawn mower your Pa
pushed after supper on a warm June night, pipe lighted, shirt
sleeves rolled up. Mowing our grass had the sound of home and
peace and broiled baby mackerel we'd had for dinner, asparagus
if they were selling it for a dime a bunch, strawberries if the
huckster drove by and wanted to get rid of what he hadn't sold.
The mackerel Papa had bought off the boat tied up at T wharf
in Boston on his way to the train home. Swimming around in
Massachusetts Bay that morning, now wrapped up in a newspaper and handed over to Papa for twenty-one cents to ride to
Quincy, Mass.

Live long enough and you'll come into pensions, a lovely thing. Presents every month from people you didn't know cared. More or less business acquaintances and mostly a telephone voice or a letter. Pensions and after what age is it you can have pensions and don't have to retire?

Papa was glad to retire and get his pension given him as foreman of the Mellin's Food Company for twenty years or more at $37.50 per week. Six days a week, 7 A.M. to 6 P.M., in latter years half a day on Saturday. His pension was ten dollars a week, later reduced, later dropped. No doctor's bills looked after as late as 1931.

1979, what a harvest. Close to the first of the month Social Security sends me over $500. Actors' Equity Association $135, and for the month's finish $195.50 from Screen Actors Guild.

Writes my bank, they don't want me to be troubled depositing it and sends me a nuisance of an envelope. "Send it to us," writes Morgan Guaranty Trust, "we'll deposit it," but I'm not that blasé, I get a kick out of making a bank deposit. All I ask of you, Morgan Guaranty, is look after it.

Anyone can be talented. To want to be talented is the first step. The second is, be selfish. They go together, it's give and take. Take when you're starting out, give when you've got it. Careers give actors a chance. Maude Adams let me join her company when I had no experience. My first year on the stage was in the admired Maude Adams Company. In memory of her, Garson and I engage a beginner to play a part in each production we do. Be selfish, be successful, be talented, *then* don't forget.

Along the way to civilization have you stuck to your old loves or did you outgrow some? I outgrew cats. Big black Cudah was my first. Then came Billy, half coon, also black, a beauty we brought from Christmas Cove. He got out of his box and ran around the grand saloon of the *City of Bath,* the Bath-to-Boston boat. He looked cute climbing up the leg of a red velvet chair, but some passengers didn't like it. We got him home, then something went wrong with his fur, it fell out and before winter he was no more. Next came Punk, a tough tiger. Didn't give a damn about Mama and me, knew we couldn't deal with him, but took a shine to Papa, recognized tough when he saw it.

I've passed up cats, except for the big tiger that sleeps afternoons in the Superette Grocery Store window, corner of Seventh Avenue and West Fifty-eighth Street. Pints of Perrier water form a wall behind him, piled up boxes of Ritz Crackers are a barrier from the rest of the store. Whatever grocery gives him his privacy he is curled up, lost to New York noise, gas fumes, skateboard kids, heat, cold, he ignores the facts.

When the assistant stage manager calls half-hour before a performance, have your makeup on, be in costume, wig, then run through your part. I do, but no one else I know does except Lynn Fontanne. Astonished at my asking her, "Doesn't everybody?" she asked.

Be prepared. Before I go on the stage, before I do an interview, before a Mike Douglas show, before I give a dinner, I'm prepared. To make it at the last minute is not how I do my best. Assemble myself, my dress, my jewelry or not-jewelry, my makeup, my hair-do, my thoughts, my anticipation, my dread, my inspiration and when the cue comes, when the guest comes, when the director says, "Roll," I don't have to wait for inspiration, I'm ready. Go!

Ever say, "Throng"? I never said it, but I'm going to write places that throng my memory. Every summer I know I'll see Christmas Cove. Every summer I'm going to the Asticou Inn, Bar Harbor, where I never was. What's the pull? Was it because Mary Roberts Rinehart had a house there? Stylish like Edith Wharton, like Edith Wharton she wrote the biggest successes, you still can find Edith Wharton, but no Mary Roberts Rinehart unless her son who's the Rinehart in Holt, Something and Rinehart would have some. Why don't people stay famous? Why Edith Wharton and Henry James, Thomas Hardy, but not Edna Ferber or George Meredith or Arnold Bennett. Read his *The Old Wives' Tale,* then write me why he got dropped overboard. And write me why do I want to go to Bar Harbor. And to return to St. Tropez. Places always lie just ahead. Very much changed, say all, but I see the places I look to see. Bar Harbor is all in my vision, but en route to St. Tropez I'll see the gray town of Cogolin up there and St. Maxim, the leafy houses, just before St. Tropez and the old port and Freddie Vachon. Are he and his gallery there and his mother's shop? The time I saw Picasso he looked as though he'd got his far-out clothes at Madame Vachon's, then went over to Freddie's gallery to have a look-see.

Why can't I get to Paris? Paris is a part of me. To walk the streets, remember, feel the pangs, the heights, put up with what has replaced what. In 1921, everybody said, "If you didn't see it before the war, it's nothing." Each generation gets that. I've been there poor, I've been there rich, I've seen snow on the mansard roofs, I've felt the heat, loved the rain, more beautiful in Paris than anywhere.

"No sun till January twenty-fifth," said one-armed elevator man at the Hotel Raphael, his confidence muscle working fine.

"How can you know it will be the twenty-fifth, not the twenty-fourth?"

"The twenty-fifth," said he.

It was the twenty-fifth.

Rain or shine, hot or cold, rich, poor or so-so, it's Paris. I'll get there.

Nantucket, a ten-minute flight from Edgartown, why don't I step on the plane? At 'Sconset on Nantucket was a theatrical colony, old Mrs. Gilbert, young Madge Kennedy, Patricia Collinge, Frank Gillmore, daughters Margalo and Ruth, DeWolf Hopper. Hard to get there, but actors loved it and got there with a contract signed for rehearsals starting Labor Day. You could enjoy the sun and sand and sea with a contract for next season locked up in your Taylor trunks.

Theodora, in a book I had to part with on Cornhill, went to 'Sconset. What a picture of her and her pretty daughter, sitting out on the sand, another of sister Phoebe bicycling over the dunes!

My next door neighbor on West Twelfth Street wrote a book about 'Sconset. "The sky was the color of an old gray nickel."

I go here, I go there, what keeps me from Bar Harbor, Paris, St. Tropez, Nantucket? I've intended a lot of things and got them. Maybe this summer, juice up my intender!

If William Gillette's play *Too Much Johnson* were still playing I'd buy a ticket just for that title alone.

William Gillette was handsome, could act better than most
anybody, wrote hits, lived in a castle in Connecticut, had his
own steam train, wrote a novel called, *The Amazing Crime on
the Torrington Road.* Anyone who could think up that title
could think up what to go with it.

A title I thought up was *23 Beekman Place.* I wrote the out-
line of a comedy to go with it.

23 Beekman Place, Act I, takes place in a brownstone house
where Katharine Cornell and husband and director Guthrie
McClintic lived. It was beautiful and not like anybody else's
house, all the furniture had been used in their plays. One success
after another, then one wasn't. Nor the next. How about take
down the front wall of 23 Beekman Place? Wouldn't what went
on there interest people? I wrote down what maybe went on and
sent it over to Kit and Guthrie. A good rule in show business is
make use of what you've got to offer. The McClintics had
plenty.

ACT I
The theatre curtain is the
facade of 23 Beekman Place,
one of a row of brownstone
houses. It rises and we see
Kit and Guthrie's room. Emma,
their maid, has brought up
their breakfast. The year is 1945.

"Here, Hon," she says to Kit. "This is you, Shug," to Guth.
(Shug is short for sugar.) The two dachshunds, Elau and
Looney, are lying at the end of the bed. Gert arrives with Porgy,
her French poodle, bringing the mail and papers. Gert is Gertrude Macy, manager of Cornell-McClintic Productions. The
mail is enormous, four or five scripts as well. Lists of phone calls.
Guthrie's manager, Stanley Gilkey drops in. Kit is passing a

bowl of Shredded Wheat to Elau, who has gotten under the bed-clothes at the bottom of the bed. Koussevitzky, conductor of the Boston Symphony, rings up from Boston. Lillian Hellman rings up from her summer home in Vineyard Haven. Guth reads out loud the New York *Times* drama notes and talk concentrates on who has a play and who hasn't and where are the plays coming from. The room is stacked with scripts, but there isn't one among them. *School for Scandal* is wrong for now, and where are the playwrights? Bob Sherwood is in the Army, worse than useless as far as theatre goes, Sam Behrman hasn't got an idea, Max Anderson has locked himself in and no one knows *what* he is doing, Sidney Kingsley is in the Army and Clifford Odets has taken to directing, Marc Connelly is getting up benefits, Ben Hecht is staging pageants and writing a screenplay of the life of Sarah Bernhardt with modern-day significance. Charlie MacArthur is a colonel, George S. Kaufman is apprehensive, Moss Hart is tired, Tallu is opening in a show they have read. Some good lines but no good as a whole. Helen Hayes says she hasn't read anything this season and Ina Claire has read three hundred and sixty-one and not pleased with any. Ruth Gordon had to write one for herself and some people say her husband wrote it for her and everyone says Kaufman put in the funny lines. English actress Constance Collier rings up and wants them to listen to an idea she has.

"It's probably to do a revival of *Our Betters*," says Guth, and does his imitation of Constance.

Gert says why don't they go ahead with *The Bible Story*, and Stanley says he doesn't think people are ready for it.

"F'gawd sakes, it's been a best-seller for years," says Guth.

Kit has to get up and get dressed because she is having lunch with Molnár, who has an idea for a play.

Gert wonders if Maugham would care to write *The Bible Story*, it would give it a good angle, Guth says, "He retired."

"How old is he?" asks Stanley.

"Seventy, but he's yellow."

Kit is gone to take a shower. Actor Clifton Webb and his mother drop in. Clifton says he has been reading the most divine book he ever read, *Zuleika Dobson,* and society leader Helen Astor Hull says it would make the most wonderful play for Kit and him.

"It would be divine," says Mabelle, "and Main could do the clothes. I won't wear a stitch that isn't made by Mainbocher, and Fulco could do the jewelry, it would be the chic-est thing in town, everyone would come to see it, they'd *have* to, it would be a must and Luigi Luccione could do the scenery, he'd do it for Clifton. And it would kill everyone it would be so beautiful and if they wanted to have a divine Agnes de Mille ballet—I can hardly bear to go, but Antoine is going to give me a new hair-do and will kill me if I'm not there."

Clifton has had a letter from Noel and Clifton says, "It must be divine to be where the war actually *is,* and not have it like here with no excitement, but just getting in people's way." His farm is a pain in the ass to get help and fertilizer and seed and paint, plus the fact that how can you pay for everything if there aren't plays? "And Noel writes London is booming and everything is a hit, but all are like *Flare Path,* it goes in London and lays an egg on Forty-fifth Street."

David Selznick rings up and wants Kit to do a picture. Gert says Kit is out and makes a sign for everyone to keep quiet and she says why doesn't he send over the script and Selznick says could he speak to McClintic and Guth pantomimes he is out. And Kit rushes in from her shower and Clifton says he never thought of it before, but she looks so harum-scarum in her wrapper with her hair flapping loose, what about doing *Pygmalion*? She would be divine and Leslie's part would be wonderful for *him.* And if she would say yes, he would then phone and order delivered to his farm one hundred Plymouth Rocks guaranteed to be the finest layers since what's-her-name left town.

The Cornell-McClintic office calls up and says the new Terence Rattigan play has arrived. Talk of this and that and finally all agree to go ahead with *The Bible Story*. Even in its present version, it's the best thing to do and Clifton says it would be divine, and should they do it stylized and Gert says, "What about an Agnes de Mille ballet?" And Clifton says he guesses he will order only fifty Plymouth Rocks. And they wonder if Kit would go for a ballet. And Constance Collier arrives with her dog, Jennifer, and *does* want them to do *Our Betters,* but instead they all agree she would be great for Miriam the rug cutter in *The Bible Story* or Solomon's mother, who got in the hair of most of his wives. And Constance, talking just like Guth's previous imitation of her, says, well, darling, she'll leave it to Guth's judgment and knows he will never advise her wrong.

"It isn't anything like *Herod and Mariamne,* is it?" asks Stanley. Their last play and it didn't go.

Guth hollers at him to spit out the window three times, take off his coat and put it on backwards for one minute and whatever harm he has done may have a *chance* of being set right.

Constance helps distract Guth's attention by getting him to do his imitation of wonderful British actress Haidee Wright and in the middle of it Pauline Lord rings up and says, "Where do you get a play?" as Emma brings in a new script just left at the door.

The phone rings, it's Moss Hart wants to know if Kit would mind singing? He has an idea for a musical.

ACT II
Rehearsal of *The Bible Story*
in the parlor of 23 Beekman Place

Constance is in it and Clifton. Kit is wonderful. They are feeling pretty good about the play and somewhere in it there is a touching, dreamy scene that comes out of the chaos and takes fire even in rehearsal due to Kit and her wonderfulness.

The Motleys, who are doing the scenery and costumes, are in and out. They found the purest little Jerusalem oil jug up on 245th Street, and they have a cashmere shawl from Palestine they got from a merchant marine they ran into and know where to get the only olive tree in New York City, but it belongs to Mr. Goldfarb, the florist's father, who is attached to it.

"That sounds like a story by John Collier," says Guthrie.

More rehearsal stuff, and Gert says, "Boston phoned, there was a line for *The Bible Story* down to Tremont Street when the Colonial Theatre box office opened this morning." And in comes Aaron Copland to play a phrase of the incidental music. . . . And Koussevitzky rings up to say he is only going to play sacred music at the symphony the week of Kit's opening. And the press agent says the Mayor of Boston will present her with the key of the city if she will let him and says the Mayor *knows* it's their hard and fast rule to say no, but if she could make an exception this once he could land a lot of pictures because the Mayor agreed the key of Boston can be an exact copy of the key of Damascus borrowed from Mrs. Jack Gardner's museum, and it would tie up so great with the scene in the garden at Damascus that opens the show, and Kit says she thinks they better not but, "make it clear there is nothing against Boston personally. She has to say no to all the cities." And Constance says, "Dear Ellen could never be made to take a key and it sometimes irked dear Henry, but Ellen would just laugh her golden laugh and say, 'Dear Henry.' I don't say he wouldn't sulk a bit, but of course that was Henry Irving."

The last act gown comes for Kit and she and the Motleys go upstairs to try it on. And all through the earlier part of the play there has been talk about dieting and being careful about preserving one's figure, for until a play is chosen, you don't know whether it will be a hoopskirter and then it would be all right to eat peanut butter and chop suey or anything, but if it's a play with a slim-waisted part, then be careful. Also how an actress can't cut her hair till she signs the contract because she never knows whether to leave enough for her to pin pieces to for costume-style or whether she would wear a wig and have Charles of the Ritz cut off most of it to give it the latest do, and somewhere is the story of did she ever wear a wedding ring? "Only in *Can-*

dida," Kit replies. And somewhere here Guth tells about the threepenny bit he wears in his shoe for luck. And after Boston they will play Toronto and when they mention Canada, they always say Candida, sometimes correcting themselves afterwards. Last night Guth told the story of "On the sixtieth anniversary of Candida-Canada they lighted bonfires all over Candida," and down comes Kit looking absolutely magic and everyone is so happy and rehearsal knocks off and off go a lot of actors and the press man and the Motleys.

Only staying are the actors in the Last Supper, which they are going down to the dining room to rehearse and of course Kit is not in that. Emma has put a tray of tempting sandwiches on the parlor table for Guth and Gert to have later. For Kit two RyKrisps and a glass of cold water. Alone, Kit looks into one of the beautiful sandwiches and there is gorgeous crab meat oozing out all over the place. She looks around furtively, from downstairs come sounds of the Last Supper scene, with Guth chiming in. Their dining room where so many scenes have been laid out, the supper scene in *Ethan Frome,* Mother God Damn's banquet from *The Shanghai Gesture,* the scene *à deux* in *The Green Hat.* Kit listens and feels safe, Guth has taken over the part of Simon called Peter, she takes a little dab of mayonnaise and spreads it sparingly over the crab meat, takes a bite. Great! She looks at herself in the mirror, it doesn't show. Another bite, but she knows she is doing one hell of a wicked thing. In the grip, she can't resist more mayonnaise, salt and in the middle of a gorgeous mouthful, the door opens, it's Guth and before he has a chance to open his mouth she hollers she doesn't give a *damn* what he says, that she has a right to *eat.* He tries to say something, she shuts him up, doesn't care *what* he has to say. Gert rushes in and says they can hear her out in the garden and quickly closes the window, but Kit keeps hollering she's only had cold meat and salad for days and Gert says, "But look how *wonderful* you look!" and Kit says she has got to look wonderful and still *eat,* and bursts into sobs that just rack her. She starts to go upstairs but sinks down on the second step. Guth comes over to her, puts his arms around her, she just sobs and sobs, he gets down on his knees and tries to comfort her, but she just can't be, and he starts to cry too, says *of course* it was all wrong, *of course* she had to eat, and they would right now go to the back room of the Plaza or "21" and eat everything there was, but she just cries and cries and he says she was never going to hear him say don't eat anything again, but would she just do one thing for him, he didn't care *what* she ate, nor how much, if she would only weep like that in Act IV.

ACT III

A replica of Act I, but instead
of it being Beekman Place, it is
the bedroom of their suite at
the Boston Ritz. *The Bible
Story* has opened the night before,
notices are no good.

Emma is serving them their breakfast, having dismissed the Ritz waiter. She has come up to take in the opening and pay her annual visit to the Mother Church. Elau and Looney are on hand and the Shredded Wheat fits fine into the Boston bed. Gert is in her pajamas and a raincoat looking for quotes in the notices, Porgy at her feet. They have all the Boston papers and Guth and Gert are rereading and debating the notices. Constance drops in with Jennifer, and in her conversation there crop up some veiled references to closing and doing *Our Betters*.

Clifton and Mabelle come in and Mabelle says she wishes she had known everyone was going to bring their dogs, she wouldn't have left theirs at home. And Mabelle says their friends, the Welds, who *are* Boston, think it is just Boston, those reviews, and Mainbocher rings up and thinks it's not only Boston but the lighting. And all agree Kit is terrific, but Clifton says *he* thinks people want to be entertained and with the income tax and rationing and nowhere to go at all they don't want to think much.

Koussevitzky rings and tells them, "Look what they did to Wagner when *his* music was first played."

"Wagner didn't have Kit's and Clifton's salaries to pay," points out Gert, "let alone backstage bills and trucking and hauling." And Selznick rings up and wants to know what they are going to do about his script and Guthrie can't remember what he did with it and Emma says she thinks it's the one she read to put her to sleep the night before she came up here and they ask her if it is about Russian people and she says, "It could have been."

Two bellboys carry in a six-foot fan made of pink roses and nestling at the foot of it is a small package which turns out to be a very small Renoir and it is from Billy Rose with a note asking Kit if she would care to star in *The Seven Lively Arts,* his new show, or if she didn't care to do that, would she be interested in Donald Ogden Stewart's *Emily Brady,* or else a wonderful comedy he has with a great part which at present is for a man, but that was only the way it was written and if she likes the idea at all, he could have it *re*written by Friday, as a starring vehicle for her and if that didn't appeal, what about her doing all the wives in *Henry the Eighth,* and Moss Hart phones and wants to know if he could come up with Kurt Weill to play her some numbers from their sequel *Lady in the Light,* which is designed for her and her *only,* and it is the kind of thing Guth directs best of anything in the world, plus which Paramount will buy it for three hundred and fifty-*one* thousand dollars and hasn't even seen a script.

Meanwhile, Kit is mulling over in her mind the script of that play she can't remember. Guth is sure it is *Magic,* but she knows it isn't and Constance, who already has said she was engaged to Sir Herbert Beerbohm Tree, Sir Max Beerbohm, and Somerset Maugham, looks winsome and confides to Gert that she and G. K. Chesterton once had a little something on the fire. Kit has got up and got dressed, she has to cut the ribbon across the newly widened Frog Pond to keep Boston quiet since they couldn't give her the key to the city, when in comes Behrman, who says it's hopeless, the play will be a seven-day-wonder-of-a-flop-out-of-town, but they *must not go in with it,* and Kit is glorious, but it isn't the right thing for her to do, the Last Supper ran away with the show and he doesn't care *how* it's rewritten, the Last Supper will *always* run away with the show, and Kit is a fable, a legend not only to the public, but to people she knows, to her friends, what she does is news, because she has become part of the life of her times. People got engaged the night they saw her in *A Bill of Divorcement,* now take their son or daughter to see her in whatever is her latest play. "Home ties are woven in with your career. 'Going home to Summit your mother and I got engaged on the Delaware and Lackawanna the night we saw you in a play abut the old war,' says Papa. '*A Bill of Divorcement,*' it was called.

" 'That was Katharine Hepburn, Papa,' says their stupid daughter.

" 'No, it was *not* Katharine Hepburn, she may have acted in the picture, but your mother and I went to see Katharine *Cornell* in the play, *A Bill of Divorcement,* and it was riding home I asked your mother to be my wife.' "

And, continued Behrman, "There is something about *real* stuff, I don't know why, it doesn't have to be interesting but it holds interest. Look, if you happen to get cut in on a busy wire, probably no one is saying anything important, but you don't ring off. You listen. Or sometimes through the wall of hotel room when you hear voices, don't you listen? Well, suppose they took down the fourth wall of Beekman Place and people could look *and* listen, Cornell-McClintic Productions could sell standing room for as long as you care to run! And it wouldn't even have to be interesting, just Kit having dinner or sitting around talking about people or things or what they're going to do next, or even talking about how there just aren't any plays."

And Constance joins in and says it would have been divine for Sacha and Yvonne and wonders why they never thought to do it.

"They didn't have to *think* to do it," says Guth, looking straight at Behrman. "Sacha Guitry always could think up a *play.*"

"You'd be wonderful in it, Guthrie," continues Constance, "and with your talent it's wasteful for you not to act. And, darling, I'd fit in, too, I know I would."

And Selznick rings back to see what they have decided about the script and Gert says their ace playreader is giving it her undivided attention and soon as she can be contacted they will give him an answer.

And Behrman says, "Everyone is too rattled to think of a play and what's the harm of doing something real? After all, even Shakespeare wrote Henry's First, Second, Third, Fourth, Fifth, Sixth, skip Seventh, and Eighth."

"Later! Not when the folks were *alive,*" says Guth.

"Well, what the hell," says Behrman, "that was *those* days."

"Those days everything was a hit!" sighs Guthrie.

Kit, looking at him full of love, "Let's order up some crab meat salad sandwiches."

CURTAIN

It could have worked. It could now. Actors do a lot of plays that have no relation to them or to you or me. Why? Perhaps it's the best script that's come along. Perhaps in comparison it seems good, but is it about anything you or anyone else is interested in?

Woollcott said when anyone bores you get them on the subject of themselves. Oneself is a subject everybody is good on.

23 Beekman Place, Noel or Garson or I should have written it. Today when I walk past Kit and Guthrie's former house I block out scaffolding and workmen. Someone is building three up-to-date stories on top of forever memories.

Out in Connecticut what are they building on Gillette's castle? Or his train? Bricks and rocks and steel don't wear as well as ideas, remember we started with *Too much Johnson*? *The Amazing Crime on the Torrington Road*? That leads us to *23 Beekman Place,* just a piece of real estate to you who aren't of the chosen.

"The day was in tune," said Dr. Gustav Eckstein.

A day that wasn't in tune, or maybe it was, was a day I died in Burlington, Iowa, where I'd played two performances. It was almost the end of 1916, for two months I'd been the leading lady of *Fair and Warmer*. There were seven companies playing all over the country, only one worse than ours, but I was a leading lady! I loved my adorable part wearing beautiful costumes I didn't have to lie about, because they really *were* beautiful. A different town every night and after living eighteen New England years now I was sleeping in Ohio, Indiana, Illinois, Michigan, Wisconsin, Iowa, Minnesota, North and South Dakota in a different hotel every night except for Burlington, Iowa, where I spent six nights in their hospital.

Handsome tan boots bought in Fremont, Ohio, had brought a blister on my heel, I put peroxide on, it got worse, hurt more. Gretchen, who played the comedy maid, looked up a doctor in the phone book, God led her eyes to Dr. Thomas Boyd. "I'll drive you to the hospital," he said.

Pay a Sunday afternoon call on a doctor and he says he'll drive me to a hospital? We had a hospital in Quincy past the Faxon mansion, where no one we knew ever went. Aunt Ada's doctor wanted Mama to go and be operated on for appendicitis or ceetis, we didn't even know how to pronounce it, but our Dr. Adams said better have flaxseed from Mr. Copeland's drugstore made into poultices by Mrs. Dunham, practical nurse who lived down the street. The swelling came down and Frank Dunham and I felt embarrassed at our mothers. He had the desk across from me in the fifth row.

Flaxseed poultices, mustard plaster, quinine, Antiphlogistin, castor oil, aconite, laudanum, hot lemonade, Guinness stout, elderberry wine, Smith Brothers lozenges, a recently removed stocking pinned around your throat were tried before a hospital. People got born at home, got sick, got well, died there, funeral in the parlor, chairs brought by Mr. Fay after he'd placed the coffin, moved the sofa, hung the purple ribbon on the front door. When they carried the coffin out across the front porch, down the steps Mr. Fay picked up chairs and purple ribbon for next time.

"I'll drive you to the hospital," was the second worse thing I'd ever heard.

"Get out, you'll never work again," was the worst, but I didn't believe him.

"I'll drive you to the hospital."

Did I hear right? "My things are at the hotel." I sounded cool.

"Your friend will bring them."

Gretchen nodded.

"Put on your stocking, I'll let you have a warm slipper."

We drove off. "Never go with strangers," Mama had warned.

The hospital was large, up-to-date, white-uniformed nurses, men in white coats. I registered, got in the elevator. My private room had a window looking out on a side street. It was nice. A pleasant nurse listened to what Doctor told her.

"You get her things," Doctor told Gretchen.

"I'll be right back." She winked, but she always did that, she'd be right back, and tomorrow night when she played my part in Iowa City would she be better than me? Nurse handed me a hospital nightgown. In bed she raised my leg onto a sort of trapeze.

"Blood poisoning has started," said Doctor, "we have to drain it."

"What if it doesn't drain?"

"You'd lose the leg, gangrene."

Gretchen came back with my suitcase packed. Our trunks were never brought to the hotel, only to dressing rooms.

"My trunk key is in my pocketbook."

Gretchen found it, though what use? I was small, she was tall. My costumes couldn't get on her, but giving her my key was behaving right.

"You better be alone," said Nurse, "we'll be doing hot compresses and tests. Your friend will understand."

"Tell Mr. Ryder," I said. Mr. Ryder was our company manager.

Tomorrow morning the company would leave on the 7 A.M. train. I'd been with them only since Thanksgiving in Hillsborough, Ohio, then three nights later open in Circleville, but time in show business isn't time you can measure, a company is a family.

Gretchen was gone, my leg was up in the air. Gangrene? But I didn't die until 7 A.M. Were the company getting on the train? My leg up, red scratches still red, still hurting, compresses growing cool. A winter Monday morning, *Fair and Warmer* was leaving Burlington for Iowa City and I dropped out of my life. Through the door came an unlikable breakfast, at noon an unlikable lunch. Then a box of flowers the company had taken up a collection for. "Get well and hurry back," signed:

"Gretchen, John, Grace, Billy, Mr. Ryder, Claude, Jack, Bessie."

Flowers, but my people were gone.

"Miss Ruth Gordon?" A short dark-haired man stood at my door.

"Never speak to strangers," said Mama.

"Yes?"

"I brought this for your dinner." He took the white cotton napkin off his grape basket. Under the napkin, a raw steak, a baking potato, little boiling onions, a piece of lemon pie. "I'm Mr. Reilly of Reilly's Cafe, the troupe was in for breakfast and paying his check your leading man said, 'Our leading lady is left behind in the hospital, any courtesy you show her is appreciated by the profession.'"

I *didn't* die. The company had told Mr. Reilly to be my friend. He came every afternoon, basket in hand, napkin over a chicken, carrots, apple pie. Next day, napkin over two lamb chops, veg, a cup custard.

Doctor's wife brought me a small Christmas tree. From a friend of Doctor's came a bowl of china lilies.

"The red scratches have gone down," said a pleasant nurse, "but if you don't have a bowel movement, I'll have to give you an enema."

Gangrene? Enema? No one in my family ever had either. Nurse went out and I got my leg off the trapeze against orders, hopped to the bureau on my good leg, got the Pluto Water Gretchen had brought from the hotel, drank most of it. Back in bed, worried, got up and drank the rest.

The Sunday after I entered the hospital I left on the 5 A.M. train. The day before, Doctor had let me go in a taxi to buy white satin slippers to wear in the show. Doctor had told the shoe man to take out the stiffening over the heel.

One foot in a comfy slipper I started the long ride to Sioux Falls, South Dakota. The company said they were glad I was back, but the way they said it, Gretchen had been better.

Four years later, a hot summer night, Gregory and I in Booth Tarkington's *Clarence* played Burlington. Mr. Reilly closed Reilly's Cafe after dinner, he and Mrs. Reilly came to the show with Dr. and Mrs. Boyd. After the performance they brought Gregory and me back to Reilly's Cafe where, shutters closed, a sign on the door, NOT OPEN TONIGHT, Mr. and Mrs. Reilly served Dr. and Mrs. Boyd, Gregory and me after the theatre.

"Any courtesy you show her is appreciated by the profession."

Remember the spring day your mother didn't make you wear long woolen underwear?

For refinement do you have to go through marriage, children, career, money, no money, health, L. B. Mayer, who was head of Metro-Goldwyn-Mayer, summer stock, winter stock, children's careers, children's children getting born, what to wear? What to eat? Try that new skin food? I tried it first when I was twenty-four, playing Savannah, Georgia. I had written to a place called Elizabeth Arden in New York and at the Desoto Hotel, Savannah, a package arrived. Venetian skin food to be patted on the face with Elizabeth Arden's costly version of a small flyswatter, covered with chamois.

I spread Venetian skin food on my face, patted each side a hundred pats. Did I keep it up? Should I do it now? Should *you?*

All the cares that infest the day *and* night and out of all the joy and fright and worry and hope and wondering and counting on and faith and symptoms and getting let down and making both ends meet and making a hit, calming down, pepping up, be on time, out of all that comes refinement. I don't know what comes from Venetian skin food.

Out of the whirling snow in Central Park, no jogger in sight, no stroller, no taxi, out of the white world came a present. On the wrapping paper were printed yellow tulips, wide open pink pink roses, clusters of little pink flowers, a yellow butterfly, two cosmos, scarlet poppies, a bright pink silk ribbon tied in a bow. I was writing this book and didn't stop, but after dinner said to Gar, "Maureen sent me a present." It was the English girl's diary with her pretty drawings, scattered over the page of the appropriate months, tansy for May, roses and peonies for June, November chrysanthemums and autumn leaves, in March two sturdy farm horses pulling the plow, with a quote from Tennyson, for October a quote from Matthew Arnold.

"I know you will love this," writes Maureen O'Sullivan.

Is that often true of a present? George Cukor gave me an antique brooch, chrysoprase in a Tiffany box. "It's not from Tiffany's," wrote George, "but it's valuable."

I sent it to Katherine, my schoolhood friend in Quincy. "Why don't you ever wear it?" asked George. Some people send a present and that's that, George doesn't take an effuse thank-you. Katherine mailed it back to me, I wore it, pointed out to George how beautiful it was, how I loved it and him, sent it back to Katherine, insured, George might be right about valuable. "I know you will love this," wrote Maureen, who has been through everything and come out with not only refinement but with knowing how to send a present I love.

The last time I graduated was June 24, 1914, this June 22 I'll be coming back for our reunion. It'll be at The Neighborhood Club on Presidents' Hill in Quincy. I'll fly from New York or our home on Martha's Vineyard, where we didn't secede from the Commonwealth.

Long before the event I'll have mailed in my check for eight dollars and fifty cents, marked a cross where it says, "Do you want baked chicken or scrod?"

Our English teacher, Miss Sally Dawes, a stickler for language meaning what you mean it to mean, would ask, "Is 'want' the correct choice of verb? Or would it be more exact, 'Mark a cross opposite which you hate least?'" In third-year English, Miss Dawes explained "L'Allegro." I never liked it much after that.

Seventeen of our class will show up, the same photos are scattered around, copies of our school magazine *The Goldenrod* will be on exhibit, it won't be very interesting, but it would be very *un*interesting to miss it. 1914 to 1979, we have come one helluva long way.

"Are you?" asked the lady following me.

"Yes."

Her face lit up. "Lillian Gish!"

"No."

Her smile faded.

Couldn't I have said, "Yes"? Who would *that* have hurt!

"Plus ça change," forget it! Some things last, some disappear, get lost, go broke, quit, but look for the Algonquin Hotel, it's still there. Frank Case and Bertha don't run it anymore, the elevator boy that ran the elevator for thirty-one years isn't running it, but it's the same elevator, at the desk pleasant Mr. Mitchell isn't shuffling papers and pleasing guests. Miss Bush isn't smiling and waving from the switchboard, Alexander Woollcott and Harold Ross and George S. Kaufman and Marc Connelly and Frank Adams and Dotty Parker, Bob Benchley, Robert E. Sherwood don't lunch at the round table, but the table's still round and in the Rose Room. It didn't use to have a name, it was just a table in the unpopular dining room. Mrs. George S. Kaufman hired it one night, a party for her analyst, and everybody was surprised to be in there not at the big table and not lunch.

My first time at the Algonquin Hotel was years before I knew all the above. Olive Templeton took me there. I was going to be eighteen years old any minute. She was an actress who looked me up because her mother in Brookline told her to. In 1914 we sat in the long narrow dining room, the popular one, where Frank Case had a big black woman playing Aunt Jemima in calico, kerchief and cap. She cut hunks of chocolate, coconut or caramel layer cake. Olive Templeton and I sat at a booth to the right of Aunt J. "John Drew stays here," said Olive, making sure I knew what a grand place she was taking me when she could have just crossed West Eighty-fifth Street and had dinner with me in the Three Arts Club where I lived and she was a non-resident member. After our grand dinner we walked down Sixth Avenue to Thirty-ninth Street's Maxine Elliott Theatre, where she was acting in *The Rented Earl,* starring Lawrence D'Orsay. "Would you like to come to my dressing room?" she asked.

After she got made up and in her costume, she let me stand behind the scenes with her, introduced me to one of the actors, told him this was my first time backstage.

"Excuse me," he said, "I must get into my part," stepped off a way and did gymnastics gestures, strange movements, his cue came, he went on.

After the play I told Olive that at dramatic school they hadn't taught us that, how did he know what to do?

"Well, dear, I guess he was just joshing you."

I thought a long time about it. Maybe it would be a good thing to really do. *Not* go from offstage conversation into a scene, but bring something on with me, a different mood, a different feeling that would cut me off from the real world.

Anywhere I go I'm likely to learn things and backstage at the Maxine Elliott Theatre, Albert Brown taught me what to do before every play, every movie, before *Where's Poppa?*, *Mrs. Warren's Profession*, *Harold and Maude*.

Everybody has to find his own cutoff from the world, mine is Arnold's:

> Go, for they call you, Shepherd,
> from the hill . . .

Sometimes that's it, sometimes I keep on. Coventry Patmore's:

> It was not like your great and gracious ways! . . .

And his:

> My little Son, who look'd from thoughtful eyes . . .

And his:

> Here, ever since you went abroad . . .

And after the poetry when I've gone out on the set, before assistant director says, "Roll 'em," I'm off to one side, not doing Albert Brown's gestures, but a cutoff from studio, director, makeup girl or fellow, hairdresser smoothing down or poking up my hair, I'm off working up feeling. Whether my part is sad or wild I have to feel feeling.

> I only walk our wanted road,
> the road is only walked by me . . .

What has that got to do with *Inside Daisy Clover*?

Feeling begets feeling.

Backstage at *Mrs. Partridge Presents* the company asked Guthrie McClintic why was I so stuck-up? Why wouldn't I talk to people?

"She's not stuck-up, she's reading poetry to make her cry."

"She's not playing a sad part, her part's funny."

"I don't know *why* she does it, I'm just telling you she does."

A lot can change in one evening. With Olive Templeton I got introduced to the Algonquin and backstage at the Maxine Elliott Theatre how I'd prepare for every performance I'd ever play. Before that night I never knew you had to prepare and since that night no one has ever told me.

The hotels in New York I'd heard of were the Waldorf-Astoria, big and sprawly and terra cotta color, where the Empire State Building is now, the Astor Hotel in Times Square, the Ritz Hotel, so stylish it didn't have a sign on it and I was so green I didn't think to look in a phone book.

A hotel where "John Drew stays" was something to know and still is. Today it's where Laurence Olivier stays. Mr. and Mrs. Bodne, the owners, live in the tenth-floor suite where Gregory and I lived, only now those two rooms and the two rooms where Clifton and Mabelle Webb welcomed Marilyn Miller and Jeanne Eagels and Ethel Barrymore and Laurette Taylor are part of one grand suite plus the single across the hall where Ralph Forbes stayed when he left London to make his New York debut in *Havoc*.

From the lobby, climb the steep iron staircase between the bar and ladies, turn sharp left at the top and through the door on the end went Woollcott to write his next morning's review for the New York *Times*. Same stairs, same door into the same suite, doorknobs look the same, but so does everything. That's the Bodne touch, paint and repaint and repair so it looks as if nothing changed.

Looking downtown, Gimbel's is where it was and Macy's and Altman's. You can still see the Flatiron Building whose picture was on Mama's jigsaw puzzle she had plenty of time to work on at Mrs. Gould's Nursing Home, East Milton, while I was job hunting on Broadway and for one night having grand food at the Algonquin. Olive suggested we start with oysters on the half shell. How do I remember I did that in 1914? They were the first I ever saw served in the shell on a plate of crushed ice. Sometimes Papa brought a dozen home from the Boston Market in a watertight box. Mama wouldn't eat them raw, but Papa and I liked them with a little vinegar, lemons cost money.

On Fifth Avenue, Lord and Taylor's had come up from Twenty-eighth Street, elegant Franklin Simon's was where Something and Something Sloane's furniture store is and Bonwit's was across the street, Tiffany's was on the same side between Bonwit's and Altman's. And catty-corner across Fifth Avenue was Mary Elizabeth's Tea Room for lunch and tea, not one thing served that wasn't perfect.

Perfect Lady Baltimore cake and perfect crullers and perfect vanilla éclairs and ice cream like you made in the White Mountain freezer, turning the crank and adding ice and rock salt, biscuit shortcake when strawberries came to town, chicken salad with nothing in it to doubt! Shrimp salad, lobster salad if anybody could afford it, hot fudge sauce, hot gingerbread, with lashings of hand-whipped cream not flavored with vanilla.

Up at Forty-second Street was the Public Library. Hours could go by reading *Theatre Magazine*.

"Look over anybody's shoulder there," said Thornton Wilder, "and ten percent are reading about the occult, ten percent, religion."

ABOUT
EVERY-
THING

Reading *Theatre Magazine* I didn't know what anyone was reading.

Coming up Fifth Avenue after Forty-second Street nothing is the same until St. Patrick's. Then nothing till Central Park. The only grand dress store still doing business at the same stand is Henri Bendel, whose doorman is the same since 1934. How do they stay in business and not Sallie Milgrim? Or Lucile, Lady Duff-Gordon? Or Giddings or Hollander or Herman Patrick Tappé or Nathan Gibson Clark or Madam Frances? Cammeyer or Slater or Dean's or Stein and Blaine or Ferlé Heller? Wouldn't you like a hat from Ferlé Heller? You bet you would!

Plus ça change, why no more Japanese Garden restaurant at the Ritz? Why no Ritz? Why no Castle Cave with oysters on the half shell served in glowing ashes down Seventh Avenue somewhere. Why no Billy the Oysterman? Why no Dinty Moore's where if you ordered a hamburger without onion he asked you to leave? Why no green double-decker Fifth Avenue buses, top open to the sky? Why no Maillard's for hot chocolate, nor Huyler's for ice cream soda, no Child's for butter cakes or wheat cakes and maple syrup? Why no Sixth Avenue Rotisserie? Why no Brevoort Hotel with the great restaurant? Why no Lafayette, small and unobtrusive and obviously not the famed restaurant you were looking for, but eat there and you thought you had died and got into heaven. In the hall a picture of French actor Coquelin, who stayed there when he came over with Sarah Bernhardt. Where does stuff get lost to? *Plus ça change* it never comes back.

Why no Forty-fourth Street Delmonico's with *everything* great? Why part with East Forty-eighth Street's small elegant Crillon Hotel? Did you ever have a Welsh rarebit at Mock's on Eighth Avenue and Forty-eighth Street next to the fire station? Where's Pirolle next to the Lyceum Theatre? What chocolate and vanilla éclairs! On Forty-fifth Street the Lyceum is there, sometimes it's a long time between shows. "Do you honor the profession?" I asked the company manager, and showed him my new printed card:

RUTH GORDON
CHARLES FROHMAN MANAGEMENT
PETER PAN
THE LITTLE MINISTER

That was 1916, only one card left. Why no cards like that now, *plus ça change* it's harder to get a pass.

The manager wrote "Okay" and his initials, box office man gave me a pass to enjoy Ethel Barrymore in *Our Mrs. McChesney,* by Edna Ferber. Why doesn't anybody read her books?

Up over the Lyceum was the rehearsal room where two girls and I practiced the pillow dance for the part of Nibs in *Peter Pan* and that night Maude Adams' director, Homer St. Gaudens, rang me up at the Three Arts Club and said the single greatest thing I ever heard, "You're the worst dancer, but you've got the job."

Hurrah for when luck turns! It will if you don't drop dead. Now I wasn't *going* on the stage, I was *on* the stage!

Did someone say words to you that changed your life? When
Papa said, "What makes you think you got the stuff it takes?"
his ten words opened the way. I'd have been an actress anyway,
but when he said that I could surface and ask for help, could
write for the American Academy of Dramatic Arts catalogue,
ask Papa for the twenty-five-dollar application fee, request a
room for next October at the Three Arts Club, reserve passage
on the Fall River Line boat, tell everybody. Tell everybody!
How would you like to live at 14 Elmwood Avenue and when
somebody said, "What are you going to do, Ruth?" say "I'm
going on the stage."

"She *talks* of going on the stage," said Mama, "but it's a long
time off yet and people have been known to change their mind."

Not people named Ruth Gordon Jones, who'd seen *The Pink
Lady* and gotten a letter from Hazel Dawn. *Plus ça change,* I'd
still find a way to go on the stage.

Plus ça change, what change was going to take place if
Ruthie Selwyn couldn't find a backer? I'd told her I'd do *Here
Today* in a revival and now if she dug up the money I'd have
had to turn down the offer from RKO, the movie company, to
play Mrs. Lincoln in Sherwood's *Abe Lincoln in Illinois.* I
hadn't been in a movie since I was an extra at Fort Lee, New
Jersey. Now opportunity had knocked at 60 West Twelfth
Street, where Thornton Wilder and I sat out on the front steps
or in the parlor and decided what to do next in my career. Now
opportunity rang the doorbell at 60 West Twelfth, but I'd given
my damn word to Ruthie Selwyn. "Do you think you'll get the
money?" I asked her.

"I think Stuart Scheftel will put it up."

"Who's he?" Her answer went out the window. What if he
did and I couldn't be in the movie?

"You can't be a damn fool *all* your life, just say you won't do
it." That was former lover Jed Harris.

"Stuart won't do it." That was producer Ruthie Selwyn. "I'll
get someone else."

"Ruthie, I'm not going to do it. I'm going to California to be in *Abe Lincoln*."

Draw the veil.

In London, the summer before, Sherwood had brought the script of his play for me to read at the Savoy Hotel. It was going to be the newly formed Playwrights Company's first production, to start rehearsing in New York, early September.

"I love it," I told Sherwood and Madeline at Great Enton, their house in Witley, Surrey. "Who will play Mrs. Lincoln?"

"I hoped *you* would," said Bob.

Should I have? I'd just played Nora in *A Doll's House*, Marjorie Pinchwife in *The Country Wife*, Mattie Silver in *Ethan Frome*, and now a supporting part? Maybe better to do than *The Birds Stop Singing*, where I was the whole show and got that end of the stick, but now I had the part in the movie.

An actor's life is hard, but there are days when things let up.

"Max Winslow who's been associated with Irving Berlin for years will represent you," phoned Jed from the Coast. "Say you won't make a test. If you do, you'll lose the job and right now they *want* you. Say your salary is two thousand a week, don't take less, Max Winslow will handle it."

Sherwood and Madeline had already gone out to the Coast. Shooting on *Abe Lincoln in Illinois* had started up in Oregon.

"They want you for Mary Todd." That was Max Winslow long distance from Hollywood, a nice voice, not hurried. "They want you for two thousand and you billed second to Massey, a drawing room New York to L.A. and return, four weeks' guaranty. They're up in Oregon, they'll be back before Labor Day and need you right after."

When the cup runneth over, say thank you.

Madeline called up to ask should they reserve a sitting room and bedroom for me where they were? The Chateau Elysee was a spacious family hotel on Gower Street, the bottom of the hill was the RKO Studio.

Jed phoned. "When Jones comes back from camp at Orleans

I want him to come out to California till Friends Seminary starts. Miss Ryan can bring him, maybe bring Richard Bray."

In show business, money coming in changing lives, mine, my son's, his father's, his governess', his friend Richard, who lived just behind us, on West Eleventh Street. A movie career starting up takes in a lot of lives, gives a lot of help, opens a lot of new chances.

Drawing room to Chicago on the Twentieth Century, in Chicago a drawing room on Super Chief. Everything super but the scary news, war any minute. Marlene Dietrich's drawing room was next to mine, she got out for the ten-minute stop at Trinidad in Colorado and strode up and down. Town folks had come down to the station to watch the grand train. A mother holding her little girl's hand watched Marlene.

"Would you want her to be like that?" asked the woman standing beside her.

"Noooooo!"

Why was a life up in the Rockies in Trinidad better than Marlene's?

Jed met me at Pasadena. RKO had a limousine to meet me and a photographer whom Jed brushed aside. RKO didn't care for that, but settled down. I drove with Jed, the RKO car brought my luggage.

Jed had ordered lunch at the Chateau Elysee for us and Bob and Madeline. Hotel pleasant, suite fine, food no treat.

In the afternoon, chauffeur Leo Proust drove the Tanner limousine I'd hired for my stay down Gower to the studio. Fittings for my wonderfully beautiful costumes Walter Plunkett had designed. His last picture job was Vivien's clothes in *Gone With The Wind*. A hair color discussion with Hazel Rogers, who'd be in charge of my hair. Massey and I kissed, I was introduced to director John Cromwell, who later said he'd heard I was hard to direct and meant to cut me down. "I want your hair Chinese black."

Dark hair, but why Chinese black? I drove in to Saks Fifth

Avenue in Beverly Hills and talked to their Miss Parker, who
knew all there was to know about making you auburn, blonde,
brunette, chestnut. "It could wreck your hair, Chinese black dye
gets inside a hair and nothing's ever the same. Very dark is all
right, but for Chinese black wear a wig, I wouldn't dye it."

Back to the studio. Mel Burns, head makeup man, said they'd
do it there, but I believed Miss Parker. She had her oddities, "If
you cut your hair and it's a new moon, your hair will surprise
you."

My hired limousine, my chauffeur at the wheel, drove me to
Max Factor's, who had an order to get my Chinese black wig
out *fast*.

Nothing more that day, Madeline suggested we go to
Farmer's Market. She'd been my best friend for nine years and
I'd never been to market with her, but anyone would want to go
to this one. Booths of everything, everything that you'd want.
Peas, corn, spinach, endive, romaine, chives, radishes, potatoes,
sweet or white or the little pink ones, artichokes, avocados, carrots, scallions, strawberries, blueberries, watercress, raspberries,
loganberries, gooseberries, every kind of apples, pineapples, every
kind of pears, grapes, honey, fudge, salted nuts, bread from San
Francisco, bread from France, Norwegian bread, Jewish rye,
whole wheat, graham bread, loaves the size of sofa cushions,
loaves the size of a roll, the Farmer's Market has it and don't
forget the fish stands, the butcher, the sausage, the cheese, the
counter where they squeeze fresh carrot and fresh coconut juice.

No wonder Madeline liked it. She had been a Mack Sennett
girl and Ben Turpin's leading lady and if you've been an actress
you can cook. "I feel like cooking dinner," she said and picked
out a lot of potatoes. Dinner was potato soup, mashed potato, a
sweet potato dessert. My best friend now for forty-nine years,
whom I've visited at her apartment in the Elysee Hotel, New
York, the Chateau Elysee in Hollywood, her English home,
Great Enton at Witley in Surrey, 25 Sutton Place, the house at
East Hampton, her apartment in the East Sixties, but the potato

dinner was the only one I ever saw her cook. Without being Mrs. Lincoln would I have known what my best friend could do with a bag of potatoes?

"Everyone has more to them than what surfaces," spoke Zarathustra, who gets it right more often than not.

Next night Sherwood took us to dinner at Chasen's and he and they got it right. Fittings and interviews and the studio had me worn out. "I'm tired," I said. "I've never been to Chasen's and I know it's the place, but I don't think I can even talk."

"Have a vodka," recommended Madeline.

"Will it rest me?"

"Yes, and you'll *love* to talk."

True.

Back at Twelfth and Eleventh Street, Jones; Richard, his classmate at Friends Seminary: his governess, Miss Ryan, were getting things packed to come to California.

"They'll come to the Grosvenor with me, then we'll take off," said Jones' dad.

At Gower Street, my first day's shooting was the scene where Mary Todd, soon to be Mrs. Lincoln, was visiting her sister in Springfield, Illinois, receiving afternoon callers, among them Mr. Lincoln. I wore the beautiful dress Walter Plunkett designed, pink silk with a black trim. The Chinese black wig was ready, not easy to wear, but elegant. The scene was good.

John Cromwell stopped the rehearsal, cut a line. To cut a line isn't bad, but to snip one out of the middle of a long speech makes it hard. Was that how he'd cut me down? He'd been an actor and actors know that's hard.

Start again. I got mixed up, got scared, did it. On! Now another snip and I went up. Now I really was scared. They told Massey we wouldn't get to the scene with him; he went home, we nightmared on. Every take I got mixed up. We got the scene on the fifty-seventh take. Had he cut me down?

When we became friends John told me he'd felt he should cut me down.

Draw the veil, but if anybody can cut anybody *permanently* down, you really are not anybody. Give yourself leeway on the day it's going on, get through it, then take stock after. I didn't have to wait, while it was happening I *knew* it was his fault. That night he sent a mass of expensive flowers, I hated him even more, also the flowers.

"Be generous with yourself," the book says.

"Don't face the facts," say I.

"Don't be helpless," said Mama. My built-in confidence muscle worked.

The Sherwoods went back to New York. Things were going fine. Every night I went over to the Garden of Allah, where Elsa and Charles Laughton had a bungalow. Charles was making *The Hunchback of Notre Dame*. At dinner, he talked about *his* day, I talked about mine, and Elsa told her side of things. Maybe Marc Connelly stopped by, maybe Bob Benchley, Dotty Parker.

"Early call tomorrow," was the sign-off.

"See you tomorrow."

"See you tomorrow."

Making a picture, there's no time for outsiders or for outside life, it's go to bed, get up, be in Makeup Room at 7 A.M. At the RKO Studio, Makeup was up a flight, Jim Barker just finishing Lucille Ball tackled me. 8 A.M., Hazel Rogers braided my hair in numberless skinny braids, wound them round my head, held them in place with bands of flesh-colored net, then slid my black wig on, adjusted it, put pins to keep it in place, went with me over to the set to get into a beautiful costume. I loved it.

One Sunday, chauffeur Leo Proust drove me to Beverly Hills for lunch with Laurence Olivier and Vivien Leigh. I'd met them in London, where it was whispered there was a romance. Ursula Jeans had gotten me invited to Olivier's house on Cheyne Walk. He was married to Jill Esmond, baby Tarquin was in the nursery. At the Old Vic, Lilian Baylis had asked me to act the balcony scene with Olivier for the Shakespeare Birthday Night at the Vic.

I asked Edith Evans' advice.

"I wouldn't, dear. You've never done it and it takes a bit of doing, y'know, and why find out if you can in front of an audience that admires you?"

At Cheyne Walk, Jill said, "You're going to do the scene with Larry."

"No."

"Lilian said you were."

"No, I'm not."

"Then who is?"

"I think Jessica Tandy."

"Well, that's *too* much! She gets Katherine in *Henry Five* and the balcony scene I don't think!" Shakespeare's Birthday Night Jill Esmond looked over the balcony at Larry.

Ursula promised I'd adore Vivien Leigh and after *Bats in the Bellfry* at the St. Martin's, starring Lilian Braithwaite and Vivien Leigh, she took me backstage.

Vivien saw us only a minute, she had a prior engagement. Now those chapters were over, they were together in Hollywood, Larry shooting *Rebecca,* Vivien had finished *Gone With The Wind*. They'd rented Reggie Gardiner's house, which had been Leslie Howard's. In Beverly Hills everybody's house has been somebody else's. For phone calls and mail and propriety, Larry kept a room at the Beverly Wilshire Hotel. Sunday I arrived on time, a maid opened the door and looked surprised. I said I was expected and she disappeared. From above, I heard a knock on a door, muffled voices, then the sound of two people jumping out of bed. Some houses are built like that.

In no time both beautiful people were apologizing. They offered something, then led the way to sausage and mash, two beautiful and adorable people. That afternoon all the English dropped in, Sir Aubrey Smith, Dame May Whitty, everybody laughed a lot, but no one forgot about the war. Larry hated *Rebecca* and did scenes from it, we laughed, then got back to the war. Larry and Vivien were going back, but might do

Romeo and Juliet on the stage. It should have been the greatest, what happened? A few days after I'd seen it I sat next to Captain Joe Patterson at lunch. "I saw you at the *Romeo and Juliet* matinee," I said, glad to have a subject to discuss with the founder and owner of the New York *Daily News,* who wasn't talkative.

"Yes," he said.

"What did you think?"

Nothing had been panned worse, but the Captain drove a new nail. "I thought *his* costumes very coarse."

The doublet was short-short and where Romeo's privates bulged under his tights swung two distracting golden tassels.

It *was* distracting. New York's *Daily News* was founded by one able to express himself and if Shakespeare had seen the performance I bet *he'd* have been distracted.

Out at the RKO ranch in the Valley we were shooting Springfield, Illinois, at night, the torchlight parade for Lincoln. Mrs. Lincoln and the little boys watched from a balcony and waved when Abe looked up from the procession.

"Is that all?" I asked John Cromwell.

"Yes, that was fine."

"That's all," I told Hazel Rogers. "Tell Leo to bring the car up and we can go." I'd dressed at RKO on Gower Street and I'd go back to take my costume and wig off there.

Hazel helped me into the limousine, pushed the big crinoline-lined skirt in after me. We started off at a good clip. Was it about fifteen minutes? A car shot ahead of us, made an idiotic U-turn and barred our path. Leo pulled up, brakes screeching, assistant director got out. "You're not dismissed," he yelled.

"John said that was all."

"He meant for *that scene.*"

We turned round. Glad they were to see me with costume and makeup still on! What if I'd taken off for some night joint? They'd have had to bring the whole outfit out again for a whole other night!

"The director can't dismiss you, only *I* can," said the assistant. And that's the way it is, even before Walter Cronkite said so.

A comfort to get solvent, to have a good part, a comfort to have people say I was good. I believed them and didn't go to the rushes. Two thousand dollars a week for four weeks could pay off Helen Hayes and Lillian Gish. Everybody on the picture was lovely except one louse. Hazel Rogers told him to settle down. Everybody else was someone to look forward to. Jim Barker at 7 A.M., some mornings even earlier, between gulps of coffee and a sweet roll, telling a saga and patting Max Factor greasepaint on me, powdering over, shading-in pronounced eyebrows like Mary Todd's picture propped on his makeup table, handing me the cosmetic brush for me to darken my own eyelashes, a light dusting of rouge to accent cheek hollows, he delivers the saga's punch line, hands the lip rouge for me to do my own, while he says the punch line over again, then with *his* brush straightens out what I started.

Across the hall to Hazel Rogers to hear about how her walnut ranch is doing while she braided the braids and wrapped the gauze band over my own hairline, ready to take the wig off the wig block, another beautiful dress, Hazel's skillful hands easing it over my gauze-wrapped braids and the walnut ranch story reminding her of what Vivien Leigh said. Hazel had done Scarlett's hair. A black hairpin here, another there, a gulp of coffee and a promise, "I'll bring you some walnuts when they're ripe." Down the stairs out on the lot and walk over to Stage 8 or Stage 4 where everybody was lovely and where I was getting two thousand dollars a week to act. Is this a visceral myth?

Weekends Dorothy and Ray Massey took me to dinner or John Cromwell and his wife, actress Kay Johnson, had a party at their beautiful house in Bel Air, or Max Gordon our producer and his wife Millie took me to dinner and all week nights to the Garden of Allah, Elsa Lanchester's English cook offering boiled fowl, a trifle, a raspberry fool and we all discussed why was it vegetable marrow doesn't grow in America and problems like that.

The heat was breaking all records, not an electric fan to be bought, Charles boasted the thermometer rose to 135 degrees out in the Valley, where they were shooting *The Hunchback,* his makeup kept running off. Not a complaint, an appreciation of what art can surmount. He loved movie acting, he loved California, he felt he'd come home. He was born at Scarborough, in the north part of England, his feet felt native when they touched California soil. "It's a place actors couldn't dream up," he said, enjoying the light fading back of the Hollywood Hills.

One noon I ran into him on the RKO lot. Charles was with William Dieterle, director of *The Hunchback of Notre Dame.* Dieterle was German born and raised, had acted in the Reinhardt theatre, directed plays, films and came with wife and mother-in-law to live in Burbank on a hill above Cahuenga Pass, five minutes' drive to Warner Brothers Studio, where he carved his name in film fame with *The Story of Louis Pasteur, The Life of Emile Zola, Juarez.* Charles admitted Dieterle's prowess, but with all directors he had his differences.

"This is Bill Dieterle, Ruth. Bill, this is Ruth Gordon, our great actress." He said it in a throwaway tone as though he were above all that.

Tall, El Greco Dieterle, handsome, elegant, bowed, said no word.

No wonder. Charles had irritated him plenty and this hot day he proclaimed some five-foot nobody in a yellow linen dress, hair in braids pinned around her head, "our great actress."

Lesson on how to get into a movie: be wherever is the place to be on the right day and be "our great actress"!

Whose great actress? My luck and his Teutonic tenacity sent film director William Dieterle to a projection room. "Let me see the *Abe Lincoln* outtakes," he commanded.

Later at the Chateau Elysee the phone rang. "This is Max Winslow, Warners wants you for Mrs. Ehrlich in *Dr. Ehrlich's Magic Bullet,* starting the last week in October. They'll pay you two thousand a week, a four-week guaranty, first feature billing, Edward G. Robinson starring, William Dieterle directing."

What a feeling! Board Super Chief at Union Station, Los Angeles, say au revoir to Leo Proust, who had driven my hired limousine all during *Abe* and would meet me at Pasadena two weeks later and drive me back to my same suite at the Chateau and this time to Warner Brothers Studio off Cahuenga to play Mrs. Dr. Ehrlich! I love a train ride and even more with a movie contract.

Sixty West Twelfth Street was fine. I'd missed Jones' birthday party at the Rodeo in Madison Square Garden, then back to the house for supper, birthday cake and ice cream. Sorry to miss it, sorry to miss mine, but for two thousand a week, a good good part, a foot in the door to being a movie actress, skip a birthday cake.

Debts paid, money in the bank, go to Hattie Carnegie's, a place with a heart.

"That price is all right for Mrs. William Randolph Hearst but not for me." Miss Penn, in charge of ready-to-wear, went off somewhere and came back. "You got it." Then she noticed my coat. "You need a new coat."

My old mink was turning pink. I'd bought it in *Serena Blandish*. Who dug up that furrier!

"Buy one," said Gert Macy. "Kit bought one. I have, he's giving them to us cheap."

Did I pay eleven hundred?

"Some of the skins are good," said Bergdorf's Mr. Feldman when I sent it to storage, "some aren't. Look at this one."

Anyway it was mink, everybody had one and so did I. It was mink and warm and had lasted ten years.

"You can't go out in that!" said Miss Penn, and had the furrier come down. "What can you do for Miss Gordon? She's starring with Edward G. Robinson in a new movie at Warner Brothers. She's taking the train Monday, she can't go out wearing *that*." Miss Penn threw my coat on a chair as though it was the floor.

"Want to come up and we'll look?"

"Yes," said Miss Penn.

I bought a beauty. Mink.

"Never tell what it cost," warned the furrier, "Miss Carnegie likes you, she'll look the other way. Take it for a thousand, but don't tell."

That one I wore till Garson bought me one for ten thousand dollars the day *Born Yesterday* opened in New York. Next time I was in Boston I passed the Carnegie mink on to beautiful Miss Elizabeth Irene O'Neill, who had taught me to read Virgil, taught me how to learn how to learn. Back at Carnegie's before all that, I bought another. Was it bear fur? It was dark brown thick fur, full length, good for a rainy day. Not sable like Mrs. Joe Patterson's, who came with the Captain to a matinee of *The Three Sisters*. I couldn't keep my mind on what we were saying. "Is your coat sable?" I asked.

"Yes," she said, "it's a rainy day."

Figurez-vous! Mine cost three hundred dollars and would take the wear and tear off my new mink and it felt grand to have two fur coats.

To wear under the new mink, Miss Penn had a chic wool dress of beige and black plaid. "Just the thing under that divine coat!" said Miss P. Three years later, I wore it to get married to Garson, where it wasn't at *all* the thing, but it was my best. What happens to money?

Goodbye, goodbye, off to California in my secondbest fur coat! Cross the red carpet onto the Twentieth Century, grand dinner in the diner, how did I decide not to have a cigarette? I was astonished. Astonished further when I went to sleep without one. After breakfast none, none in Chicago. Maybe I *could* give it up. None in my drawing room on Super Chief, none after breakfast going through Colorado, none when we stopped at Albuquerque for twenty minutes and I walked back and forth and bought newspapers and turquoise Indian jewelry. None when I got out for the night air at Flagstaff in Arizona and got back in lest I freeze to death, none after breakfast riding through the orange groves from San Bernardino to Pasadena, none in Pasadena. Leo Proust put the bags in the limousine, drove to the Chateau Elysee, same suite, drove to Cahuenga Pass and turned off at Burbank to the grand Warner Brothers Studio, my favorite of all.

In the days of Harry and Jack Warner it was a luxey place and I was with a luxey outfit. No one higher than Edward G. Robinson and William Dieterle. My dressing room was a sitting room, bedroom and bath. On the stage, a portable dressing room. To look after all our wants, Bill Robinson, who looked like the famous Bill Robinson, had the same name, but instead of starring at the Cotton Club or tap dancing with Shirley Temple, he was there to do anything he could for us. A cup of tea? Bill brought it. A cup of coffee? Bill. A tray of breakfast? Bill. Another chair? Bill. Kleenex? Bill. A darling guy.

Another darling guy was Mr. Dieterle. Alarmingly tall, dignified as an oil painting with a warm heart. They said he was a health nut and went home every day to lunch. At home the food was not only healthy but delicious, I was invited one Sunday for lunch. His assistant, Peter Berneis, also adorable, called for me at the Chateau Elysee and took me to the house looking over Burbank. I wore my new mink coat and my perfect beige and black plaid. Mrs. Dieterle was adorable, mother-in-law ditto. They were from Munich.

After luncheon, we talked about theatre and Reinhardt and Shakespeare and I told him about the production of *Henry V* at the Old Vic with Laurence Olivier as Henry and the staging by Tyrone Guthrie. Mr. Dieterle got a copy of it down from the shelves. I found the "Once more unto the breach . . ." and the "St. Crispin's Day." Everybody in the house on the hill looking across the Cahuenga Pass loved each other and Shakespeare and acting and theatre and nobody was German and nobody was

from Quincy, we were all worshipful of talent, aware we had
some.

At the studio when Mr. Dieterle came on the set, he wore
white cotton gloves. Some said superstition, some said to avoid
dirt. He said he got his hand infected from something on the set,
so he wore white cotton gloves and changed them often.

He was conscious of the stars in the sky and what numbers
were right and when. He started a picture only if the date was
the right number. What made it right? He knew. All his pictures were successes.

It was good that Eddie Robinson took to me, he had things
his way. He'd been on the New York stage, acted in Theatre
Guild plays, *The Brothers Karamazov* when Alfred Lunt played
it. Woollcott had asked what the G. stood for. Eddie told him it
was an adopted name. He'd seen it somewhere and admired it
and took it for his stage name. Alec was convulsed by the idea
that of all the names in the English language "Edward G. Robinson" would appeal to a young Romanian.

Eddie had seen me in plays, I'd seen him, but we'd never met,
we liked each other right away. We had to, I'm apt to speak out.
Do I do it to make people laugh? To speak out for the sake of
speaking out? To not feel I have to kiss Mr. Doliber, head of the
Mellin's Food Company, but I wouldn't kiss him. It made
Mama cry. Papa said why should I?

Rehearsing a scene, Eddie got some words mixed up.

"You're such a big star, why can't you say your line straight?"
I asked.

The surrounding group tensed, then Eddie laughed, then they
laughed, then we all laughed, then we were friends. For Thanksgiving he asked me to dinner at his home in Beverly Hills, his
gallery built beside it for the collection of Manet and Monet and
Cézanne and the wonderful others.

"Do you know Horowitz?" he asked. "Vladimir and Wanda
are having Thanksgiving dinner with us."

Some things you can't believe are being said to you.

Thanksgiving morning I took the trolley down to Los Angeles. I love a trolley ride, I love a city and every once in a while I have to hook up to reality. I had lunch at Clifton's Cafeteria on Hill Street, everybody enjoying turkey. Good food, cheap and no matter what you ordered, you were given a glass of free green water. You could have water-colored water, but most of us drank green.

At seven, to Eddie's fine house. A sumptuous dinner, then we crossed the driveway to the gallery and the paintings. After the paintings, Horowitz played.

Truth would have outshone any elaborate lies. Everything seemed to go right. Shooting this picture was a uniquely happy time.

"Go to Lantz, they have beautiful clothes," advised Anita Loos. "Inexpensive, but beautiful."

I went. In her play *The Fall of Eve,* she had taken me to the Place Vendôme to Cheruit and to Faubourg St. Honoré to Madame Lanvin; now she liked Lantz on Wilshire Boulevard, Los Angeles. I got carried away and bought some. At Bullock's I bought a grand red coat and told Lillian Gish to buy the beige one. It felt good to advise people I'd owed thousands to, to throw their money around.

Eddie's contract stipulated he quit filming at six. "Come to dinner tonight," he said. "We'll drive back here to see what we've done."

Good dinner, then into the car, "The studio," Eddie told his chauffeur.

A studio at night is lighted up and no one is there to be lit, the same quiet as a graveyard. Mystery and no one around but the policemen.

At the front gate they waved the barrier up, the car drove through to projection room number whatever. No more deference in the world than that paid a reigning screen star or Mr.

Lee Shubert when he went to his theatres. I never went out with
royalty, but it couldn't bring more reaction than a studio's toward Edward G. Robinson, Tyrone Power, Greta Garbo.

Eddie gave permission to start. We ran about half, maybe a
little more of *Dr. Ehrlich*, it held us riveted. No background
music, just what is called "the rough cut," but Dieterle's direction, Eddie's performance of the doctor and the great Basserman
playing the great scientist.

Mr. Dieterle had brought Basserman over from Europe. The
day he had been called, I wasn't in the scene, but got there at 9
A.M., the start of the day. Mr. Dieterle conducted Basserman
onto the set and introduced him, a scholarly, elegant, simple
man. Dieterle said that when Basserman toured in a play in Germany, a town would declare a holiday, people would line the
streets to see him pass.

On the sidelines, I stood watching. His scene was when Dr.
Ehrlich showed him the discovery of what could be the serum to
cure syphilis. In Dr. Ehrlich's laboratory other doctors and scien-
tists had gathered. Some believed, some doubted. Dr. Ehrlich
welcomed the master scientist, explained, then stepped aside and
offered him his place at the microscope. That is a moment for a
great actor. The scientist had come here knowing that Dr.
Ehrlich thought his 606 serum was the cure for the heretofore
uncurable. Many doctors *think* they have a cure, then disappointment. Would this be another?

Basserman, tall, not thin, not sturdy, frock coat, wing collar,
beard, listened to Dr. Ehrlich, then stepped to the microscope,
put his eye to the lens, looked in, looked in, looked in, looked in,
looked in, then sighed. Another step had been taken, another
barrier downed, another chapter in progress.

The circle we made, back of cameraman James Wong Howe's
camera, learned a lesson in acting.

In the projection room, Eddie and I sat awed. In a foreign
land, in a foreign language, he *was* the scientist, he *was* convinced.

Driving home, we felt contented. We knew it was good and *we* were. Kiss-kiss, "See you tomorrow."

Next morning on the set, I waited to speak to Mr. Dieterle. "It is just great."

"What is?"

"The film."

"The film?"

"What we're doing."

"You saw it?"

"Oh yes, Eddie invited me to see it last night."

"Where did you see it?"

"In a projection room."

Eddie hadn't told me not to tell. All hell broke loose, Dieterle thought it was the most highhanded behavior he'd met with.

I told Eddie I was sorry.

"Don't be," he said. A reigning movie star reigns.

The picture was finishing. Warners' offered me another. Wolfgang Reinhardt gave me a script. He was the producer of it. "It's an Academy Award part." It was called *Mama Ravioli,* also the name of the character I would play, a big, hefty Italian mother like in the funny papers.

I didn't like the script and the part was too far away from me. Wolfgang pleaded.

What a good feeling. Not only to *want* me, but for two thousand a week. But Mama Ravioli was not for me. I can do a lot, but not a big, stout, overwhelming Mama Ravioli.

Warners' gave me another script. No wonder it's my favorite studio! This part was far away from me, too, but I could do it, Queen Victoria from seventeen years old to the old lady of Benjamin Disraeli days. The script was called *Disraeli,* Laurence Olivier would play Disraeli. Two thousand a week, would I just make a little test?

No.

They wanted to be sure they could get a likeness on film.

No.

Anna Wheaton took the pistol and shot the letter but didn't get the movie. "I don't make tests."

"Don't you trust yourself?"

"I can act it, but I don't know if I can look it, if I'm signed, you'll *make* me look it."

Zarathustra, maybe take a lesson?

Disraeli wasn't much of a script, but would have more work done on it. Larry would be tremendous.

They waived the test and I signed.

On a day I wasn't called for *Dr. Ehrlich* I made the makeup and wig tests for Victoria, but now that I was signed the studio had to come through. Perc Westmore called up. Perc was king. The head of Makeup at Warners', and total genius. All the Westmore brothers were, but none equaled Perc. Ernie was head of Makeup at 20th Century, Wally at Paramount, Bud handled Universal and one more ran their Hollywood beauty parlor.

Perc sized up my face, called up the Ehrlich set to find out when he could make a cast of my head, made it. "Don't sneeze," "Don't wink." It worked. An adorable man, Perc, who thought life began and ended with makeup. Why not? The *Encyclopaedia Britannica* asked him to write their article on it.

To speed up things he called me in on Saturday morning. For Victoria at seventeen, he'd try pulling my face up, I was forty-three. "I have to shave two spots on top of your head, as big as a quarter."

Who said no to Perc Westmore?

He shaved two round spots, attached a pad to each end of a tape, put spirit gum on, applied one to my hairline above the left ear, the other to one of the shaven spots, then did the same on the other side, pulled the two tapes up tight, my cheeks became smooth as youth. The tapes dropped off the shaven spots. Perc tried again, pulled, they dropped. "Goddam it, you got the same goddam skin Paul Muni has, it won't stick to him either."

From Wardrobe came a message, Milo had to fit my Victoria

costume. Milo was head of Wardrobe for Warner Brothers. "Perc has ordered a new costume made. The okay has come through. I have to first make a foundation. The young Victoria we can pull something out of wardrobe, Perc says, but for eighty she's got to look *right*. Right jewelry, right decorations. He's having Factor's make the wig."

That could only happen when you're signed and only for Perc Westmore.

Costume fitted and finished, wigs fitted and delivered, jewelry and decorations approved by Perc, he booked two days of makeup. The young Victoria didn't take a full day, the call for the eighty-year-old was right after Perc put on Eddie Robinson's makeup, beard, mustache, wig, sent him off to shoot. He looked at me, gave a groan, swallowed half a cup of black coffee, said a prayer and "Sit down."

At lunchtime, they brought me something skimpy that I could suck through a straw. About four o'clock, Perc said get Milo. Milo and assistants and girl with the jewelry took over after an almost total swoon at Perc's makeup. Even ears that sagged from all the diamonds worn in them. The throat sagged under pearls, the breasts sagged under the Kohinoor diamond, and the Order of the Garter, the hands were old and jeweled, wrinkled and big-knuckled.

"Ready," said Perc. Milo lifted the train, we stepped through Perc's open door. Can you imagine if some Stuart Scheftel had put up the money for Ruthie Selwyn to put on *Here Today*?

"Can you walk?" asked Perc.

I was wondering.

"My God!" It was Pat O'Brien crossing our path. "My God!"

"Don't talk to her, she'll crack the makeup."

Without Perc holding onto me could I walk? If I spoke, I'd crack the makeup, how would I say to Disraeli, "Arise, Lord Beaconsfield"?

We needed only to cross the studio street to the test studio, everyone was ready, no dialogue spoken, just front view, side and back.

Test cameraman could hardly believe what he looked at. Two days before, he'd shot the young Victoria. Two days and she was eighty. Perc directed the lights, camera angle, the shots.

The test was over and I was full of fear. *How* could I act with that on? How could anyone? And with Larry, who had admired me at the Old Vic? Perc and Milo steered me back to the makeup room.

"I'm looking at it at four today." Perc sounded tense on the phone.

"I'll be there."

We walked down the street to a projection room. Perc grabbed my arm. "Say a prayer." It came out so tense it sounded like a threat.

"Okay?" asked the projectionist.

"Go."

The young Victoria came on the screen. Very good. Not pretty, not *not* pretty. My own amber-colored hair parted in the middle and rolled in rosettes over each ear. No acting, just trying to *be* the young Victoria who would become a someone. How had Perc created the foreign look? On the screen I was foreign.

Perc didn't give a damn about that one. That one wasn't why he was head of Warner Brothers Makeup, why he was in charge of Bette Davis, Edward G. Robinson, Paul Muni, Errol Flynn, Humphrey Bogart.

The screen lighted up again:

TEST NUMBER 796
SECOND PART
RUTH GORDON as
QUEEN VICTORIA
for DISRAELI
PERC WESTMORE
MAKEUP

Perc grabbed my arm like a clamp. Then! Were we looking at it or imagining it? Victoria, friend of and beloved of Benjamin Disraeli. Victoria old but not an old lady, old and full of power. The queen who went to Balmoral, who became Scottish, though retaining her German strain, the queen who entertained the Empress Eugénie and it was noted that when Victoria sat down she didn't look to see if a chair was there, she sat knowing it would be. Empress Eugénie *looked*. At dinner, Victoria, still in her riding habit, had pinned on the Kohinoor diamond and Order of the Garter. On the screen we were looking at that sagging bosom, great girth held tightly upright, crepey neck with the ropes of pearl not concealing wrinkles, accenting them, ears dragged low by the heavy diamonds, the ribbon of the Garter worn by one who gave it out, face old, undefeated, tired, powerful.

"*Give* it to me!" shouted exultant Perc. The reel under his arm, he kissed me. "I'm taking it to Jack Warner, no one's going to show *this* to him but me." He ran out like Man o' War.

Look in the *Encyclopaedia Britannica,* the still of Victoria illustrates the article on makeup.

Goodbye, goodbye, the Dr. Ehrlich film was over. Mr. and Mrs. Dieterle gave a farewell party at Perino's newly opened restaurant opposite the Beverly Wilshire Hotel in Beverly Hills. In screen language it's called a wrap-up party. The crew, the cast, everybody but Eddie Robinson. Why was that? Mr. Dieterle gave me a beautiful George III silver box. I gave him *Les Filles d'Elisa*, illustrated so beautifully.

Everybody knew our Ehrlich film was going to be great, Otto Kruger, whom I'd scraped acquaintance with at the Stratford Hotel in Chicago when I was playing the Babytalk Lady in Booth Tarkington's *Seventeen,* was there with his wife Sue. Basserman had gone back to his native land, but we remembered the wonder of watching him. Peter Berneis, and Irving Rapper, our dialogue director, and Jimmy Howe, who was opening a Chinese restaurant in the Valley, along with continuing his Academy Award-winning career as a cameraman. Why wasn't Eddie there?

Goodbye.

Goodbye.

Home for Christmas. Back to do *Disraeli*.

Leo Proust pulled up at Pasadena station. Behind us, a fine car stopped, Eddie got out.

"Going to New York?" I asked.

"San Bernardino."

He sat in my drawing room. The conductor looked surprised. "I didn't expect you on board, Mr. Robinson."

"I'm getting off at San Bernardino."

The conductor looked pleased, but what a scandal going through Kansas if Edward G. Robinson and his leading lady were sleeping together!

New York, Twelfth Street going fine, the little house looked lovely, ditto New York. Did it look lovelier because my Warner Brothers contract for my third movie meant two thousand a week?

A telegram from Warner Brothers. *Disraeli* would not be done. Instead they would transfer my contract to *Reuters Ltd.*, which was going to be Dieterle's next film. I would be Mrs. Reuter, the salary two thousand a week, a four week guaranty. Script on the way.

Script arrived, it was harmless, something you might do betweentimes, Mrs. Reuter not as good as a Mrs. Ehrlich.

"Do it if you want to," said Jed, "but make them pay you for *Disraeli*."

"I don't think they want to. They want me to do this instead."

"What do you care what *they* want? They owe you eight thousand dollars. After they pay you, make a new deal, but they can't make you."

Legal, but is that how you build relationships? Warners' was for me. Now what?

"Nothing doing."

I was for accepting, Jed was adamant. Right, from a point of principle, wrong, for continuing good relations. Warners paid the eight thousand dollars. I tried to get into *Reuters Ltd.*, but Jack Warner said he'd see that I never worked again. I worked and for Warners, but there was a long period in between. Jack and I were good friends and his widow sent me a bottle of Dom Perignon for Thanksgiving. Be as honest as you can without denting your chances. In business probably nobody knows what to do about anything, but some don't know what to do more than others.

Movie careers not only help pay bills, but bring invitations from the White House. *Abe Lincoln* would have its first showing for the President of the United States. Dinner with President and Mrs. Franklin Delano Roosevelt!

At Hattie Carnegie's they went into action. Miss Penn got the grand evening dresses assembled. We chose a dark green and silver brocade with White House written all over it. Elegance itself. Miss Penn went over to jewelry and chose three rows of cut emeralds as a necklace. Emeralds or a reasonable facsimile thereof. I wore my own diamond bracelets, square diamond ring, out of hock due to solvency. Gregory had bought it from a fence in Chicago introduced to him by Georgie Jessel introduced to Georgie by Fanny Brice. My diamond engagement ring Gregory had had made at Ratterman's, Cincinnati, the center stone of which was the one-karat diamond in Mama's engagement ring she lost and found under our potato basket. My circlet of square diamonds wedding ring Gregory bought at Tiffany's like Mary Miller's only better. Beautiful for dinner at the White House! How elegant my Carnegie mink coat! "Don't be helpless, Ruth." I hadn't been. Hadn't I got the part in the picture? Hadn't I lived through the first day's fifty-seven takes! Hadn't the outtakes been so good I got another movie part? Hadn't Miss Penn pulled out the most elegant clothes for Washington? Mrs. Robert E. Sherwood, Mrs. Raymond Massey, Mrs. Max Gordon with all their money could have no better. Board the Washington train with my Louis Vuitton suitcase and forget *Disraeli* or *Reuters Ltd.* or Jack Warner, enjoy the moment!

At Union Station, RKO had a limousine that would be with
me for the trip. Call the number, he'd be there. He dropped me
at the Carlton Hotel. Up to an expensive suite, meet the press,
meet Carol Frink, reporter on the Chicago-Hearst paper, remember not to think entirely of myself, maybe suggest we talk
about Mary Howard, who played Ann Rutledge. In Carol
Frink's interview with me for the Chicago *Examiner* she told
about how this was my first picture, how much I'd learned,
then, "Ruth Gordon said, 'Let's talk about Mary Howard a
while.'"

"You didn't learn *that* in Hollywood, Ruth," wrote Charlie
MacArthur's first wife.

The press left about five o'clock. I called up Joe Alsop.

"What are you doing here? Can you have dinner?" he asked.

"Great! I'm here for . . ." Then I told him.

"Come at seven. I'm having Justice and Mrs. Frankfurter.
You'll adore them. I'm at Dumbarton, near Thirtieth Street,
Georgetown."

"RKO has given me a car, I'll be there."

Wear my beautiful two-piece black wool, black velvet appli-
qué, priced mercifully by Miss Penn. Mink coat over it and off
to Georgetown. Where was it? Over a bridge and there. Like
Quincy, pass the Adams house and meadow and there you are.
Like Quincy in position, unlike it in anything else. In Georgetown, back of every lace curtain somebody is running something.

The limousine stopped in front of Joe's, the opposite side of
Dumbarton from the one he lives in today. Small and, like
anyplace Joe lives, perfect. Same for his menu. We began with
broiled mushrooms on toast, but what mushrooms! What toast!

"Where did you get such a cook?" I asked.

"He was a taxi driver."

Seem logical?

It is, if you know Joe Alsop. With a Filipino miracle worker
in the kitchen, dinner was a glory, the company more so. Justice

Frankfurter had read my "Look in the Glass" articles in *Atlantic Monthly*. He'd read each installment aloud to Mrs. They loved them.

Joe I'd loved since his visits to Woollcott's island. After one of the visits he was going back to Washington via Hyde Park.

"I envy you," I said.

"Come with me."

Can you imagine dropping in on the President and Mrs. Roosevelt?

"They'd love it."

"I wish you had come," wrote Mrs. Roosevelt, "we're that informal."

At table, talk was brisk. Joe likes to talk, the Justice liked to, Mrs. Frankfurter wasn't one to clam up and I like to get on. What made me think of beloved friend, wonderful playwright Ned Sheldon?

"I'm glad I met you, Mr. Justice. You're going to have Ned Sheldon's case come up. I'd like to tell you about it."

Do I sound like Chicken Little?

"Don't discuss it!" shouted the Justice.

It was the Letty Lynton plagiarism suit. MGM made a film about the famous Scottish murderess, Madeline Smith, after Ned and Margaret Ayer Barnes had written *Dishonored Lady,* which Kit had played. In the film were big chunks of Ned's and Mrs. Barnes's improvisations. They sued.

"I know a lot about it," I explained.

"Don't discuss it!" he shouted louder. "Or I will have to leave."

"But I should think you would want to know about it if you're going to hear the case."

A backward Chicken Little.

The Justice put his hands over his ears and Mrs. Frankfurter and Joe convinced me that a case coming up could not be discussed over the dinner table. I *guess* they convinced me, it didn't convince Ned. When the court did hand down the decision, it was in favor of Ned and Mrs. B. but the sum paid was ridiculous. Too bad the Justice put his hands over his ears.

Over the phone, Joe had said, "If you're free tomorrow, I'd like to have a luncheon for you."

Once we got past Supreme Court restrictions, I loved Joe's guests, "Will you ask them to lunch tomorrow?" I asked.

"I can't."

"Why not?"

"You can't ask them two days in a row."

"Why can't you?" asked the Justice, who had overheard. "What is it? We'll come."

The evening ended with us all driving around the corner to the Frankfurter house on Thirtieth Street. The Justice ran upstairs and brought down a photo he wanted to show me. What photo was it? Overwhelmed by the company I was in I've forgotten the photo.

Outside waited the limousine. "It's RKO gives it to me," I apologized.

"*Arceo Daniisque ferante dona,*" quoted the Justice. I'd been a Latin star, but it had to be explained to me that the Justice was making a pun on "I fear the Greeks bringing gifts."

Joe's next day luncheon, lovely people, all somebodies or they wouldn't be at Joe's, but my choice was again Justice and Mrs. Frankfurter. Start of a long friendship with the Justice. With Mrs., not.

After the luncheon, John Cromwell came to pick me up, a radio broadcast scheduled for Ray and me and John and Mary Howard.

Sunday! The day! Everybody telephoned everybody to check arrangements. Everybody verified everything. The phone rang again. It was the Justice. "I've spoken to Missy LeHand, she'll see that you tell the President the story you told us last night about Mr. Collins."

"Oh, I couldn't tell him that."

"Why, of course you can." A verdict.

"It's a good story, but nothing to walk up to the President of the United States and say, 'Mr. President, I'd like to tell you a three-minute story about the principal of Quincy High School working his way to Hamburg and back as a common seaman."

"He'll love it. Missy will see that you tell it to him. Goodbye." Click.

The big RKO limousine stopped at the gate, the chauffeur gave my name, he waved us to the front steps of the White House. The first one in my family to go in. My mink coat came off. How? Somehow. The usher showed a table plan, told me to look and see where I sat. Then pointed the way to the Red Room to await Mrs. Roosevelt. The President would receive us seated in the State Dining Room.

In a circle as directed, stood Sherwood, Madeline, Ray Massey, Dorothy, Max Gordon, Mary Howard, John Cromwell and I, everybody looking appropriate, everybody feeling nervous when from the hall came an infectious laugh.

"Mrs. Roosevelt," announced the usher, and we almost relaxed. An event and maybe not an ordeal, at the White House they laughed? Maybe *we'd* have a good time, too.

In came Mrs. Roosevelt. At first impression, she seemed one big smile and not putting it on. That smile had everything going for it.

The usher introduced each of us, she knew who we were, gave the feeling she was glad we came. Her long evening dress was like a part of her, like the robe on a statue and not out of Bergdorf's or *Vogue*.

"We'll go in to dinner. Franklin is waiting."

The usher didn't exactly point the way, but didn't exactly not. We filed through the big door out into the broad hall, passed the entrance doors where we'd come in. Passed and kept on to the State Dining Room at the end. Big. Somber, elegant, patriotic, on its dark wooden walls, the painting of Lincoln. The table, U-shaped, chairs placed only on the outside of the U. Midway on the left side of the U sat the President. Was he the handsomest man anyone ever saw? Suntanned, though it was winter, smiling as though he loved this affair. Madeline sat on his right, Dorothy on his left. Across the U, Mrs. Roosevelt, Max Gordon and Sherwood on either side.

The food was not memorable, but nobody would have chosen to be anywhere but there. The man next to me said, "Did you notice how the silver is marked?"

Instead of initials or an insignia, it was engraved, "The President's House."

"Franklin." It was Mrs. Roosevelt. The whole table stopped talking except the President. "Franklin," repeated that unmistakable voice. The President looked toward her. "Mr. Gordon has such an amusing story. You must hear it. Please tell it, Mr. Gordon."

That worst moment when someone asks you to tell a story over again! What would happen to Max? Maybe his greatest quality was he never got thrown by conditions. When the big turntable for the scenery broke at the dress rehearsal of his musical comedy, *Three Waltzes*, thousands of dollars riding, Max, standing in the back of the theatre watching, said, "Well, I can't do anything about *that!* and went home. Millie says he went to sleep.

Around the U-table, all eyes were upon him, he didn't look terrified, looked the way he always did. "Well, Mr. President, it's the one about the two bums standing in front of the Palace Theatre.

" 'You going to vote for Roosevelt?' asks one.

" 'Not *me.*'

" 'Why not?'

" 'What's the matter with the one that's in there now?' "
Roosevelt had just started his third term in office. Everybody laughed.

Thank God, it was the *other* Gordon they wanted to tell a story.

After dinner, up the great flight of stairs to the upper hall where the film would be shown. Mrs. Roosevelt led the way, the President would go in the elevator.

In the hall, rows of chairs, an open space for the President's big wheelchair, center of the first row. On one side sat Sherwood, the other side Max Gordon, the rest of us distributed ourselves behind them, lights dimmed down, the screen lighted up:

ABE LINCOLN IN ILLINOIS

Trepidation. I'd seen it at the second preview, Huntington Park, in California, I thought the audience hated it. At least they didn't react warmly and I froze. It's never the way *you* think it's going to be.

At that preview, I thought the early scenes shot in Oregon would never end. The stuff with the pigs went on ad infinitum and longer. By the time Mary Todd came to visit in Springfield, events were stiff as new cards.

It was over and John Cromwell looked at me with a confident smile. Had he been watching the same movie? I struggled for something to say, but it was so lame that *he* froze. "You're just not used to previews," he said. If you're in a movie and don't have any control over it, best not to go to previews, buy a ticket and sit with regular customers. Why had I come to Huntington Park? Some days you know what you're doing, others you're just winging it.

Tonight at the White House none of us watched the picture, we watched the President and Mrs. Roosevelt.

The lights came up, the screen faded out. He was moved and spoke at length. The President turned to Sherwood. Great praise, great eloquence, great appreciation of the patriotism involved. Then he turned to Max, "You have produced," he said, "a monumental work."

"But will it get a quarter?"

The ice broke, everybody laughed, everybody relaxed, felt comfortable.

Mrs. Roosevelt led the way to the Oval Room. We followed, the President in his chair.

Miss LeHand came up to me. "Justice Frankfurter says you have a story to tell the President."

"Oh, I couldn't."

"The Justice says the President will enjoy it."

"Oh, no, it's very long. It wouldn't be right."

"The Justice thinks it would. He wants me to see that you tell it."

"Oh, I couldn't. I'm sorry, I couldn't."

"Well, perhaps later."

I just shook my head.

The President talked with everyone, gave the impression he really had enjoyed it. A gift to enjoy things. He and Mrs. Roosevelt had it. Now we were all enjoying it.

"Miss Gordon, I'm going to bring you over to the President." Mrs. Roosevelt took my arm. "He'll want to hear your story."

"Oh, I couldn't."

"Come along." Her hand on my arm brooked no resistance. She guided me to the President's chair.

"I'd really rather not."

"Franklin, this is Miss Gordon. Felix says she has a story to tell you."

The President looked up at me with that beguiling smile, that dazzling expression that conquered what came in its way. "Felix is a great talker himself. If he says it's good, it must be."

"Oh, it's nothing."

"Felix talks more than anyone I ever knew except Herbert Bayard Swope. Do you know him?"

"I lived with him," I blurted out. I meant to say, "I lived with *them*."

He looked a little startled, then someone else came up and I was back on the fringe.

The evening was over. We couldn't bear to part, so most of us went to the Grill Room of the Carlton to fasten the occasion in our memory.

Next night was the public showing. We were announced to make an appearance. In the first limousine rode Mrs. Roosevelt, Ray Massey and I. In front of the big movie theatre was a picket line. Mrs. Roosevelt was shocked. "No one told me. I've never crossed a picket line, I'm sorry," she said to the pickets, and stepped out. "Nobody told me, but I must go in. I'm sorry."

Great to be in the movies, great to meet a great lady. Great to find the courage the day I said, "I don't test."

This page is lilac color.

A dark green brocade dress from Hattie Carnegie's can afford to be without trimming, but ribbons and buttons mean a lot when you're poor. You can afford them, cloth you can't unless you come on a good remnant.

"Swiss muslin," murmured Mama as though it was a poem by Wordsworth.

"Batiste," another piece of poetry.

"Handkerchief linen," a kind of lady's prayer.

To Mama linen was like honor: you had it or you didn't. Once in summer a man came to our back door. "I'm tired. You can have this bolt of linen for two dollars, I'm tired and want to go on home."

It was heavy white Irish linen. What suits she could make! One for me, one for her. What skirts! What a Sunday school dress!

"It's my last bolt and I want to go home. You know what real linen costs, take it, it's two dollars."

There was only a dollar and one nickel in the house.

"It was too darn bad," said Mama. "Twenty yards on a bolt for two dollars. I wish I had it, it was dreadful not to be able to find two dollars."

When Papa got home, she told him.

"Why is linen so great?"

"Why, Clinton!" She just looked at him. It was the nearest she ever came to a rebuke.

I love linen, money, pine trees, hard chairs, spruce trees, elm trees, apple trees, steamed clams, money, sunflowers, hats, cinnamon pinks, any Cézanne, an open trolley, old Vuitton luggage, a Matisse, orange blossoms, orange cake, money, velvet carriage boots, nasturtiums, silk not nylon stockings, Lady Baltimore cake, not a fortune, but money, egg roll, Horace Pippin's paintings, country lilacs, lace, Boston fern, batiste, hot chocolate, French percale, country lily-of-the-valley, Julianne's madeleines', money. By the way, that *plus ça change* stuff is okay. I thought it was an old chestnut, then editor Ken McCormick and Anne and boy came to lunch at Edgartown. Their boy showed me a sharp black something. "Is it a stone?" I asked.

"It's a shark's tooth," said John.

"A shark's tooth! Where did you get it?"

"Oh, if you look" said Ken, "they come up quite often in the sand."

I thought back when Papa and I went for a Sunday afternoon walk in Quincy, we might come home with an Indian's arrowhead. Maybe in the rough ground going up Third Hill before it was built over, maybe on the backbone of the world, before it and the peat bog were done in, maybe on the links of the Montclair Golf Club. "Put it back," said Papa, "we're trespassing, only millionaires are members."

No smoking peat bog, no backbone, Third Hill built up, but the Montclair Golf links look the same. Have they still millionaires and their own arrowheads?

"The waves on Martha's Vineyard beaches wash up sharks' old teeth," said Ken.

People come to lunch and screw up your convictions, so okay, "The more things change the more they stay the same" is a correct chestnut. Or maybe only sharks' teeth and arrowheads stay the same. Ice cream doesn't and mayonnaise and prices and starch being all right in food and men's shirts. Anonymous sayings are mostly ridiculous. Maybe make up some sayings for yourself.

No matter the troubles I've had in Providence, Providence is all right. Pay attention to any city who names its main street Weybosset Street. That shows it knows better than to look for the easy way. Ralph Waldo Emerson didn't mention Providence but said, "The child of New England if he can live through the heat of August dog days, the December northeaster knows life is hard and if he can survive our weather will succeed."

In Providence not only the weather, but Weybosset Street teaches the Providence child nothing is easy.

I wish Robert E. Sherwood had written a play about the Adams family. He captured Abe Lincoln in Illinois, why not Abigail Adams in Quincy, Washington, Paris, London? What a part!

Adrianne Allen talked Sherwood into working on Helen Jerome's play made from *Pride and Prejudice* when Ade acted Elizabeth Bennet. Why didn't I talk Sherwood into the Adamses?

Thornton Wilder said, "The world is made up of doers and ooers."

And thinking up stuff too late. Sherwood died and who else can write Abigail Adams, wife of a President of the United States and mother of one?

Are you still the one your husband asked to marry him?

Think it over.

Maybe never mind if you're the one, but want to consider, if you cooled and he took a decent interval would you be the one?

How about drop the subject. Life is rough enough without tuning in on after death.

AN OPEN BOOK

Why do I think I can learn how to do *anything?* I learned how to act, how to write, how to stand on a platform and speak.

Thornton and Garson and I were discussing if everyone *can* learn to. In Edgartown early spring look for mayflowers by day, in the evening discuss. Our mayflowers were in a tumbler on the parlor table, we were discussing. When you write a book ought you to get out and talk about it?

"When I wrote *The Bridge,* I was asked to go to bookstores and sign my book for anyone who bought it," said Thornton. "There was quite a nervous pause between strokes of the pen."

"Nobody's asked me to do that yet, but my publisher has asked me to meet the press and speak at a luncheon at Sardi's, will I know how to do it?"

Thornton thought about that. "Gertrude Stein said, 'It's very important everyone find out what his solitude or gregariousness quotient is.' *My* solitude quotient is very high. I don't sparkle before five p.m."

It's good I do or I couldn't have talked at that Sardi luncheon for critics. Perhaps everybody wouldn't define that as being gre-

garious, but to me gregariousness means speaking and not getting paid. Most Wednesday and Saturday afternoons I've spent
with a thousand people and was paid to, but that's not gregariousness, that's show business.

For show business if your solitude quotient is high, get it lowered and boost your gregariousness. I think I *should* go out and
talk about my book. Maybe something I say can be of help. My
solitude quotient wasn't high when I needed people, why now?
People helped me. "Can you always write when you want to?" I
asked Somerset Maugham.

"Oh, yes. If I can't think of anything, I write 'Somerset
Maugham' until something occurs to me."

An adorable man, he answered any question asked him, he
wanted to be helpful.

"What is your preoccupation with society?"

"Ah, they have such beautiful houses. To see Millicent Sutherland receive at the head of the stairs of Sutherland House was
worth an evening out."

"What's a *trouvaille?*"

"It's what Balzac found to end *Père Goriot.*"

A *trouvaille* for me was the publishers gave their luncheon for
the critics not just anywhere but at Sardi's where I've been going
since it was a brownstone that served whiskey or gin in coffee
cups. In back was a garden, in summer dinner was served and
you met almost anyone, Mr. and Mrs. Sardi fed the profession.
If you paid, that was all right, if you didn't, you would.

When Guthrie McClintic died, his wife, Katharine Cornell,
named Mr. and Mrs. Sardi to sit in for Guthrie's family. A
trouvaille! They were everybody's family.

When their son, Vincent, opened the Belasco Room on the
second floor of Sardi's I gave him a letter Mr. Belasco wrote me.
I thought there should be something in the room that really had
come from Mr. Belasco and spoke Zarathustra: "There's a time
people give you things, a time you give them to people."

It was a help to know what to write if nothing occurred to me, a help to know what a *trouvaille* is, a help to know why people go to parties, a help to meet the book critics at Sardi's where sometimes Mr. and Mrs. Sardi had picked up the check until I went to work again. Atheneum Publishers picked up *this* check, but if they hadn't, probably Vincent Sardi would. Only the other day a big star now not so big must have felt Sardi's was still family. Bill collector sent star his Sardi bill for about six thousand dollars. No reply. Collector showed Vincent the bill. Collector said, "We'll sue him."

Vincent looked at the bill. "He owes no bill here," and tore it up.

I know this not from Vincent, but from a friend.

Language not heard around Sardi's. Mrs. Booth Tarkington
came to lunch with us at Ogunquit's Whistling Oyster, stepped
outside looked east and west, "I must find my Jehu. Ah, here he
is."

Gar and I stopped off at the public library, looked under the
letter J.

Would you know what Jehu means?

Now I know I'd like to use it, but I don't think I'm there yet.

If you've been poor you've learned a lot of inexpensive ways
to pass the time. At small cost I started with the proposition I
was always right. When it went wrong it would not be me.
What a surprise when it was!

I've had a lot of surprises and still know I'm right. And I *am*
right more times than if I didn't think I was and started to fluff
around uncertain.

Who appeals to you? Someone undecided or someone crash-
ing ahead who blows it, but acts like a winner and sometimes is?

"Be *for* things," said Thornton. "Don't be *against* things, it's so wearing. Of course, you have to be against Nazis and the Klu-Klux Klan, but don't be against anything you don't *have* to."

Our housekeeper came from the Argentine, her little girl was born in the land of the free. They were watching Garson and me on the Mike Douglas Show. "Why don't they ever come over to *our* house?" seven-year-old hospitable Vivien asked her pretty mother.

Decide you're different and you have to fundamentally go it alone. I was thirteen when I knew I better guard my thoughts. I decided after the visit to my friend Martha Robinson's aunts, who lived in a beautiful Brookline apartment. That night I told Mama and Papa, "Then the Auntie Etta's girl put a cut-glass bowl with water and a little geranium leaf in front of each of us and the Auntie Etta and the Auntie Sue put their fingers in and wiped across their mouths."

"We've got finger bowls."

"But ours are way up on the top shelf and, Mama, theirs are beautiful, *everything* there is beautiful and that's how I want things to be."

After the luncheon at Auntie Etta and Auntie Sue's I knew I would have them and I knew not to share ideas except for just the surface. I was different and different is mostly misunderstood.

Different, too, were Auntie Etta and Auntie Sue and Auntie Sue's friend, Mr. Basset. When I went on the stage with the grand Maude Adams Company, Mr. Fred Tyler's London suits made me see Mr. Basset strolling down Standish Avenue in Quincy, with beautifully dressed Auntie Etta and beautifully dressed Auntie Sue on their weekly visit to their plain sister, Agnes. The sisters were different and so was Miss Clarens, who chose me out of the whole Maude Adams Company to invite to tea. We were different and Mr. Fred Tyler was. In *The Little Minister,* he played Lady Babbie's father, elegant Lord Rintoul, his performance as the Judge in *The Legend of Leonora* was considered very fine by the troupe.

He stopped beside Miss Clarens in the dining car. Miss Clarens' hazel eyes smiled up at him. "Will you share our cinnamon toast?"

Once after a matinee at the Empire Theatre I'd seen Mr. Tyler's wife and daughters come backstage. "In the winter they live in New York," said old Mrs. Ada Boshell, "and in summer on Shelter Island."

"Thank you, no," said Freddie. "Tea only and I'll swaller it neat. My first visit to the Garrick Club, old Miles, the steward, advised me to 'not dawdle and drink it neat.'"

Mr. Tyler brought London to the tea table rushing through Iowa wheat fields.

The waiter brought tea and Miss Clarens poured. "When we close, Ruth, where will you stay in New York?" she asked.

"I haven't really decided."

"Perhaps you might like to try the Hotel Richmond on Forty-sixth Street between Fifth Avenue and Sixth. Freddie, write down Hotel Richmond for Ruth. That is where I stay."

"Oh, thank you." How could I afford to live where Miss Clarens lived? Would she discover I was nobody?

"Write them at once, my dear, otherwise they might be full up."

Pray they would be! Their reply was an answered prayer, but a surprise. "Theatrical rates begin at a dollar and a quarter a day for room with hot and cold running water." Cheaper than I dreamed and how stylish it would sound in Quincy, "Hotel Richmond, just off Fifth Avenue!"

When Miss Clarens inquired later if I had written the hotel, I said "Papa's dippy over having one be chaperoned." Miss Clarens referred to herself as "one."

I went back to the Three Arts Club, everybody nice, but, taken up with her own affairs, Ruth Johnston had left to marry Roger Wisner. Edith McClellan was going to marry Otto Torrington and had a new best friend. What if I moved out and stayed at a downtown hotel? Much more convenient to look for a job.

I went down to West Forty-eighth Street and asked to see a single room at the Bristol Hotel next to the Playhouse. Someone said the Bristol was the cheapest. The room they showed me wasn't made up, a spurt of courage sent me over to West Forty-sixth Street, no debts and two hundred dollars pinned to my corset cover. The Hotel Richmond had an outside room that barely cleared the Hotel Deauville's roof, I couldn't see Fifth Avenue, but looked toward it. The bathroom window of the room next to mine looked catty-corner into my room, but rise above it? "Rise above it" became my motto or maybe it had always been and waited to surface at the Hotel Richmond.

One hot night a man unfurled a roll of toilet paper to let it blow into my room. "Come and see me," was written on it. I pulled the shade down and rose above it.

"Don't be helpless, Ruth."

I say I can learn anything, but why does it take me so long? I was never going to lie again and a year and a half later I did.

After our Saturday matinee, rich Mary Miller asked me up to the Plaza with her fiancé and his friend. Mary had been in my class at dramatic school, but only for something to do, she wasn't going to be an actress, her mother and grandmother were rich and lived in a big suite at the Plaza Hotel. Mary had a suite of her own.

The tea dance was fun, but I had to have dinner before the show.

"Have it upstairs," said Mary, and gave me her key. "We're going to Reuben's, then after the show we'll pick you up, we're driving out to Shanley's Yonkers." Lovely to be rich, tell everyone what to do and expect everybody to fit in!

The waiter brought a menu, I ordered. On the side table a big green bottle of Poland Water looked rich. At Martin's Theatrical at 227 West Forty-fifth Street all our water came out of the faucet. Lovely to be extravagant! On the table by the couch was *La Vie Parisienne*. The girls wore nothing but lingerie where everything showed through. One girl went without any. Had Mary's fiancé seen *her* without any? If you're engaged is it all right to?

A knock at the door.

"Come in."

The waiter rolled in a white damask-covered table, a busboy rolled in another with a spirit lamp and a tray of French pastry. In Quincy I'd never heard of it.

What lamb chops, what green peas! Martin's green peas were gray, these looked like ones from Aunt Ela's garden. The pat of sweet butter melted. In Quincy I'd never had sweet butter.

In front of me on the silver plate, each pastry was in paper lace. Should I choose the chocolate éclair? At Cooke, the caterer in Boston, Mama and I blew in thirty cents to have an éclair after shopping.

When I'd be a star I'd have French lamb chops, French pastry and green peas two or three nights a week. Should I choose the cream puff with powdered sugar like Mama made when I had the measles? Or the vanilla-frosted oblong cake with half a maraschino? The strawberry tart with yellow cream underneath? That chocolate éclair like Pirolle's next to the Lyceum Theatre? This one was better than Pirolle's. Better than Cooke's. Have the other one.

The door opened. "It's me, sweetie, I forgot something." Mary disappeared in the bathroom.

The waiter came with the check.

"I'll sign," called Mary.

The waiter looked at the French pastry tray. "Two."

Mary came out. "No, I didn't have any."

The waiter looked at me. "Two," he said.

"One. Miss Miller didn't have any."

"*You* have two?"

"One."

"She had one." Mary sounded impatient.

"I bring six on the tray, now is four."

"You made a mistake," said Mary. Rich people have conviction.

"No mistake, room service put six." He turned to me. "You take *two?*" he asked, politely.

"One."

Wouldn't anything teach me not to lie? A year and a half ago that terrible scene at Miss Clarens', I'll never lie again I swore, now for a chocolate éclair I'd done it.

Miss Clarens had rented an apartment. "Come and have dinner with an Australian friend who's going out to California to act in films," she said.

I'd never met anybody from Australia, I'd never met anybody from California. I was a movie extra in Fort Lee, New Jersey, but Miss Clarens' friend was the first I knew going to be a California movie star.

Miss Clarens had engaged a couple to cook and serve, and what a dinner! How polite everyone was, how like you read about!

"It was perfect, Elise." Miss Bennett put her arm around Miss Clarens. "I hate to say goodbye."

So did I. Reluctantly I put on my hat.

"What a beauty!" exclaimed Miss Clarens.

A beauty that had cost me fourteen dollars at Stern Brothers' untrimmed hat counter.

"May I try it on?"

"Please do." I handed her my dark blue velvet tricorn, a ribbon rosette I had sewed on the side like Ninon Lacey's hat I'd admired, sitting back of it at our Quincy Unitarian Church.

"I love a tricorn, where did you buy it?"

"Henri Bendel's."

"No wonder it's a beauty!"

"Bendel's?" asked Miss Bennett.

"Just off Fifth Avenue on West Fifty-seventh Street." Miss Clarens looked at the hat, gave it back and opened the door. "Mind the stairs," she warned.

"We will. Good night, Elise."

"Good night, Enid. Good luck in the films."

"Good night, Miss Clarens."

Two days later the elevator boy shoved a pearl-gray envelope under my door.

> 132 West 34th Street
> New York
> 18, August, 1916

Dear Ruth,
  Your guest card for the Gamut Club expired
last Saturday,

                                   Elise Clarens

Each word was clear, why did it sound strange? Read it again.

>Dear Ruth,
>   Your guest card for the Gamut Club . . .

She had told me I'd be elected any day and it was all right to go. Did this letter sound as though I was *not* to? Was it unfriendly or did it just sound so?

Don't be helpless, leave my washing in a damp lump and get dressed.

"Taxi." Extravagant but I had to feel right again. "One thirty-two West Thirty-fourth Street."

I ran up the first flight, up the second, the dark hall had a flaring gas lamp. Up the third, the hall was lighted by a skylight, Miss Clarens' door was opposite the head of the stairs. I knocked. "What are you doing out so early?" she'd exclaim in that lovely English voice. "I got your letter." "My dear, it's a matter of form. I'm sitting down to my second cup of tea. Have a cup with me, you'll be elected at tomorrow's meeting." "Thank you, the letter really did scare me." "Silly child, have some tea." The door hadn't opened. Knock again, a firm knock.

It opened a crack, Miss Clarens peered out. "What do you want?" Her voice was icy.

Words stuck in my throat. "Miss Clarens, your letter—" The words stuck.

"Don't come here anymore." The door closed.

Along the way to civilization some agony grows less, some almost is forgotten, some you lose motion, I sat on the top step and held onto the bannister. Three flights to go, just sit and hold on.

The door opened a crack, Miss Clarens glared at me. "Go away!"

I got down the stairs, got across Thirty-fourth Street and up Sixth Avenue. Back in my room I sat on the edge of the bed, gave the operator Angela Ogden's number. Angela was the best actress in Miss Adams' company. "Don't let it be busy, God, let it answer."

"Hello?"

"Angela, can you come over? Angela, can you? Angela, listen Angela, can I come over *there*? Angela, I have to talk to you, I can't tell you over the phone. Angela, something terrible has . . ."

How endless can a half hour be?

Angela sat straight-backed in my armchair.

"She just opened the door a *little* and looked at me like she hated me, then she said, 'Go away!' You *know* how great she's always treated me. Angela, I never did one thing wrong to her."

"Ruthie, *collect* yourself. Nothing is solved by having a fit."

"But—"

"Stop talking and listen to me."

"I—"

"Ruth, shut up! You asked for help and I'm going to give it to you. I don't think it's your fault. I don't *know* any more than you do, but I feel this isn't anything you deserve."

"She must have *heard* something. I told her about Mr. Archie Selwyn acting as if he was going to kiss me. Maybe she thought there was more." I burst into tears. "Maybe she thinks I'm living with him."

"Don't be a baby, Ruth. It's a jolt when people turn on you, but I think Elise is trying to get rid of you."

"Trying to get rid of me? She just had me to dinner!"

"I think you were a little troublesome, dear."

"How *could* I? I *love* her."

"Yes, dear, but being underfoot."

"She *likes* me with her, she even put me up for the Gamut Club so we could go there *together*."

"When was that?"

"Two weeks ago."

"That might not be convenient anymore."

"But why wouldn't she *say* that?"

"Perhaps it wouldn't be convenient, it's not easy to tell somebody they're in the way."

"But she had me to dinner with her Australian friend, Miss Enid Bennett that's going to California to be a movie star."

"That was before."

"Before what?"

"Before Freddie Tyler got back. He was on Shelter Island with his family, now he's back in town."

"But Mr. Tyler likes me."

"That may be, dear, but he likes Elise better. Ruth, dear, pay attention. Elise is having an affair with Freddie Tyler."

Are you a believer? Sometimes it's hard.

August 19, 1916

HOTEL RICHMOND
Forty-Sixth Street
off Fifth Avenue
New York
Egbert B. Seaman

Dear Miss Clarens,
    I will not bother you, but could you please tell me if I have done anything you don't like?

Yours truly,
Ruth

Another gray envelope under the door.

132 West 34th Street
21 August, 1916

Dear Ruth,
    Don't give it another thought.

Best wishes,
Elise Clarens

P.S. Did you ever hear the old English music hall song, "Where Did You Get That Hat?"?

When she took off my hat she noticed it had no lining. A hat from Henri Bendel would have a silk lining.

Hadn't that taught me not to lie? Didn't I believe if someone would teach me, I could learn? Now I'd told the waiter, "One."

"Two are gone," he said to Mary.

"I choose to believe my friend." How haughty the rich can be! "Tell room service to correct the check and I'll sign it at breakfast."

The waiter looked troubled. He wheeled away the tables.

Mary shrugged. "I'm sorry, sweetie. They're stupid when they get old! See you tonight. Jimmy Phipps is crazy about you, isn't he a whiz?"

At the stage door a word for the doorman. "When Lieutenant Phipps asks for me after the show, say, 'Her father arrived and surprised her.' And Wilbur, *don't* make a mistake."

" 'He surprised her,' " wrote Wilbur on his pad.

"Remember, Wilbur, I *beg* you."

"How many times did your father surprise you and how many mistakes did I make?"

I kissed Wilbur's cheek and felt discouraged. *Could* I learn to be an actress when I couldn't even learn not to lie?

Know anybody named Egbert?

Three years ago I went back to lying. Maybe in the old days, but today I don't see it.

Success is tough on everybody. Even a cat. The opening night of my play *Years Ago* was a wonderful opening. The earlier version that we'd tried out was called *Miss Jones,* now it was rewritten. Fredric March would star in it, the title was changed and so was the cast. All but the cat. Opening night of *Years Ago* the only member from *Miss Jones* carried off the honors in his scene. Mrs. Jones carried him across the stage with a spray of Boston fern in his mouth. He liked Boston fern and when the property man gave it to him, hung onto it.

"Punk, you're a bad cat," scolded Mrs. Jones as she carried him across the stage. "You've been eating my Boston fern again."

"Meee-ow!" The audience applauded. After the opening the property man rode him home. He had a bowl of milk and died.

What's the lesson? Fredric March had a much bigger part, made a much bigger hit and didn't die. Do you notice there are things there's no answer to?

Subject of dying, I'm thinking of writing a letter to the New York *Times* obit department, some stuff ought to get straightened out. Their obit for Mabel Taliaferro tells about a play she played in, *Mr. Wiggs in the Cabbage Patch.*

Dear Obit Writer,

Let me read my obit. Or if you don't want to, when I go leave a line or two and head it, "Unlisted Number."

"Mrs. Wiggs *of* the Cabbage Patch," the star was Mrs. Eleanor Belmont's mother, Madge Carr Cook, a beloved actress. Lovey Mary was the next best part to *Mrs.* W. I saw it when I was six years old and can still cry when the horse lies stricken and Mrs. Wiggs pours a quart of warm soup down his throat.

Mrs. August Belmont, you had a dandy mother and I wish you and I were taking in a matinee of "Mrs. Wiggs of the Cabbage Patch."

At least, obit writer, you didn't write *Ms.* Wiggs. Thanks for that.

Ruth Gordon

After I quit thinking, I wrote it. It's Sunday afternoon around three. It will get in the mailbox, but then what if I die before it gets delivered?

"The dreaming soul of the human race . . ."

Do you dream or do you take potluck and trust in the postal system?

Obit writer did not reply.

Did you ever notice trouble is no respecter of age? "A happy childhood," say many. I wonder. Everything going fine then would you think a butterscotch ball could do harm? Six for a penny wrapped in yellow wax paper, but they melt in summer and stick to the paper. Carrying my red mercerized sunshade with the bamboo handle I pulled the yellow paper off, tossed it away, nobody ever heard of don't litter and when I got home Mama asked, "What's that on your lovely parasol?"

With all the Commonwealth of Massachusetts to land in six sticky butterscotch papers had stained my red mercerized parasol.

Don't send me flowers that have wires on their stems. Don't send me any if you order by phone or Western Union, they're full of lemon leaves, button chrysanthemums, gladiolus, asparagus fern or that rubbery fern that looks like plastic. Maidenhair fern, but where is any? Vivien Leigh could choose flowers. She asked us to do a heartrending favor for her and sent us masses of pale straw-colored daffodils and black tulips. Little Vivien! She knew what to do about everything except find a reason to live.

"Poor everybody," said Leonora Hornblow.

She says *I* said it. I wish nobody had to say it, but if anybody's going to have to I wish it would be me.

In Sunday school they said a lot about hell. In church, also. I did wicked things, was wicked, but hell is for bad people and I was never bad.

I don't think hell is devils and red-hot pitchforks. Hell is to get left in the cemetery with no more chances and the gladiolus and set pieces curling up.

"In my Father's house are many mansions," says the good book, and I don't like to be in anyone's mansion. I hope heaven is like the Swopes', where even your first visit you felt at home and everybody enjoyed themselves.

Heaven is where the quilt is warm enough, where the blind doesn't creak, where the bathroom works, where things are the way you want them, so are the people.

I bet I'll get there even though I've broken all the Commandments but three. I never worshiped graven images, I never killed anyone, I never coveted my neighbor's wife.

I don't blame me, the Commandments should be more in tune with the times.

Do you go for the short cut? With me it doesn't work.

Do you go for the short cut? With me it doesn't work.

Do you say, "I happen to like bananas?" "I happened to walk in the park?" "I happen to not like cats?"

What does "happen" have to do with it? Cut out some, like Noel Coward had to cut out a lot of verys. He had left the galleys of his new book with Alexander Woollcott.

"Too many verys," wired Woollcott.

Back came a telegram, "VERY VERY VERY . . ." seventy-five of them, signed "NOEL."

Once he sent another telegram, first night good wishes signed "FIORELLO LA GUARDIA."

"You can't sign that," said the Western Union clerk.

"Why not?"

"Because you're not Fiorello LaGuardia."

He signed it "NOEL COWARD."

"You can*not* sign that."

"But I *am* Noel Coward."

"You *are!*"

"Yes."

"Well, then, you can sign it 'FIORELLO LAGUARDIA.' "

Get famous, cut out "happens," use less verys.

Instead of very, maybe pick up a useful word?

"Skeeky," said Glady Bain when she described flowers she had to throw away and *had* to tell someone. An auto horn honked, I put my thumb over the line in Virgil, looked out at Gladys driving. "I have to see you!" she shouted. Gladys Bain was a junior at Wellesley College and had more style than anybody.

"Mama, I'm going out with Glady Bain." I rushed downstairs.

The Peerless took off almost before I got in. "My mother is on this train coming in, I told her I was having lunch at a girl's house and would come home on this train, then nipped up Commonwealth Avenue to the Algonquin Club where a fellow I was meeting was in an open Stutz, horizon blue with nickel mudguards, 'Get in,' he said, went up Commonwealth with a noise like giant firecrackers and pulled up in front of a nifty gray stone *apartment house!*"

"My *God!*"

"What could I say?"

"What *did* you?"

"I went *in!*"

"My *God!*"

"Nifty elevator, my heart going like the Stutz, a *Jap* servant opened the door!"

"My *God!*"

"He bowed as if old Corlew taught him, took my coat, bowed and *there* was the table for two!"

"My dear!"

"Lace table cover, silver with big gobby monograms, silver vase with a circle of cupids, bright orange skeeky flowers, my God, after lunch what could *happen?*"

"My God!"

"We got back in the Stutz and ratatat to the South Station with the flowers."

"Where are they?"

"In a trash can. I *can't* let Mama know I was in a man's apartment and where *else* would be those skeeky flowers? Only the Jap there and just one little cuddle and kiss, we came out of it and he said, 'Next week.' I'll make Mama think she told me the three-ten and by the time *you* go home, she'll forget."

"My God, couldn't you have kept *one* flower?"

"A flower like that you couldn't explain!"

"Really skeeky?"

"Really!"

Where it fits there's no other word.

"Get up early in the morning before everybody has breathed up all the good air," Thornton Wilder said. He says I said it.

"*You* did, Thornton."

"I *never* said it. It's much more like you than me." He didn't make it sound like a compliment.

When you got solvent what were the penalties? Was one getting acquisitive? We *had* to have a country house. We drove out I don't know how many times with how many real estate agents, then we found it. Fairfield, Connecticut.

Life isn't country houses but when solvency sets in, it *is*, and here it was, tranquil, gentle, no view, just trees and lawn and lilac and wygelia and forsythia bushes. On a dirt road life would smooth out.

The real estate agent was pleased for us, drove with us in our Packard limousine giving directions to Chapman, our chauffeur for eighteen years who in all those years hardly ever could find the place we were going. Lady agent guided him back to the village to sign the preliminary papers at her office. What a pleasant ride after looking and looking and disagreeing, compromising, now Garson loved the house, I loved it, it was the right distance from New York, the house was right, the grounds were right, the price was right, how lovely, how unusual!

"And you'll feel so good here, it's restricted, you know."

"Restricted from what?"

"Well, restricted." She smiled a ladylike smile.

"But restricted from what? Restricted means it's restricted from something." The thought dawned. "What's it restricted *from?*"

Then she knew! "Well, it's restricted from—er—from people crossing your lawn." She got out at the real estate office and we turned where the sign said Merritt Parkway. Goodby Fairfield, it was nice while it lasted. Or was it?

God was on our side. He found us the best house he had vacant.

Not restricted, not anything but glorious total perfection and we owned it, a house in the country. That brought on weekend guests. And walks up our hill that halfway up became the Gilbert Millers' hill, their house on top. We walked into the drawing room, was it Connecticut or Park Avenue? Woods and fields and winter twilight were curtained over. Lamps, and wall brackets gleamed on elegance. On the walls hung paintings, objets d'art were scattered over polished tables, an Aubusson carpet softened our tread. Was it designed to shut out life?

At the far end sat Sandor Ince, faithful companion of Gilbert. Pince-nez adjusted, he read at arm's length a rumpled manuscript. Or was he taking a Sunday nap? Kitty Miller, smartly turned out, country jewelry gold and semiprecious, listlessly turned the pages of *Vogue*. A scraggly valuable dog, too big for a rat and too small for a possum, lay dead in front of the hearth.

Garson and I walked in and doggie came to life resentfully, let out shrieks. Ince glanced up, a ray of hope lit his face. Kitty and he greeted us with such enthusiasm we saw what a dull Sunday this had been. "Ruth!" exclaimed Kitty, delighted.

"My dear!" Ince rushed forward.

The nor-rat-nor-possum let out more short shrieks.

Gilbert gave a grunt meant to sound hospitable. We were somebodies and besides he almost liked us, especially Garson, a man who could write a hit.

Everybody moved about, pushed chairs, adjusted lights like dragonflies darting here and there over a pool. They gradually alighted.

"What a divine day!"

"Did you walk?"

"The relief of a sunny weekend!"

"How beautiful you look, darling."

"Aren't you too warm near the fire?"

"Sit by the fire. You must be frozen."

"What a divine color."

Glen wheeled the tea tray in. Delicate cups rattled delicately, the tea service shone.

"Sugar, dear?"

"No sugar."

"Lemon, darling, one sugar on the side."

"Strong for me."

"As it comes."

"A drop of milk, darling?"

Glen moved, silent and dexterous between hostess and guests. Kitty poured, Glen made it work. On the tea table were small frosted cakes, frosting spun round and around to a silver sugar candy. They were for the guests; for Gilbert, a plate of Ry-Krisps, a plate of Swedish-non-fatteners, a plate of zwieback.

"Glen." He snapped his fingers.

Glen was by his side.

"A biscuit."

Glen offered the RyKrisps almost before the word was out.

"A *biscuit*," Gilbert repeated, irked.

Glen offered the something from Sweden.

"A biscuit," bellowed Gilbert, "a biscuit, my dear fellow, a *biscuit*."

Glen swooped the zwieback toward him and strove to read his master's visage.

"Goddam it, a biscuit! A biscuit! A biscuit!"

For the first time Glen was tentative. He offered the silver tipped cakes. Gilbert lunged at them. "God," he moaned, "what makes you so stupid, Glen?"

"Yes, sir." Glen moved nimbly away.

Once solvency drove us to a country home we found time to write a movie script to lead to further solvency. We sold it to Harry Cohn, the head of Columbia Pictures, took the train to California and were invited to Harry Cohn's for dinner. Coffee was served in the big projection room before he showed a movie. I'd never been to a dinner at a movie tycoon's, around me swished the conversation. "My little boy's five and a half, I took him to Paris this summer."

"They got nothin' but fairies in the State Department."

"We loved Paris. He said 'Mummy, let's live here all the time and bring our house and garden.' He loved Paris but he did want his own garden."

"You all right?" Harry Cohn glared at me. I was Gar's wife so I was somebody.

"Yes, thanks!"

He knew I was lying and moved on.

"Gave me some lousy gold cuff links. What do I want of gold cuff links?"

Where was Garson? The butler was giving him coffee. "I put up twenty-seven dollars and got back fifty-three! He wasn't even the favorite."

Garson never saw a horse race, why should the butler confide in him?

"I was always scared, but this trip with my little boy I was supposed to fly the Hollywood Special from Le Bourget. They booked me on the ten o'clock, but I said, 'Put me on the ten-thirty, the Hollywood Special,' but I *was* booked on the *ten o'clock,* so I said only on the Hollywood Special, and when my driver came to meet me at Burbank, they told him the plane was lost so he thought I was lost but *I* came on the Hollywood . . ."

Maybe walk over to Garson, beside Mrs. Harry Cohn talking to the wife of renowned French cameraman. Mrs. Cohn saying:

"How much'd you pay for that dress? Of course, you're French. Where'd you get that?"

Do you think sometimes that it will never be time to go home? Then do you notice it *does* come time. What if we hadn't bought our house in the country and hadn't written that screenplay that brought us to California and hadn't sold it to Harry, where would I be that evening? When money starts pouring in, think it over.

First loves: My light blue silk parasol from Cousin Mabel. I was four years old. Where did that ever get lost? Mama hardly ever let me use it and never on a sunny day. Blue fades quicker than any other color, at least that's what she said, but I say what became of my parasol?

Do you bring the bad days with you and enjoy them because they're no longer going on, things are going great?

Do you stir up mischief to remind you of days that didn't look as if they'd get solved, but now the mischief you've thought up you can straighten out?

Is happiness too much to take? You've got the engine going to fight off trouble and now there isn't any.

Hard to believe that days when everything is going well can be too much to take.

Can anybody endure steady happiness or steady trouble?

We all have our own remedy. Sometimes I go in for wild flowers and gingham dresses with closets full of Chanel, Dior and try to live my childhood life along with my mature life, which doesn't strike me as all that mature. I want to bring my poor years side by side with the rich ones. Is that why people who don't have to, love to cook? Reminder of when they had to? Why people who can afford a log cabin with four bathrooms camp in the woods? Recollections of the old days, knowing they can quit and return to comfort?

Why do tycoons have their Ma's picture on their desks while screwing up someone in front of it? Would Ma have thought how far her boy or girl had strayed or would she have wondered where did *she* lose courage to do the same? Do people get moral when they don't get ahead?

VISCERAL MYTHS REPRISE

Sometimes I got back to Quincy to touch base. 14 Elmwood Avenue still looks the same. It takes me a minute before I can walk up to the place where I connected with myself. At 41 Winthrop Avenue I left without anything in mind, the same when I walked downstairs at 41 Marion Street, but when I walked down the 14 Elmwood Avenue front steps I was on my way. Do *you* have an address where the world shifted and went the other way? Mine was this gray house that was red when we moved in, red when my second grade teacher, Miss Ida Cameron, came to lunch and played our piano and I loved her, then, sometime between red and when they painted the house gray I knew what I wanted to do. And still do. Is that *your* definition of lucky?

This house full of worry, what would I do, what would I be, and one day I had the answer. I knew. Knew what I wanted, knew nothing would stop me, learned to accept trouble, learned to live with it, learned to get what I wanted, learned the need for confidence and built it in, learned not to accept facts, learned to believe. Even without talent, that could swing a career. What

I didn't have in this house was the goodness to think of someone else. That came only with success.

Do you know the British "I've got mine, Jack?"

I don't say it has to be, but I had to succeed before I knew there were more than two kinds of people: those who could help me and those who could get in my way.

Darling W. Somerset,

Why don't you let anyone call you Somerset? How are you celebrating Ash Wednesday? Buying dresses at Mainbocher is my penance. Did you ever see his bills? I'm glad I grew up irresponsible. For a while it looked as if I was going to have character. Thank God I rose above it! People with character can turn out gloomy, I'm loose in my ways and take the trouble to enjoy myself.

Do you love possessions? I fought it, but I've given in. A load off my poitrine! And speaking of same when do we dear people meet? Would Alan rather we came to visit you or would he rather you two visit us? We could offer Alan a lovely suite and a sort of shakedown for you. From your books you're always so obliging, run here, run there, sleep anywhere, anything to accommodate, so what do you say? If you don't want to come to us, we can show up at Villa Mauresque any date after quatorze Juillet when I plan to dance my heart out in the old port of St. Tropez.

Love,
Ruth

Have you learned patience? You have to or give up getting civilized. My patience grew stronger when Quincy celebrated its three hundred fiftieth anniversary. I was invited to sit on the dais. Breakfast in Atlanta, then Eastern Airlines to Logan Airport in Boston and that night dinner at the Chateau de Ville, Randolph, the next town to Quincy where I lived the first seventeen years of my life, knew there was a place named Randolph but never was there. What was there was the Chateau de Ville that could feed a thousand of us.

Eastern pre-boarded me, I took the first-row window seat. When the passengers came on, the aisle seat was taken by a man who looked like Alec Guinness playing a diplomat. He went to work on his papers, I started planning what would I say on the dais, when a cute stewardess knelt down beside the dip, talked to me across his letters and papers, "We got a bet going in the cockpit whether you're Helen Hayes or Ruth Gordon."

"I'm Ruth Gordon."

"Great!" she shouted. "That's my bet!" And rushed into the cockpit.

"What kind of fame is it," I asked my seatmate "when they know you, but don't know who you are?"

"The best kind." A dip for sure.

George Abdon, with the big gray limo, met me at Logan, we kissed. He's from Quincy, has three limos marked "Abdon 1," "Abdon 2," "Abdon 3," he drove me to the Ritz to dress and eat an early dinner up in my room, a must before a banquet. God knows what they'll serve and when!

"Room service, at five o'clock, send me up a filet mignon, rare, baked potato, not opened, spinach, strawberry ice cream."

Quincy's three hundred fiftieth doesn't come cheap: seat on the plane, George's limo bill, a night at the Ritz and a seventeen-dollar dinner, but there's only one three hundred fiftieth anniversary of the city I was born in to sit on the dais.

Bathe, make up, eat filet mignon, baked potato, spinach, ice cream, dress the way Mama would want me to, turquoise blue satin from Givenchy, diamonds, pearls. "Mama, I looked like an actress and also like *you* would like," long sleeves, high neck, a small train. I'd ordered it for when I won the Golden Globe for my performance in *Inside Daisy Clover*.

In the gray limo George headed for Randolph. As we neared the Chateau, traffic, traffic, but we had allowed time for it. A sea of parked cars and still traffic from all directions.

"Pick you up right here," said George. "I'll squeeze inside the ballroom and when I see you start to go I'll meet you right here with the car. Remember this exit now!"

An official met me, got me through the fans up the grand staircase. "I want to look in at the dais, see where I sit, how many steps when we march in and where I speak." The first banquet you spoke at did you think of stuff like that?

Great sight an empty dining room. Empty except for the army of waitresses knowing just what they're doing. They waved, I waved, counted two steps up, the podium, stand up to it, too high. "I have to have a little something to stand on." Found my seat, two beyond the podium, next to our hired professional Master of Ceremonies. Fine! Now go back where dais sitters were drinking cocktails in a room shut off from paying diners.

Before I speak I don't have a drink, I hold a glass of soda with a slice of lemon so they won't keep asking what I want to drink. I fought off a shoulder corsage, met the this-generation Adams, Charles Francis, and his elegant, young Mrs., met the Mayor, met the everybody.

The letter requesting me to appear had asked me to speak. "Yes and for how long?" I wrote back.

"We'd love to hear you reminisce," came the reply.

"That could take two or three days. How long should I actually be at the mike?"

"Maybe half an hour? Whatever you feel."

Half hour I'd planned, but on the dais I noted the number of speakers' chairs and thought, "Cut it down to twenty minutes. Even though I'll be the highlight, be practical but don't skimp."

Master of Ceremonies came up, lifted his glass to me, paid me
a list of compliments.

"Thanks," then back to practicalities. "When you introduce
me who do I follow?"

He looked over his list. "You follow Chairman of the School
Board."

A good spot.

Time for the lineup. A lady said she'd hold my chinchilla
coat, so I could march in unencumbered. Everybody was asked
to see where their name was on chairs set out to match the
chairs on the dais with our names on a card in each seat. We
found ourselves, waited, then the orchestra whooped up our entrance number, everybody stood in position, marched from a
gently lighted room into spotlights. Glad I had been on the
Johnny Carson show, where they have bright bright lights! Also
glad I knew where I was going, when suddenly our leader
goofed and didn't do the serpentine around the front of the dais
to show us off, did he get blinded or stage fright? He led us
straight up on the dais, entering from the left. Eventually we got
sorted out, stood for the ovation, not too overwhelming, then sat.

On each plate was a fruit cup, beside it a roll and butter. In
front of me people came up to the dais, asked me to sign this or
that, behind me a steady procession came up to our Master of
Ceremonies: "You have to introduce the heads of all Quincy's
wards."

"I've got a big list," demurred the M. of C.

"They have to be introduced."

"Okay." He wrote another note.

"When do the intros start?" I asked.

"*Star-Spangled,* then priest, rabbi, Protestant, honored guests,
officeholders, people from the audience."

"A long list. How long would you like me to speak?"

"Well—" He looked anxious.

"Should I cut it down to five minutes?"

He squeezed my hand.

Twenty minutes snipped to five takes a little thinking.

The loudspeaker blared out, "This is Chief of Police of Randolph. If your license plate is X-600, 241-609, F 42-833, 076, LA 2-77, G2-984 move 'em or they'll get towed."

Move them where? When George and I drove up, it looked as though all Randolph was paved with cars!

The band played, a lot of people danced, eight young girls danced a round dance. Why did I think of Ibsen?

"This is Councilman Reilly, Ruth, and Councilman Horan."

We talked, then a talk with Father Farren, Monsignor Carey. "We used to go over Saturdays and play with the Curley kids." Mayor Curley lived at Jamaica Plain.

"Near Jamaica Pond."

"You should see it *now,* Ruth!"

"Was it Emerson said about Jamaica Pond, it was perfection? The shape, the proportion, the setting?"

"I never heard that. They're talking of tearing down your old high school, Ruth," said Chairman of the School Board.

"Good." Memories don't get destroyed, the building wasn't what we remember. Room 24's architecture wasn't what brought us to life. Beautiful Miss O'Neill was killed over twenty years ago, but lives on vividly with her pupils.

People kept coming up to the dais. "I'm Marion Edwards' daughter."

"We were such friends!"

"She's told me. This is my husband."

"I don't know if you'll remember, but we met in Ogunquit, when Garson's play was there and Mike Todd was the producer and did you know what happened? The company was supposed to go back to New York from Ogunquit, but the theatre in Fairhaven wanted them to play there, so you all went from Ogunquit to Fairhaven and a few days later Mike's general manager sent him a bill from Ogunquit to New York. Somebody forgot to cancel it."

I don't know what I said.

"My mother says she went to Maine with you and your mother one summer," said Marion's daughter.

People were waiting to talk to me.

"I have some snapshots of us at Christmas Cove and one day we went over to Squirrel Island to spend the day with Mr. and Mrs. Emery, your *great*-grandmother and *great*-grandfather."

Her husband is trying to look with it, it takes patience to go through a three hundred fiftieth.

"They had a house on Adams Street right opposite the President's house. And Marion took me to spend the night there. But who *I* loved was your grandmother, Marion's mother."

Her husband gave a little tug to her arm. His trek to civilization was getting a *real* patience workout.

"Mrs. Alice Edwards, she lived in that lovely house on Greenleaf Street."

"My Uncle Ken's daughter lives in it."

"Edwardses *still* live in that Greenleaf house?"

Husband getting restless.

If Garson had been there, he'd have given me a hint to break it off, but he was still in Atlanta.

"In that house one Saturday your grandmother served us the greatest sausages called Newport. I never served any other kind until the firm went out of business. Why didn't Marion come with you tonight?" Quincy's three hundred fiftieth and I have to tell about sausages?

"Deep arthritis, we moved her from Hingham down to where we are at Cotuit on the Cape."

Other people's reminiscences are only interesting if you shared them and husband didn't.

A handsome, elegant man with a lady stopped in front of me. "I'm Lee Remick's father."

"Mr. Remick!"

Remick's store in Quincy Square, the best of Quincy stores! Mr. Remick, gentle and gray-haired and young-looking, introduced me to his wife. "Lee was so sad she couldn't come, she's in London."

"Through you we heard about the Hotel Belmont at West Harwich. Do you still have your place on the Cape? Through you, Thornton Wilder and Garson and I went, loved it and stayed till we were asked to leave to make way for the New England Post Masters Convention."

Master of Ceremonies introduced each councilman from all the wards, the Superintendent of Schools, head of the Historical Society and through it people kept coming up to talk to me.

A pretty blond lady said, "My husband loves you." And there was her husband, nodding his head.

"Did you see *Harold and Maude?*"

"Yes, but the one *we* love is *Where's Poppa?*"

Master of Ceremonies introduced City Clerk, State Senator, Associate Justice on the Massachusetts Supreme Court, the Mayor's wife, the Mayor. Over on the left that whole section couldn't hear and gave up trying, talked, laughed, had a fine time of their own, made a clatter along with the waitresses passing out individual plates of roast beef, bowls of string beans, bowls of potatoes, clearing fruit cups, everybody talking to everybody, while more and more intros were going on.

Then the *Star-Spangled Banner*. Pleasure to stand up, next the rabbi, next the priest, next the Unitarian minister, then first speaker. Up to the microphone came Dr. Priscilla White, in strawberry-ice-cream pink satin crepe. "I came to Quincy in 1907," she commenced.

She must have been seven, and I was eleven years old. Mrs. White, her son Leon, and Priscilla lived on Farrington Street, a brook limped along between Mrs. White's house and Dr. Adams' stable, except in summer, then it dried up. In March it showed action, the rest of the time it was a brook because Brook Street was called Brook Street and ran parallel.

Waitress put a plate of roast beef in front of me, but I'd had my dinner and was looking at Priscilla and remembering the home she'd lived in, dark green, shingled. Did it have a withdrawn look? Mrs. White, stout and pleasant, could have been pretty once. Her son, Leon, was good-looking in a big-boned

blond way, went in for athletics. He was a year or two years
older than I. Priscilla was chubby. If she weren't so pretty she'd
have been fat, but when pretty it's called chubby. I loved her
and so did Mama. And Mama liked Mrs. White.

I don't think we got asked to the Whites' house, but Priscilla
came to see us and on the seventeenth of March Mama made a
birthday cake for Priscilla and we carried it over to Farrington
Street. Angel food made in the big round cake pan that had a
round hole. An angel cake takes the whites of a dozen eggs, a lot
of eggs when you have to go easy on Mr. Backus' grocery bill
and mid-March eggs are an item.

At 14 Elmwood we were stuck with a golden cake, no favorite, but we had to use up the twelve yolks. Mama made a boiled
frosting for Priscilla's cake, golden cake like a poundcake, has no
frosting. Who makes rules?

The boiled frosting Mama colored pale green with pistachio
coloring. In the hole in the center she put two sprays of our
asparagus fern. I wish I had some, but it was Priscilla's. Her
mother thought a birthday cake spoiled a child.

Priscilla read on. It looked as though she had quite a few
pages more for us, but they didn't seem as interesting as old
thoughts that came back to me.

Her father was a great Boston doctor, he and her mother were
divorced. Mrs. White was the only person *we* knew who had a
divorce. Something stylish about it, I admired it. I don't think
Mrs. White did, I think she never forgave the doctor. "Forgive
and forget," they say. Forgive yes, do you ever forget?

Priscilla's pink satin dress rolled over some bulges. For school
she wore a middy blouse and pleated skirt. Blue serge in winter,
in summer white drill blouse and navy blue galatea skirt. Whatever became of fine cotton? Galatea and drill, percale, nainsook,
lawn, dimity? They still sell Fruit of the Loom, can you still buy
Pride of the West?

Pink satin tonight but when she lived on Brook Street only for
dancing school did Priscilla wear frills. She danced with style,
lots of bends and bows and in a white muslin with pale blue

satin sash, she looked like Cupid dressed in dotted muslin.
Would anyone know she was going to grow up and be voted one
of the ten greatest doctors in the world? Greatest authority on
child diabetes, head of the Joslin Clinic when old Dr. Joslin retired.

When she was nine her aunt in Paris sent her the prettiest hat
I ever saw. I've had hats made at Dior, at Rose Descat, famous
for the cloche, Douglas Pollard at Mainbocher, Miss Jessica at
Bergdorf's, Nathan Gibson Clark, who told the Governor of
Massachusetts' wife to go home and put on another dress, he
wouldn't have *that* color red in his store. No one made hats like
Nathan Gibson Clark so the Governor's lady changed her dress
and Nate let her order hats, but even his were not as beautiful as
Priscilla's floppy soft straw with its crown of cream chiffon,
round and round which was gathered cream color Val lace,
circled by white velvet ribbon not cream and over it a wreath of
white daisy-sized daisies, two discreet streamers falling over the
brim.

"That's the prettiest hat I ever saw," Mama told Mrs. White.

"It's from her aunt in Paris."

Talking to Mrs. White, Mama changed life for Priscilla.
Maybe better? Maybe not?

"I can't wait to see Priscilla's dress for the dancing school
ball."

Does that give you a picture of what *else* Mama had to look
forward to? Priscilla White's dancing school ball dress she
couldn't wait for? Each of us kept our dress a secret till the
event, but guileless Priscilla spilled the beans to me and I told
Mama and she told Mrs. White. Did that nip Priscilla's secret
hope of becoming an actress?

"Why, how do you know what Priscilla's going to wear, Mrs.
Jones?"

"Priscilla told Ruth."

Mrs. White's face turned stony. "Well, I shall put an end to
all *that*."

Mama was dismayed at what was back of the words. Priscilla

hadn't told me not to tell and why wouldn't I tell Mama and why wouldn't Mama tell Mrs. White how happy she'd be to see it?

Was she making too much of it? Back to my yellow silk muslin trimmed with white silk soutache braid sewn on in a circular pattern and a soft yellow messaline sash worn low around the hips. Yellow satin slippers, yellow hair ribbon, white ostrich feather fan, there were no yellow! It took a lot of squeezing out the money, but what gave us courage would be my splendor and the splendor of the other children one at a time coming through the door far right, the long walk across the ballroom floor in Braintree's Cochato Club to Miss Corlew, our teacher, "Dancing and Deportment," and the line of patronesses standing beside her, my mother, Mrs. Johnson, Mrs. Alden, Mrs. Glover, Mrs. Streeter. Through the door came Anna Witham, pale yellow embroidered chiffon over apricot messaline. Yellow over *apricot?* It *looked* pretty, but was it right? It must be right, made on Boylston Street in Boston, but yellow over apricot?

Through the door came Howard Johnson's sister, Barbara, in pale green silk muslin and gold slippers. Gold? Gold. Gold *color?* Gold leather like gold. Very unusual. Through the door came Priscilla in white drill middy blouse and blue pleated galatea skirt!

Had anyone *seen* such a thing? Mrs. White told Mama it was to teach Priscilla not to talk about clothes.

When in later years Priscilla told me that she'd wanted to be an actress I didn't ask why she thought she didn't become one, but I think her mother wanted to belong to another great doctor and made Priscilla one.

Did she remember the middy blouse and blue skirt? Standing at the podium she told a little about her mother, but mostly about her brother Leon and went on and on about how fine he was at athletics at high school and how he became a dentist and about his children and how when she went to high school Miss

O'Neill meant so much to her and steered her to Radcliffe College where Miss O'Neill had been, and what a great influence she was and how Priscilla had gone into medicine, but never lost touch with Miss O'Neill and Miss O'Neill had been her patient and said I'd been so good to her. "I saw Ruth in Barkington's play—Tarkington's play—*Seventeen*. Miss O'Neill said that when Ruth wrote the play that was at the Copley Theatre, Ruth saw that she had a share of the profits."

Any interest to the seventeen-dollar-per-place celebrators?

"Well, if you were handling a diabetes case," said Garson later, "you wouldn't be any good."

Waitresses were clearing away the ice cream dishes, pouring more coffee, we'd only got to our first speaker and she didn't seem to be in sight of her finish.

"Would you like me to just speak for two minutes?" I asked worried Master of Ceremonies.

He got right down on his knees and kissed my hand. What did audience think? Thought I, "What a celebrity! Twenty minutes cut to five minutes cut to two!" Worth it?

Speaker after speaker spoke, then Mr. School Board then finally me. Mama, you'd have been proud of how I looked, but not what I said. Only two minutes to be entertaining. "When I appeared on the Mike Douglas Show, Mike asked me, 'Weren't people in Quincy shocked at you becoming an actress? People in those days weren't so broad-minded.' 'No,' I said, 'only my Aunt Ada who lived on Whitney Road.'"

A cheer for local color.

"My Aunt Ada told Mama, 'For Ruth to go be an actress is like being a harlot,' 'Oh,' said Mike, 'how awful! How *dreadful!* Why, that's *terrible!*' And I heard myself say, 'Well, if you haven't tried it, don't knock it.'"

A thousand diners cheered up. I don't know how Papa knew to give me my first acting lesson: "When you stand up in meeting, you got to deliver."

Outside the entrance reliable George got me back. I'd acquired another lesson along my way to being civilized.

Personal to Sam Vaughan:

If you hold an audience's attention it's write or think up one speech if you have forty minutes to deliver it, but if you have only two minutes maybe all you can do is make an impression. For no reason do not wind up with a flat house.

Some things date and some stay appropriate.
"Did you ever sit and wonder?
Sit and ponder?
Sit and think?"
And so forth. George M. Cohan recited that at banquets and
benefits or for an encore. It still applies when you set your heart
on doing things right. The tickets for Jouvet's *L'Ecole des
Femmes* were hard to locate, but I got two pair, one pair for my
son Jones on Saturday night, one pair for Marie Brenier, my
maid, Friday night. The Saturday seats were in the last row, the
Friday row B. Could they improve the Saturday? After a lot of
trouble I got seats three rows from the back. Give Marie the Saturday night seats, let Jones have the good ones? I tossed this
around then thought why should Marie, who never sits down
front, be displaced for my son who has sat down front all his
life? I stuck to the original deal.

Jones arrived home from college on Thursday. I nearly
changed the seats, then didn't.

Friday the storm mounted to a hurricane, no taxis. Marie got
drenched, turned round and went back home, the seats weren't
used.

Next night I reminded Jones about the theatre.

"Oh, the girl I go with doesn't speak French so I turned back
the seats."

Would that suit Professor Alfred North Whitehead? "Let's
have order, but not too *much* order."

Do you start something and forget what it is? Keep going. Walk around. Pull up the window shade. Pull up the other one. Pull them down. Brush your hair while you do. Brush it on the way back. Maybe while you try to think what you forgot put on your stockings, maybe get into your dress. Keep going, you'll remember, give it time, ideas need a chance. *You* may be in a hurry, but that doesn't mean your thoughts.

And that didn't mean Sir Alexander Korda's thoughts. Was he in a hurry dressing? He and Vivien Leigh and Laurence Olivier were cruising on Alex's yacht, *The Elsewhere*. Korda told his captain to anchor off our yacht basin. Its graceful bow pointed toward La Réserve at Beaulieu.

Standing on our terrace, Alex suddenly looked startled.

"What is it?" Larry asked.

"I've forgotten to put on my drawers."

Vivien, Gar and I laughed, Larry just studied Korda. "I find that an interesting comment on you, Alex. You forget your drawers, but remember your decoration."

In Korda's lapel was the Légion d'Honneur rosette.

When you learn it's not the decoration but what you accomplished it may remind you to put on your drawers.

Ever struggle to remember that word?

Once Thornton Wilder came for Sunday dinner.

"We're going to have caramel ice cream," I boasted.

"That's a something flavor," he said, but for 'something' he said *the* right adjective. Garson and I admired, then forgot it. From time to time one of us would suggest some adjective, then it came back. "Drastic!"

"We're going to have caramel ice cream."

"That's a drastic flavor," said Thornton.

Drastic describes caramel ice cream.

Do you ever stop and consider the net result? What *you* do about success? We had M67 booked on the *Queen Elizabeth*. Vacation.

Phone rings. "Hello." It was George Cukor in California. "I need you for two weeks of revisions."

A letter from Darryl Zanuck had said Garson's screenplay *Come What May* will possibly need a few minor changes when a director is set.

George was set, we canceled our passage on the *Queen E.* and went to work. It proved more demanding than we'd foreseen. George wanted a lot of rewriting. The picture was set to start shooting May 21. We booked M67 for June 9.

Dear Diary of the Net Results, look where you and I are, Albuquerque. Garson and I got off and walked. The Chief waits twenty minutes. Indians sell turquoise jewelry and Indian beads, do they think people like that stuff? I buy some, then what?

Once Helen Hayes' mother said, "You know what they say on the Boardwalk in Atlantic City, 'Never refuse any offer on a rainy Monday morning.'" It wasn't rainy when we got to California, but it was Monday morning. Darryl Zanuck made an engagement for three-thirty. When we went into his office he told us the picture would be postponed indefinitely.

On the Boardwalk is anybody equipped to give us the net result if we hadn't agreed to postpone our sailing on the *Queen E.* M67?

"How have you got such a memory?" ask people.

"Because I forget so much."

Remembering is for what's important or interesting, if it's merely useful, don't. For ten years I've been a customer at the New San Francisco Market on Sixth Avenue, half a block from Central Park, I phone every day and each day I have to look up the number. Why keep it in my head when it's in my green leather New York phone book?

When I'm in *Mrs. Warren's Profession,* I remember my lines, we close and I don't.

Driving from Central Park South to Woods Hole to take the Martha's Vineyard ferry I remember that after we get out of Connecticut keep right driving on Route 95 or we'll find ourselves on a side road heading for East Greenwich, Rhode Island. I remember to bring five quarters to pay the tolls from Greenwich, Connecticut, to New London. I remember to bring thirty cents for that toll in New York.

I remember Papa's instruction, "Pick up your feet." Was that to save shoe leather or just good advice?

I remember to open my window, pray to God every morning, right after I turn on the gas flame under the tea kettle, but I can't remember to write Congressman Claude Pepper, who wrote me such a rewarding letter. Maybe I think that correspondence has gone as far as it will and his letter and my reply are in my head, which like my attic has unused things that connect me with myself, hook me in with the present, the future, the long ago.

I don't know our grocer's phone number, but clear as this morning are our two weeks summer vacations at French's Boarding House, Christmas Cove, Maine. Clear as this morning is the visit to old Mrs. Moore at Prides Crossing. "Did you know Oliver Wendell Holmes?" I asked the lady.

"The younger or the older?"

"Either one."

"Oh, we knew Dr. Holmes. Mr. Browning arranged it. We were dining in Venice and Mr. Browning said he'd write a letter." She turned to her son, "You remember, Paul, in Santa Barbara you presented Dr. Holmes with a nautilus shell. He said he had never seen one. I admired his poem, 'The Nautilus,' and had Mr. Tiffany set a beautiful shell in gold and little Paul presented it to Dr. Holmes."

Little Paul accepted another gin and tonic. Mrs. Moore left the past. "I shall be ninety-three on Thursday, will you come to my party?"

"I'm sorry," said Garson, "we'll be gone. I hope you have a lovely day."

"Why wouldn't I? I always have."

Ninety-two birthdays all good?

Call *hers* a good memory, clear she forgot the unnecessary.

Fine to have a place in your head where every single thing was good. In my head it's Maine. Even the people, the places have good names. Mr. Bert Thorpe of Christmas Cove, the island called Squirrel, town of Damariscotta, Heron Island, Cap'n Wells, who ran the pool tables the ice cream the dock. Mr. Sands French who ran the general store, Mrs. Flora McFarland, the Kelceys, who lived at the end of the Cove below Zion Hill and sometimes did washing for people. Mr. Wilbur Little always called Mister who worked at the Christmas Cove House, his brother Dennis, always called Dennis, who worked for Mr. Miles. Mr. Gammage, who lived next town South Bristol, Miss Lois Otis had a general store there, Mrs. Tibbets ran her boardinghouse across John's Bay at Pemaquid Harbor. Mr. Clifford in South Bristol made candy in his kitchen and sold it in his parlor. My boat I rowed was named *Bertha. Bertha,* a boat!

Only one thing wasn't good. Each summer we hoped the trip from Bath, Maine, to Christmas Cove would be on the *Nahanada,* not the *Wiwurna.* A man fell off the *Wiwurna*'s lower deck and was drowned. His heavy black rubber boots and a black rubber coat dragged him down. He was shifting trunks on the low-railed deck, a trunk got away from him and, trying to hold onto it, he went over, on shore, people mowing their grass, on the boat passengers watching, he came up and down. By the time they got the *Wiwurna* engines stopped, he didn't come up anymore.

Flag lowered to half-mast, Aunt Emma and Uncle George, waiting on the Christmas Cove dock, thought it was for me. They thought I was too different. A visceral myth? They just thought I was spoiled.

The man in the black rubber boots was the first man I ever saw die. Since him I've seen one other.

Do *you* borrow money?

Awful to ask.

Awful to be turned down.

Awful to face your debts.

Awful to receive the loan to pay them.

What did people do before the telephone? How did they know luck turned?

The phone rang. "Lewis Milestone wants you in his new film, *Edge of Darkness*." My agent's voice.

"He wants me, he's *got* me!"

"I'll have them send the script."

"Don't bother."

"It looks better."

"*You* look at it, but before you do, say yes."

There are times you can't be choosy, one time is when you need a job.

"What do you feel about fifteen hundred a week?"

"Grab it."

"You've always gotten two thousand."

"*Grab* it."

Goodbye a lot of debts! Is that the greatest feeling!

Why did Lewis Milestone want me? Because it had been planned. Hard times were in sight, the summer with no money, I called up George Cukor in Hollywood. "You said I could visit you for two weeks."

"Yes, but no more than two. When will you come?"

"June ten and not just pleasure, I have to get a job."

"We'll plan it."

I got my adorable cook Suzanne and my prize housemaid Katherine Waldron jobs at Garson's house on Sutton Place. Garson and I were courting and it had gotten too deep, I had to break it off.

"If you love me, why do you have to go away?"

"It's getting too—"

I couldn't finish.

Fortunately Jones had rebelled against camp. Lady Hardwicke wanted him and his governess to come to their big house in Beverly Hills. Little Edward Hardwicke was a year younger than Jones.

Jones, his governess, I got into a taxi to go to Grand Central, 60 West Twelfth Street locked up. Out of the taxi back window I saw Tom, our Esposito's Market man, coming with a white envelope. I knew that bill had gotten to about three hundred dollars. Who reads a script with that kind of a worry?

George Cukor's driver met me at Pasadena, Picsie Hardwicke and little Edward welcomed Jones and Miss Ryan. George's driver handed me a letter.

"Tonight dinner with the René Clairs. Pleasure.

Tomorrow night dinner at Ann and Jack Warner's. Biz.

Saturday. Go with Irene Selznick to Mr. Louis B. Mayer's birthday party at Santa Monica. Biz."

At Jack Warner's was Lewis Milestone, important movie director. He was starting *Edge of Darkness* at Warner's starring Errol Flynn and Ann Sheridan, featuring Walter Huston, Judith Anderson and I was right for Walter's wife. Through Cukor, Esposito got paid, Helen, Lillian, Lynn, Thornton, Dorothy Gish and my diamond bracelets, diamond rings, diamond pin, string of real pearls, gifts from Gregory came out of the Provident Loan Society, who by now had become my friend.

"Don't be helpless," said Mama.

"Money is an ever-loving friend," said Papa. He could have added, "And George Cukor."

Couldn't Lewis Milestone have thought of me at 60 West Twelfth? You'd think so, but casting isn't that imaginative. Be where it's going on. That is *really* imaginative.

Do you save every jar, paper bag, string, candle end, old torn nightgown. "Such lovely crepe de chine you'll use it for something?" Stamps that come on envelopes you're to reply to and don't and swore you would throw away, didn't and now they drift around, waiting to be cut off and soaked, then you have to buy some paste, then both the paste and they drift around?

Do you throw away soap when it gets smaller and cracks or wait till it breaks?

Do you throw away shoes when the uppers crack or before?

Do you keep stockings with runs?

Do you buy a chinchilla coat, regret the extravagance and use both sides of a piece of paper.

Do you think you will change?

Do you think anything will?

"The dreaming soul of the human race."

Never give up. Keep dreaming.

Keep dreaming. I felt as though I was. Backstage life at the Old Vic was nothing like backstage life in our country. "When you're away from home it's different," I said on my first visit away from home. It was the same on my first engagement in a London theatre.

We had opened and were a triumph. People advertized for tickets in the personal column of the London *Times*. Offstage I was a hit, too.

"Come for a weekend at Cecil's," said Oliver Messel. "His house in Wiltshire is pure William and Mary. I'll bring one of your dresses and Cecil will photograph you with the period background the dresses were designed for." Oliver had designed the costumes and scenery for *The Country Wife*.

"You *mustn't!*" exclaimed Edith at dinner. Between matinee and night performance, Lilian Baylis, who owned the Old Vic, arranged for dinner to be cooked in the Old Vic kitchen and served in Edith Evans' dressing room for Ursula Jeans, Edith and me. Maybe boiled fowl, veg and pudding, maybe a joint, veg and custard. After food, then conversation till time to make up again. Lovely to feel welcome in a foreign land.

"Edith is right, dear," agreed Ursula. "We all love Oliver, but he's *very* wild. And *Cecil!*"

"Who else is going?" asked Edith. "Oh, you really *mustn't*. I believe Cecil Beaton has a *very* beautiful home, but you really don't know what goes on!"

"Oliver wants his dresses photographed there, Cecil's house is William and Mary."

Edith shook her head. "When would you go? How *would* you? Wiltshire is a *long way*, dear. Oh, I *wouldn't*, if I were you."

Sunday I took the morning train. At Salisbury I pushed the window down, there was Oliver on the platform.

"Are you all right, darling? Cecil is longing to meet you. Here's a note he sent." The square white envelope had a black border.

"Is he in mourning?"

"No, he likes a black edge on his paper."

What would Edith think?

Cecil wrote how sorry he was not to be at Salisbury to welcome me, but he'd be at his door to greet me when we drove up.

"I want to show you Salisbury Cathedral, darling, it's so beautiful. Thirteenth century."

Wouldn't Edith think *that* was all right? Oliver explained how the knights were buried in the crypt, sometimes a dog at their feet, and some favored possessions. Why was no one admiring it but us? On one tomb "Mr Money" was carved on a stone in the floor. No dog, no wife beside him, no date, no explanation, "Mr Money." Oliver drove us through beautiful Wiltshire to the village of Wilton. "You know Juliet Duff. Opening night she came back with the Louis Bromfields, that's *her* place, it's the dower house to Wilton Castle. Juliet will come over to Cecil's, she's longing to see you again."

Why did Edith and Ursula worry? Conversation about dower houses and castles, Lady Juliet Duff was coming, what was wicked?

"To the right is the park to Wilton Castle. David Herbert's mom and dad live there. If we have time before the train tomorrow David wants you to stop by. He'll come to Cecil's."

"Do I know him?"

"You'll adore him. He's the younger son, the Honorable David Herbert, where they live was designed by Holbein. He designed only three houses and Henry the Eighth gave this one to the family, the deed is framed in the front hall. It's over the umbrella stand. The Palladian bridge was built by Sidney Herbert. Sidney Herbert is the name of Pembroke's heir. David's older brother is Sidney, Lord Herbert."

"Will *he* be at Cecil's?"

"No, he's rather tiresome, but you'll love David, he's great fun. I long for you to see the Palladian bridge and in the double-cube room are all the Van Dyck portraits Van Dyck painted of the Herbert family *in* that room."

Suddenly we dropped over the edge of a steep hill. Below was Ashcombe House.

"Oh, I long to see you in your dress! Maybe leaning out the window? Or sweeping leaves?" Oliver opened the front door. Through the long dim hall, outdoors on a terrace, were Cecil and other guests. Pale October sunshine lit Cecil's green velvet riding coat. Edith would have loved it. So would Ursula.

The other guests were Rolf Gerard, who'd been an assistant scenery designer of Oliver's and now designed scenery on his own. The blond young beauty was actress Lilli Palmer.

"Excuse me while I show Miss Gordon to her room." Cecil led me past a parlor, white walled with furniture upholstered in violet cloth, violet curtains edged with jet fringe.

In my room, lovely things on my dressing table, lemon perfume from J. N. Taylor on Mortimer Street across from the British Museum. In the bathroom sweet-smelling soaps and a nosegay that looked as though Cecil or Oliver had painted it.

"Show her *your* room, Cecil," urged Oliver. It had a fourposter bed, each poster topped by a marzipan mask with crepe hair whiskers. Why did I think of Hans Christian Andersen?

"Would you mind awfully if we take the pictures? The sun is uncertain, but now there's enough." Oliver had brought the green moiré corset, the white taffeta flounced petticoat with loops of red ribbon and cherries, the buckled shoes, the clocked stockings, the cherry and Nile ribbon-trimmed fontange.

"Lean out the upstairs front window," directed Cecil. "The stonework will show and half of *you*."

On the front path, the beautiful doorway for background, I swept leaves with a broom Oliver had improvised from branches tied together.

After lunch, a stroll through the woodland. Nearby was tethered Cecil's goat, gift of the Duchess of Hamilton and Brandon from her place on the hill beyond. Her daughter had come for lunch and strolled with us. In a clearing an old tree had been felled, Oliver and I let the others go on, we sat and admired the spot, it could've been the Forest of Arden. "Let's get engaged," I said. It was just the summing up of an idyllic day in idyllic weather.

"Anne and Michael got married and it's worked out." Anne is Oliver's sister and a beauty. "Michael Rosse never liked girls till he met Anne, but they're madly happy. You'll meet her. They have a baby and he's divine, but for *some* of us it works and some it doesn't. I don't think it would with me, darling."

Would you have explained? Not me.

"My mother is English," said Oliver, "and my father's father is Jewish so I guess that makes me Spanish. Isn't that what Sophie Tucker says?" We strolled after the others. Would Edith have minded a Sophie Tucker allusion? Otherwise, the day was straight Jane Austen.

For tea, grand folk from Wilton. Lady Juliet Duff, Madame Lelia Ralli, Sir Victor Cunard, Reine Pitman, who lived in her Uncle John Singer Sargent's two houses on Cheyne Walk, Poppy Jackson, daughter of Augustus John. "He lives over there." She pointed off into some scenery. "You must go over, he'd adore to meet you."

"This is Baron Ledebur," said Cecil.

"Iris Tree's husband," whispered Oliver. *Why* did Edith and Ursula say it was frightening?

Tea was on the lawn. David Herbert joined us. "You must stop by Wilton tomorrow."

"They're bringing her to lunch with *me*," said Juliet. "Lunch is early to make the train."

After dinner came the big event. "We're celebrating Guy Fawkes Day," said Cecil. "It's not till next week, but we'll have our bonfire tonight." Towering above his studio at the end of the garden, dead leaves waited to be lit. Before, Cecil and Oliver performed a sketch. David Herbert entertained, Oliver did his famous Italian whore behind a sheet. "It's too distracting if you see me," he said. His props were a bowl, a pitcher of water, behind the sheet draped across our end of the room, on our side the lights were out.

Laughs, applause, then Cecil said to file out, they lit the bonfire. David Herbert, Cecil, Oliver, Poppy Jackson put on Guy Fawkes costumes and danced around the fire.

What was wicked?

Next day we drove over to Bulbridge House on our way to Salisbury Station. A quick glimpse of the gardens and house.

"Queen Alexandra was Juliet's godmother." Oliver held a small amber box with a crown of rubies on the lid and large ruby A. "Queen Alexandra gave this to Juliet."

"What a pity you must hurry, come for a weekend, I insist," said Lady Juliet. "I shan't let you off."

How winning, welcome in a strange land! The doors opened, the hand stretched out because all the fear and worry and awfulness had come out right even in a foreign land.

Question for Thornton.

"Instead of inventing how to blow everybody's head off, why don't they invent goodness?"

"Plato was asked that," said Thornton.

"What did he say?"

"He said of all the subjects, goodness was the hardest to teach, but he still had belief it could be done."

That was the summer of 1976. How many years had I been bringing my questions to Thornton?

The author of *The Bridge of San Luis Rey,* was standing in front of the Booth Theatre during an intermission of *Uncle Vanya.* He was someone I wanted to know. Why wait till I got an intro? "Don't be helpless." It was only a short step to where he stood. "Mr. Wilder, I'm Ruth Gordon."

That was the spring of 1930. Start of a friendship that forty-five years later Thornton's death put a dent in, but not a finish, our loving friendship continues. I speak for him and me.

December 3 was Garson's and my thirty-third wedding anniversary. We shared it with Thornton, a worthy dinner at Orsini's, each of us choosing our favorites, wine flowed, conversation to be treasured.

Thornton liked to dine and not sit too long after. "Let's have one for the road," I suggested. We took a taxi from Fifty-sixth Street to Forty-fourth Street and the Algonquin.

One for the road and we walked along Forty-fourth Street to the Harvard Club, where as the French say Thornton had "descended."

Thornton kissed me. "Goodbye, best of Ruthies."

We loved each other, we were never in love, but he asked me to marry him. He thought the one I wanted to ask me wouldn't.

"Goodbye, best of Ruthies," but he knew that between us there never would be a goodbye.

"It takes genius to arrange a funeral," wrote Thornton Wilder in *The Woman of Andros*.

Would anybody like to see what they can do about a new model? Especially a show business funeral? For Al's the sky was gray, so were the streets, snow powdered over with cinders. I pulled the fur lap robe around me. "Campbell's," I told Chapman, who'd driven there so often it was one place he could find.

At the chapel entrance I said, "Half an hour?" Every funeral is a different length, like dreams or dress rehearsal or an earthquake or a train wreck.

A limousine pulled up just behind ours, Danny Bowman leaned out. "Hi, kid." Then he remembered the occasion. "Hello, Ruthie," he said in his gravelly voice, got out of his big foreign car and came over to me. "Lemme make an entrance with ya."

"I thought you were in Florida."

"Where do you think I got my makeup?" Deep-tanned, no hat, pale-colored polo coat draped around him, chamois gloves. "Where's Gar?"

"Rehearsing."

No ushers. Stars, producers, directors, authors found their own seats. How did the *Times* critic get his usual third row center aisle? The *Post* sat behind him.

"We rate house seats, don't we?"

In front of us were Angela Lansbury and Hal Prince. Over on the side, the house crew from Al's theatre sat slumped and glum-looking. Three character-women were tabulating how many celebrities, a committee from the Players showed dignified grief front row left, who was front row right with the widow?

Nearly full, Campbell's man gave the go-ahead. The next funeral was booked in an hour. A minute later a downcast minister took his place beside the flower-banked coffin.

"Let us pray." He made an up-motion, we stood. "Our Father who art in Heaven—" The Lord's Prayer ended and he segued into one of his own, even less appropriate.

"Who booked *that* crow?" whispered Danny.

"—You have taken unto Yourself our dear brother—"

Had Al ever been to church?

"—that he may be received at Your throne—"

Al with the big diamond ring and black fingernails? What throne was that?

The first time I met Al was at the Sixty Club. "Y'like that legit crap? Y'got a cute shape, don't get your ass tangled up in dialogue, show it! Legit's for them Bessie Knabes that hasta pull their dress down over their knees. Dialogues for if ya got a behind like the back of a—"

"I shall read from Ephesians, chapter six," droned the downbeat voice with the careful pronunciation. "Be strong in the Lord, and in the power of His might. Put on the whole armour of God, that ye may be able to stand against the wiles of the devil."

Once Al asked me, "Y'got a feller?"

"Yup."

"Is he good at it?"

"Yup."

"They're gettin' scarce as a hit, everybody turned into a fairy."

"Wherefore take unto you the whole armour of God—"

Only eleven-thirty and it was over. Usually, most of us weren't awake. Danny took my arm. "If God lets me get back to my office, I'm writing a complete blackout on any kinda session when I cool. Let's get to Sardi's for a snort."

I didn't need a theatrical funeral to call up Arnold. I'd told him my finale. He had to stick in a whereas or two and some lawyer jive, but what Arnold *says* it says is "No funeral, the bright lights I've got used to and leave the ashes in."

Across the room a beauty waved.

"Who is it?" I asked.

Garson turned. "Terrific looking."

Our guest from Paris put on her heavy dark horn-rimmed glasses. *"Quelle allure!"*

"Who is it?"

Beauty was leaving and stopped by our table, "Hello, darling." She laughed. "It's Merle."

"Of course," I said. I knew two Merles, Merle Oberon and Merle Daniels, whom I hadn't seen since graduation night at Quincy High School. Would Merle Daniels have jewels and a white mink hat? It could only be Merle Oberon or did she have a younger sister also named Merle?

"When will you be out?" It was Merle Oberon's silver voice.

"Next month," said Garson.

"Ring me."

"You bet! You know Ginette?"

"Of course. Madame Spanier, have you brought over some lovely Balmains?"

"Not this time. This time I'm lecturing and seeing friends."

"Ah, yes. Well, if you come to Beverly Hills, or Acapulco, please let me know."

"Alas, not this trip."

"Alas." She was gone.

The couple at the next table beckoned to the headwaiter. "Who was that?" asked the man, his tone rang with the righteousness of an out-of-towner demanding New York explain New York.

"That was the famous movie star, Merle Oberlin."

"Oh."

"A lot of movie stars come here," beamed the headwaiter. "Bette Davis, Katharine Hepburn." The headwaiter bowed, went to spread more cheer and misinformation.

The out-of-towner watched him go. "I don't believe a lot of movie stars come here!" he sneered. "And I don't believe Bette Davis comes. Or Katharine Hepburn. And you want to know what else I don't believe? *I* don't believe that was Merle Oberlin."

First loves: the first summer day Mama let me wear my tan sandals. Buttercups. Marian West, whom I loved because I loved her. No particular reason unless it was that she had dark brown hair, my favorite color for hair, and also she was ten years older than I was. I had celebrated my fourth birthday.

At Mr. Winthrop Ames's Little Theatre, where Gregory and I acted with Mr. Sampson in *The First Year,* I was back and I was going to walk on that stage again. Mr. Ames's theatre was changed over to accommodate TV, but I could look out front and see Frank Craven directing *The First Year* and disliking me. I lived through it and now on that stage I was saying, "Thank you, David, for letting me come on the show again." David Frost's TV talk show. "Last time I was only half on the show, because I was sitting in the audience and you picked me up. I'm lucky at that type of work, I picked up Thornton Wilder in front of the Booth Theatre in 1930. In 1941 I picked up Garson in Radio City Music Hall. This kind of thing can be very rewarding. But this time we really have met and I'm pleased you asked me on the show. I like to be in an audience, but I'm more comfortable on the stage. I left home to be and it's a comfort to have plans work. I'm glad you asked me on *tonight,* David, with your other guest André Previn. I never picked him up but he picked *me* up some years ago at Alan Pakula's dinner party, we sat next to each other, hadn't been introduced and he said 'You are great!' That doesn't make an evening disagreeable.

"André was composing the music for *Inside Daisy Clover,* which was just going to start shooting, our meeting was love at first sight and has gone on through the years and from André I learned something that has had an effect on my life. He's a stroller and I'm a stroller and one day his stroll and my stroll led to the sidewalk in front of the Beverly Hills Seed Store. Kisskiss: 'André, I admire you, it's hard enough to get one career going and keep it on the track, but *you* did, then started another! Top composer for films, people do anything to get you to compose the scores for their movies then you branch out and conduct Houston's symphony orchestra then branch out further and conduct the London orchestra.'

" 'There have to be beginnings,' he said. 'To grow, you have to keep having beginnings.'

"I learn, David, and now I want to have a beginning right on your show. Do you like your bank? I've turned against mine. Fifty years ago last October thirtieth I opened a checking account at the Fifth Avenue branch of the Morgan Guaranty Trust and for fifty years I've been depositing and writing checks and don't you think that after fifty years they should do something about it? I'm not asking for free money, but shouldn't they send me a next year's calendar? Or a get-well card? Or a wish-you-were-here? Or a get-lost? I don't think a fifty-year checking account at the same branch should be totally ignored and if anyone knows a bank that gives a present after you've had a checking account fifty years I'll leave the Morgan Guaranty tomorrow and begin another fifty years at the bank that gives a present."

The next day our apartment looked like after a first night or Campbell's funeral parlor if the obit didn't say, "Don't send flowers." Banks from all over sent flowers and presents and telegrams.

That day at the Hamburger Heaven counter, a lady on the next stool said, "Do you mind if I ask if you're Ruth Gordon?"

"Yes," I said. "I mean yes I am Ruth Gordon, I'm *pleased* you ask." And she said a more beautiful thing than what all the banks said with their flowers. "Last summer at Edgartown I and my husband sat at the next table to your husband Garson Kanin and Lillian Hellman and you, and my husband said, 'I'd like to go over and tell those people how many tears of pleasure I have shed over their work.'"

When I act in plays, some people speak to me, but since the Oscar for *Rosemary's Baby* and appearing in *Whatever Happened to Aunt Alice? Where's Poppa?* and *Harold and Maude,* everybody's a friend.

And more new fame after David Frost's show, then what a pity! The Morgan Guaranty wrote ruefully it wouldn't be fifty years for another year yet.

This page has to be lilac.

Still lilac.

When it was fifty years, what did they do?

Draw the veil. Or as Thornton used to say when he got tired of what I was saying, "Dear, my mind's wandering."

Notice the ads for diamond rings, hunks of gems at David Webb's, at Bulgari, notice the price, six, eight thousand dollars for just some fun-jewels.

"Don't economize," advised Charlie MacArthur, "earn more." His younger brother John paid attention and got on every list of billionaires. He knew to listen to brother Charlie, an impractical-looking fellow, but at Chase Manhattan and the Bowery they have practical-lookers and how many of *their* brothers are billionaires?

An honor I appreciate is to be honored by my own people. The Players club honored me in Edwin Booth's home, now called The Players, the grand house on Gramercy Park where Edwin Booth lived and died. I never saw him act, but Papa did. In San Francisco his ship tied up to unload its cargo of teak, he bought a ticket for Edwin Booth and next day signed on as a stagehand for his three nights in port so he could see Edwin Booth close to.

He did the same for Lotta Crabtree. When they ask me if I come from stage people, I say yes.

"Creative people ought to do a bit of sewing," said the best actress I ever saw, Edith Evans. "A bit of anything not demanding, not in your own line."

It works. Look around, see what you've got. Have you got a low wooden table with thirty-six inches painted along one side? Maybe use it to cut out dresses for paper dolls, color them?

Did I lose you? Maybe I'm writing this book for myself. I use my old paint box, it has every color I know and a color I didn't, crimson lac. Mama's favorite color was biscuit color, but that would make even a paper doll's dress look made over.

I learned to read seventy-five years ago in Quincy, Massachusetts. Earlier Louisa May Alcott read *her* first book in Massachusetts. So did Mr. Emerson and Mr. Thoreau. So did a lot of people I know and a lot I don't. Some nut said a dog is man's best friend, they sensibly remain anonymous. Way before a dog comes man is his best friend, then his books.

Anne, Mrs. Ken McCormick, looking at my bookcase on Cottage Street in Edgartown, picked out *My Little Dutch Cousin*, and exclaimed, "I never thought I'd see that again, was this yours when you were little?"

"It's just like mine, but I found it in a secondhand bookstore."

When I was eleven, Papa had said to sell my children's books, his pay wouldn't stretch to cover bills when Mama got the bad inflammation. Dr. Hunting wanted to operate, but Dr. Adams said keep hot flaxseed poultices on and the inflammation went away. After a while, Mrs. Dunham, the nurse, went, too. It had cost a lot of extra money and sickness isn't for the poor.

Papa's eyes rested on my bamboo bookcase beside my bed. "Snuggy, you're through with your children's books. Take 'em in to Boston to Cornhill, they have secondhand bookstores, the man will give you some money."

I took them because they were dandy books and all about a life that was not like mine. I wasn't through with them, but I packed *My Little African Cousin, My Little Dutch Cousin, Hans Brinker or the Silver Skates, Dorothy Dainty and Her Gay Good Times, The Five Little Peppers and How They Grew,* the *Theodora* books, the *Betty Wales, When Patty Went to College, The Little Colonel, When Molly Was Six, Dottie Dimple, Miss Toosie's Mission, Rebecca of Sunnybrook Farm, Little Lord Fauntleroy, Sarah Crewe or the Little Princess, The Two Sweet P's, Little Miss Boston, Palmer Cox's Brownies, Max and Maurice, Water Babies* into our big suitcase. On Cornhill the man gave me two dollars and seventy cents.

The only good thing about two dollars and seventy cents is it's better than if you haven't got two dollars and seventy cents. I promised myself I'd get them back again, not mine, but books with the same covers.

When I went on the stage and the plays went on tour I'd go to Leary's secondhand bookstore in Philadelphia, George Goodspeed's on Milk Street in Boston, Acres of Books in Cincinnati and found all my books except *Little Miss Boston* and *The Two Sweet P's*. I talk about them on TV shows and people say she'll get sent a dozen, but they have never shown up.

Nor did I ever find what Anne Parrish did strolling along Paris's Left Bank. Anne's husband sat down on a bench by the booksellers' tables that lined the quai, she turned over a book. On the flyleaf in a faded hand:

For Anne

from

Auntie May

If it could happen to Anne, it could happen to me. Anybody got my copy of *Little Miss Boston,* an adorable little orphan who was being starved by Ma'am Lunt and had to move into a church to live on stale bread the baker sold cheap after two days? Anybody got my *Two Sweet P's,* a rich little girl named Priscilla, a poor adopted little girl named Polly? Keep them, but let me know! Cottage Street, Edgartown, Mass. 02539. Thanks.

Along the way to civilization I learned what to do with myself. With no TV, radio, no movies, things had to be thought up. Things that cost no money and were enjoyable. At five years old I could interest my friend Katherine Follett to walk down Grandview Avenue to Beale Street, look out for wagons or the trolley, hold hands to cross Hancock Street to Beach Street, turn right on Willow Street left on Elm Avenue, look both ways, nothing in sight except the green lawns of the Josiah Quincy Mansion Private School, then salt marsh, then the beach with a row of rickety bathhouses where Papa paid five dollars a year for one big enough for him *or* me to get into a bathing suit. Katherine and I just waded.

Winter, a good fill-in was to scallop doilies, make sachet bags, featherstitch a duster, make a raffia basket with an eye on Christmas. Get stuff out of Mama's scrap box to make pen wipers, cover coat hangers, wrap them, mail or deliver and when I got a present, write a thank-you letter. After Christmas save up to buy valentines, homemade didn't look like valentines, meanwhile borrow *St. Nicholas Magazine,* read my own books again, borrow one from the Thomas Crane Public Library, borrow one from Martha Robinson. St. Patrick's Day wear a green hair ribbon, make green fudge, April Fool's Day think of how to fool people and not get fooled myself. Decoration Day the G.A.R. parade marched to Mount Wollaston Cemetery, where not too many years later Mama would be buried. The Grand Army marching today would soon be riding there for good. Bring a bunch of snowballs if someone would give me some, wear my new coral messaline hair ribbons and dress up.

In June, a wedding to go to or stand around and watch people go in and try to catch a glimpse of the bride. Fourth of July bring the porch rocking chairs in so boys wouldn't add them to the bonfire. At five o'clock in the morning cross the railroad tracks and be on Hancock Street to see the parade, at night bring a blanket and sit on the grass in Merrymount Park to watch fireworks. Between pinwheels, a man announced Jack

Johnson beat Jim Jeffries. Mama hoped being born in Georgia didn't make her feel sad.

An exciting something to do is get ready for vacation. August first started Papa's two-weeks, anticipation matched realization. I could sleep in an upper berth in our stateroom on the S.S. *City of Bath*. Papa stayed in the pilothouse all night because he showed his first mate's papers. Mama and I looked out the porthole to see Popham Light in Maine, daylight just coming up over the fir trees.

In Bath off the big boat onto the little steamer named *Wiwurna* or *Nahanada* and stop everywhere, the next to last stop Christmas Cove, where like the Never-Never Land everything would go right. French's Boarding House, the rowboat Papa would rent. Mama taking two-weeks membership in the Casino so I could go to the masquerade party, the children's party, Wednesday and Saturday dances. Day trips in Mr. Gee's motorboat. He lived up on the hill back of French's at Box Cottage, but his wife was stout and didn't care to cook for him and their children, Gretchen, Archie, Dick. Ten cents to see the sunfish on French's wharf and have my picture taken with it. Take the *Nelly G.* to Squirrel Island. One terrible morning we woke up in the steamy heat of Rowes Wharf, the Boston elevated clanging past, Papa went to the Mellin's Food Factory, Mama and I took the train home, no more Never-Never Land except for me. We opened all the windows, got our cat back from Mrs. Litchfield. It was horrible.

I wrote letters to everybody I'd met at French's, walked to Thomas Crane Public Library, sent fudge to the little girl named Virginia Portia Royall I met at the children's party, made lemonade, drank root beer, looked in Mama's scrap box for black cloth to make my doll a dress, Hortense's neck broke on the trip. I arranged a funeral, made her a black silk dress from a petticoat of Mama's, made a black hair bow, made the coffin out of Clark's O.N.T. thread box, covered it with Dennison black crepe paper. I learned about a funeral at Edith Gould's. Edith and I were together in the first, second, third grades, then she didn't come for a while and one morning I was sitting beside Mama looking out her parlor window at her backyard and the good pears and Concord grapes her mother let us pick and eat and today sitting in rows were neighbors where Edith and I had looked at her brother's magic lantern slides, why did I have to laugh? It wasn't the slides, what was it? I was glad when Mr. Chase got finished talking and praying, because I had to laugh. Out on South Central Avenue I could have and nobody'd hear me, but I didn't feel like it anymore.

It's a help to know what to do with yourself. I knew to cry at funerals, laugh at clowns in the circus, but why want to laugh in Edith's parlor?

Laugh or cry but feel things. If you feel things you'll know what to do with yourself. Help, love, kindness, a decent place to live are good, but not vital, Irving Berlin worked at Nigger Mike's saloon and fell into the East River, got fished out and today he's ninety-one, has more money than you do, lives in a fine New York town house looking at the East River further up town than where he fell in, a house in the Adirondacks or Catskills, whichever faith you belong to, one wife since the Twenties, who goes to Mass every day, fine children. When they were little they came with their nurse to the treasured Dr. Schloss where my little boy's nurse brought him. And one day the smallest little girl came out of Dr. Schloss's office, holding up her bandaged finger, tears pouring down her cheeks, but not acknowledging them. "I didn't *cry!*" she said.

Along the way to civilization, courage comes out top.

In the Boston *Globe,* Kevin Kelly wrote a review you dream about, the business was overwhelming. Now at the Ethel Barrymore Theatre in New York a notice on the call-board? Merrick was closing *Dreyfus in Rehearsal?*

"I love you," shouted the man who rushed down the aisle to the stage as the curtain came down. "I love you, Miss Gordon," someone shouted, cheers from the house. Playwright John Guare and director Mel Shapiro who had nothing to do with *Dreyfus in Rehearsal,* stood in my dressing room, we hugged and kissed, John was crying.

A note with a red carnation from Bud Cort. He came backstage with his mother, his grandmother, brother Joe and Joe's wife, on our night before closing at the Ethel Barrymore Theatre with two more perfs to go. Would there be a reprieve? The whole run would be twelve performances. Don't tell me *that's* show business! *That's* stinking management!

Up to and including this morning of the Ides of March I have eaten twenty-nine thousand, six hundred and thirty-eight breakfasts. Eaten them in Quincy, Massachusetts, Quincy, Florida, Quincy, Illinois, in Eastham, Mass., Windsor Locks, Hartford, Bridgeport, Middlebury, New Haven, Guilford, South Norwalk, Connecticut, where I played a one-night stand with the Maude Adams Company, Westport, where I first played *The Country Wife*, Billy Rose's island off Rowayton. Thank you, Melanie Kahane for cutting the hi-fi wire so we didn't have music twenty-four hours. Sandy Hook, where we bought Grace Moore's three-hundred-forty-seven-acre estate and all its furniture for eighty thousand dollars. Drove through Colchester where Papa was born but no breakfast. Ate it in Newport, Providence, the Crown Hotel, live past the moment, the Biltmore, an improvement, Dennis on the Cape, Chester in the Berkshires, West Harwichport, Boston, Springfield, Massachusetts, Springfield, Illinois, Worcester, Stockbridge, Atlantic Beach, where I talked with the second actress I ever met, Miss Alice Claire Elliot, Marblehead, Rockland, Edgartown, Provincetown, New York, Poughkeepsie, Newburgh, Albany, where hotel clerk phoned to ask if I had a man in my room and Gregory had to get out. Westhampton, South Hampton, Great Neck, Rome, New York, Rome, Italy, Amsterdam, strictly New York, Onteora, Syracuse, Ithaca, Utica, Nyack, Sag Harbor, Fire Island with Fanny Brice, Bill Rose and Jed Harris. "If you never slept with Jed before, you'll have to tonight," said Fanny, "there's just one room." Fanny's theatre maid Adele made the best vanilla ice cream, but it was too cold for ice cream on Fire Island. Cold Spring Harbor at Woollcott's weekend in Otto Kahn's palace. What became of fun? I don't seem to have so much. At Cold Spring Harbor, Mr. Kahn invited Woollcott every summer to invite people for a weekend. Harpo and Gregory and I and Alice Duer Miller and Neysa McMein, Benchley and Dotty Parker. Mr. Kahn invited only Marila Rowland, a darling girl and prettier than us. Oyster Bay at Ted Roosevelt's Orchard House he built for fear he'd inherit Sagamore Hill. General Marshall offered to drive me to New York, but I said no, I'd never heard of him. "He's very important," said Eleanor-Ted Roosevelt, but it was before the war. Just a few of those twenty-nine thousand breakfasts, may they go on and on. Like *The Three Sisters* who wanted to go to Moscow, I want to go to Maine and who knows when breakfast will be blueberry muffins at Bar Harbor's Asticou Inn?

Some people understand money. When Charlie MacArthur said, "Earn more," he added, "It uses up your mind to economize." He chartered a fine boat, engaged a captain, invited me to join him and Helen on a cruise from Nyack down the Hudson River through Spuyten Duyvil to some point near Sag Harbor on Long Island. At night Helen Hayes and I shared the cabin, Charlie had bought a sleeping bag and an air mattress, he lay out under the stars. Was it about three he clambered into the cabin? "I have to get in bed." Helen moved over. "That goddam Abercrombies I *knew* I should have bought the good, this cheap one got a puncture."

A straw vote among MacArthur's friends shows this is the only economy he ever practiced.

Get the best if there is a best, but when one box of Kleenex is like another box of Kleenex, would the Medes, would the Persians pay any more?

And that brings up the laws of the Medes and the Persians? What are they *and* what's the Edict of Nantes? Who were the Gadarene Swine? Alice Duer Miller could have told me and made it interesting. So could Herbert Bayard Swope. Swope's answer might not have been accurate, but would have held your attention.

Laws of the M's and P's can wait, I have my own laws. My law of economy is pay ten thousand dollars for a mink coat and wait in line at a cut-rate drugstore to buy witch hazel thirty-six cents below the regular price. I think I'm in for a change, Charlie, I think I'll earn more.

ACTING
LESSONS
II

"Never stand with your hand on your hip," said Noel Coward, "it shows defiance."

You can't have a career if you don't have a soul. You can't have a career if you don't have selfishness.

"Honor thy father and mother is fine" but not elementary.

"Honor thyself takes care of everything" is what I tell Zarathustra.

I told myself to give up superstition. I lived through the worst time of my life and hadn't walked under a ladder, no bird had flown into the room, I didn't accept a two-dollar bill, didn't sit thirteen at table, didn't see a glove lying in the street, didn't put a hat or shoes or an umbrella on the bed, didn't break a looking glass, and one phone call gave me the worst blow of my life. Years of being superstitious but that phone call decided me to give it up. A bird could fly in and I'd get it out, birds are nervous.

I could sit thirteen at table and not think I'd drop dead, I could break a looking glass and hope it wasn't expensive. If you give up stuff, really quit. It's one thing to *say* you'll give up smoking, another to give it up. I did that, now I'll give up superstition.

I put on my Lilly Pulitzer dress that wasn't really L.P., my London theatre dresser had copied it. Dody Higgins, impractical, forgetful, good dressmaker and poet with no theatre job in sight, took a job at London's department store, Swan & Edgar, made renowned by dazzling musical comedy star Elsie Janis, who scored a triumph at London's Piccadilly Circus Theatre, then rented a country house with its own lake and with the lake came two swans that Elsie named Swan and Edgar.

In the department store Dody was working, broke, blue, her heart backstage on Shaftesbury Avenue or at the Haymarket or Piccadilly Circus, but her hand was ringing up shillings and tuppence. I sent her five pounds for Easter to help till she got backstage again.

"Dear Miss Gordon," she wrote, "how generous of you. I bought some pink patent leather slippers and a pink patent leather pocketbook.

Love, Dody"

You can wear green, you can kiss the Blarney Stone, you can have Brigid O'Shaughnessy for your name, but when you're hard up, trying to squeeze by and buy pink patent leather slippers and pocketbook with naught to put in it that's the genuine Erin Go Bragh!

"I've given up superstition," I told everybody. I put on my Lilly Pulitzer Prize, buttoned it, it didn't button right, I had it on wrong side out. Could I get away with it? I was flying American Airlines with Garson. American loves me under all conditions, but the seams of my Pulitzer stuck out, also the lace that edged the hem. Would anyone notice?

"That's wrong side out," said Garson.

I took it off, I'd still be safe if I wore another, but what's the good of swearing off? I turned it *right* side out, got in the limo to LaGuardia, airport okay, got on American okay, fine flight, got off at Toronto. *That airport!* Whether you're superstitious or not, that airport is a trial! Down a flight of stairs, down some more, into Customs lineup, slow moving, inch along, identify myself to declare nothing, state how long I will spend money in their country. The first time I was there, Customs said, "Let's see your driver's license." "I don't drive." "I need identity." I showed him my American Express card that every night says Karl Malden on the TV gets you in anywhere. Not Toronto, Karl. The lady in back of me got huffy. "Don't you know who she *is?*" Lady had diamonds, gold this, gold that, Vuitton bag, authority, a lady who speaks and it works. "She's the greatest actress, she's famous."

Undisturbed Customs asked, "Why are you here?"

Now my dander hit high or is dander only in fiction? "I'm here to do the Joyce Davidson television show for which I'll get paid and take money out of country."

That grabbed him, but rich lady gave him more sharp talk. I got in.

On this non-superstitious trip I brought my passport, the photo of me looked like Carol Burnett, but Customs took it as identity. Trip going fine.

Info was, "Limo driver will meet you at the Avis desk." At
Avis desk, no limo man. Garson searched. Nobody. Limo was
paid by the TV show, taxi cost us plus tip $15.16. Would limo
man have been at Avis if my Lilly Pulitzer had been right side
out from the start? What had a Canadian limousine to do with
lace showing on my seams?

Never give up unless you *do* give up. If you give up, stay with
it.

Reservations at the Windsor Arms Hotel, the room okay for
one. Bed? Maybe three-quarters, a bed lamp on one side only.
Doesn't the Windsor Arms understand about marriage? If my
Lilly Pulitzer was on right from the start would we have got the
corner suite, double bed, twin lamps?

Interview for Gar during dinner with Toronto *Star* set for
eight o'clock, actually didn't bite into stuff till twenty-five after.
Talk, sign books, talk. Dinner is for dinner, not to discuss philosophy with your mouth full. I felt faint. "Okay I go up?"

Garson took a look. "I'll come with you." He said a snappy
goodbye, signed the check, put his arm tightly around me, got
me to the elevator, the only one and it was waiting! On the
third floor Garson sat me down on the bench.

"I want to lie down."

He got me up, key went in door on first push. On the bed. G.
got my dress undone, broke ammonia capsules under my nose,
looked in my bottle bag for honey, gave me two tablespoons and
I started back to life. Fainting may be you're fainting or dying.
It's worth it to return to life, roses back in cheeks, blood start to
warm up. Would this have happened if I had put my Lilly on
right side out? If you're a believer, believe, but do not give interviews at dinner and right side on, wrong side on, you will not
pass out!

Along the way to civilization it took me thirty-two years to discard a bathing suit. I'm not a quick starter, but if once I start I go bare-ass.

When Mama and I spent a summer day at Aunt Fan Hoyt's we took a trolley to Hough's Neck, got let off into a clutter of bouncing Bet and Queen Anne's lace, crossed the tracks, walked to Aunt Fan's at Post Island. Was it an island? Now it's called Adams Shore.

Aunt Fan's children and I went in swimming in our navy blue mercerized-cotton bathing suits, the blouse ending in bloomers with a full skirt buttoned up at the waist. Mine had a sailor collar and puffed sleeves edged with bands of white tape that soaked up Quincy Bay water. Stockings and cork sole bathing shoes laced with tape soaked up more. Any bathing suit is a drawback, but as the years go by they get less so. At Palm Beach in what Woollcott referred to as my "Lou Maguire period," I didn't go in the water because I didn't have a suit that showed me off. Florence Crozier, slim blonde from Philadelphia engaged to a Warburton, had a bathing suit that could have. Black silk, long sleeves, high neck, with it she wore black silk stockings and black silk bathing shoes and looked the way I wanted to. We both had the shape, she had the suit. Where did she buy hers?

In the summer of 1928 on the White Star liner *Majestic*, Grace Hendricks, who knew stuff, said, "There's somebody new in Paris sells bathing suits to Saks Fifth Avenue that are something and what you'll need visiting Harpo and Woollcott at Antibes. They'll cost a lot and don't be fooled by the shop, it's Rue de la Paix, but upstairs, her name's Schiaparelli."

Up a flight of stairs Mama wouldn't have let me go, I saw a bathing suit better than Florence Crozier's. Faded blue denim color before there *was* faded blue denim, thin jersey, a nothing that was totally sexy!

"How much?" I asked.

"Forty dollars in American money."

I made a fool of myself! Why pay forty dollars for a thin, plain, faded nothing in an attic store?

Poor fool, will I ever learn values? If something is just what you want and it's forty dollars, buy it, find out how to pay for it later. Enjoy money if you've got some and if you haven't you're not looking for a heart-stopping bathing suit. Never mind what Zarathustra spoke, heed Ruth Gordon Jones Kelly Kanin who opened in *Ethan Frome*, support of herself, her son, her cook, her maid, a governess, Mr. Fleischman for part-time and when the curtain went up at the Garrick, Philadelphia, owed a thousand dollars to Max Gordon, a thousand dollars to Helen Hayes, a thousand dollars to Lillian Gish, ten thousand to the Provident Loan and could count on fourteen dollars in cash, the show *had* to be a hit! When I got engaged for *Peter Pan*, I owed the Three Arts Club eighty-something dollars in rent and had thirteen cents, did that help me make a hit? Did I come by live dangerously from Papa? He sailed round the world in clipper ships, then in port blew in his cash. Gold earrings to wear when he hit the Golden Gate, a twenty-five-dollar valentine for Madame Lynch, his landlady at Le Havre. When I see perfection for forty dollars, I buy it, I've never been in a hole I could get out of for forty dollars.

I had more know-how at Elmwood Avenue, "I don't want to *think* about money, Mama, I want to be extravagant!" That was 1914 and 1928 on the Rue de la Paix, why didn't I remember it? Don't let your mind wander when you can *use* it! I crossed the Place Vendôme, turned right on the Faubourg St. Honoré to see Viola Krauss, running Lanvin.

"Do you know what you're doing, going to the Riviera in July?" she asked. "We *close* our shop at Cannes in the summer, I better phone around." She did. "Well, I don't know who they can be, but *some* people are there. They tell me all you need are bathing suits and evening clothes." She sold me some of each. The Lanvin suit was light, but not so light as the faded Schiaparelli. Lighter still is wearing nothing. That's how Phil Barry and Ellen and I and who else went in in Cannes at the Barry villa? Phil had just finished writing *Holiday* for Hope

Williams, who had made a hit in his play *Paris Bound*. And weren't we on the Riviera? And weren't we all carried away with how glamorous we were?

It was going to be midnight. "Let's swim," said Phil.

"I didn't bring a suit." Quincy girl, will you *ever* catch on?

"You don't need any." Was that the Riviera! Was that a bolt from the blue! Was that living! Plus which I looked better than if I'd bought that Schiaparelli suit.

I come from hard-working people. Mama worked hard, Papa worked hard and was tough. Frightening the things he could do and did. At 14 Elmwood Avenue below our kitchen windows is the bulkhead Papa opened to carry out the barrel of furnace ashes. In the autumn Frost's man opened the bulkhead to slide our coal down and start us worrying how we'd pay for it. And Papa rolled our free barrel of Mr. Brigham's apples down the bulkhead stairs.

Between our bulkhead and the swill house were the back steps where our lovely grocery boy delivered groceries, then one day he didn't.

"It was some trouble he got in, he was so sweet." Mama sighed.

"What trouble?" I asked.

"Oh, I don't take notice of those things. Mr. Brown was a lovely man. Life isn't easy, Ruth, you'll find that out."

"Don't be around back. I'm going to get the rat trap out of our swill house," said Papa.

At night when Mama was reading her *Unity* magazine, Papa reading *McClure's* and maybe I was deep in an A. M. and C. N. Williamson novel about life in Newport where the debutante daughter seemed to be falling in love with the chauffeur who turned out to be Lord Entonleigh, heir to the Duke of Boxburgh when through our walls we heard the scurry of rats.

"Did you set the trap, Clinton?"

"They'll eat our God damn electric wires and burn this house to the ground." He'd said not to look, but I looked. He was taking a trap of fierce squealing rats out to our driveway, then went back to the kitchen for a teakettle of boiling water. When your father says not to look, don't.

When our cat had three adorable blue-eyed wobbly little scraps of life, the next morning Papa got up fifteen minutes earlier, went across the railroad tracks with a burlap sack that mewed. He came back with a quiet sack.

When things have to be done, do them. Early I knew I had to and was always going to have to.

"When things get tough," predicted the Kennedys' father, "the tough get going."

Do you know how to forget a memory? I never tried before, but I want to forget it and there it stays.

If you don't like trouble pick up on page 293.

An ambulance waited at the door of our apartment house. Up on the nineteenth floor was a stretcher. Two men carrying me out of the bathroom along the hall, our Maria Luisa crossing herself and I wasn't frightened, I just wanted to stop being ice cold and unclench. My teeth will break, I thought, Dr. Hirschfield says they're good, but the front ones are frail. What made me think of tomorrow? Would there be a tomorrow? "Cousin Sally and Cousin Ed are coming up from Tallahassee to see the show, Garson, call Cousin Sally and Cousin Ed."

Ever go down the service elevator on a stretcher? Louis the same elevator boy who'd been running the elevator eight years tried to act as though nothing was different.

In the lobby Tommy, who'd opened and closed our door for ten years, now opened it wide the way he does when all our luggage is carried out for a trip to California only now it was Mrs. Kanin carried out and Mr. Kanin looked terrible.

Ever go clang clang down Central Park South past the New York Athletic Club, the Essex House, the Hampshire House where a lot of days I walk past and people say, "We love you." "*Harold and Maude* we saw five times." "You look better than you do on the Mike Douglas Show." "May I just tell you how much I . . . ?"

Clang clang into Central Park at the Sixth Avenue entrance.

Pass the Sixty-sixth Street playground where my grandson Jack played before he went to Edgartown, pass the tree that Dan Jenkins had had planted for Jack when he was born. Out of the park and across Seventy-second Street. Clang clang up York Avenue to where Gracie Mansion is, clang, clang, make a turn at Doctors Hospital.

All that fuss for only ptomaine poisoning. Four hours before, Garson and I had ordered the same codfish balls, corn muffins, coffee at the restaurant, now he was fine and I was going to miss three performances of *Mrs. Warren's Profession*.

At my sixty-fifth Quincy High School class reunion our class asked me to speak. "We're here for a good time," I said, "so don't tell our symptoms." I didn't tell this, but why can't I get the stretcher and Maria Luisa crossing herself and Louis and Tommy and the clang clang out of my memory? A memory's not hard to remember, but what do you do to forget?

Maybe I can't because when Cousin Sally and Cousin Ed finally did come up from Tallahassee, they sat through the sold-out matinee of *Mrs. Warren* with Cousin Sally holding a huge box of delicate pink and white and red camellias picked from her generous neighbor's garden. Only my Cousin Sally could be so persuasive. Who would part with such flowers?

And who but Cousin Ed would watch *Mrs. Warren*, holding his personally baked pecan pie made from local pecans? Anybody who said they'd eaten a better one would have to be a liar.

I think I'm going to die on a Saturday. Ever have a notion like that?

I'm going back to childhood. Not a knock, it was due to "cares that infest the day," the toilet stopped working in Gar's bathroom, our super is a man who moves slowly. Eleven hundred a month rent, but when super is likely to show would be anybody's guess. Garson had to use my bathroom to shave and bathe, then forgot and started for his own where Maria Luisa knelt fitting my new plaid skirt in front of the glass in his bathroom door.

Later he told me he wept, it was like the beginning of Act I in the play I wrote *Years Ago* about me at 14 Elmwood Avenue when I was seventeen and wanted to be an actress.

"Mama, it's all wrong!" actress Florence Eldridge in the play was kneeling on the floor fitting my tango-colored Henrietta cloth dress and I was standing on a chair in our dining room facing our big sideboard mirror.

The scene was 1913. 1979 found me at it some more. Our maid, who came for one afternoon ten years ago, agreed to come two times a week, due to my cajoling, then three, then five. She was our only one in help. Garson and I ate in restaurants. Our French cook had retired, returned to Brittany and comes back only when we keep house in California. To replace the irreplaceable Suzanne can't be done and I tackle nothing I know I can't. That is the strength of not facing facts. I do not face any facts, especially facts there's nothing to do about, though there's the one St. Elizabeth faced about bread and roses. When necessity came did the roses turn to bread or vice versa, look it up if you care, whatever she needed to happen did. It happened with Gar and me before dinner last night, everything ready for the Jack Daniels old-fashioned, I had the lemon, the orange out, a sharp knife, the ice cubes, the bitters lined up, only a little of Jack Daniels in the bottle, but faith there was more, the measuring glass, the fork to stir in the Perrier. Gar disappeared into the guest bathroom where we keep the extra Jack Daniels in a cupboard. The cupboard was bare. What what what? The cupboard was bare! Consternation, conferences, invectives.

"I'll drink vodka."

"No, no, I'll run to the liquor store."

"No, no, there's enough Jack Daniels for you."

"I have a bottle of Glenlivet scotch."

"Where is it?"

"It's somewhere."

"I'll drink the vodka, you have the Jack." He poured, there was three quarters of a jigger.

Pandemonium, confusion, now what?

Gar, a thorough man, a perfect man, an atheist, *he* thinks, but I know a child of God, went back to the bathroom cupboard, searched, noticed a big box what was it? Bread and roses in the shape of a carafe of Jack someone had given us as a present! How could we forget who? Around your house do you know what you've got? Do things turn up when needed?

Acting is where you find it. Maybe in the wonderfully kept up old Broadway theatres, maybe downtown down cellar where Gar and I went to see Katharine Houghton act in a play. I wrote her Aunt Hepburn:

Dear Kate,

Saw Kathy, she was great, she was beautiful as if Tinker-Bell had woven some gauze from all her troubles and fun and love and hatred and there it all was, I don't remember the theatre's name but it looked like a coal bin with town gossips staring at intimacy. Kathy was pure love.

Gar and I clambered backstage and down into the depths and we all cried a lot and hung onto each other. Loyal Garson mentioned your uptown shenanigans, but I said, "We don't want to talk about stuff like that!" Show biz is waiting for your December 18 *"Coco"* opening, but down cellar back of the furnace, between Men's d.r. and Ladies' d.r., sweat and talent pouring off everybody, I didn't want to talk about stuff like that. Well, I'm certainly my own girl.

And so are you.

And so is your niece.

Love,
Neighbor

10 November 1969"

If you're playing Hamlet and your fly comes open, that doesn't help your concentration on "To be or not to be." See that that zipper works before you start, see that the codpiece snapper stays snapped. Acting is inspiration *and* preparation.

At the dress rehearsal of *Saturday's Children* lovely actress Margalo Gillmore was invited to come. As I made a big exit after an emotional scene I ran into a chair by the door and hated Margalo for years because she saw me. Along the way to civilization I learned to love her again, but never forget she saw me trip over a chair.

Acting is inspiration and preparation. Get inspired and learn where the chair and door are.

Abe Einhorn, our property man for *The Matchmaker*, remembers that for the year's run instead of saying hello, I said, "Abe, are the pears ripe?" A must. If you eat on the stage, you must eat something soft. For Mr. Vandergelder's dinner at the Harmonia Gardens I had to tuck away chicken and veg, all made out of soft pears carved to look like chicken, a hard piece and I'd choke and then how would I say Thornton Wilder's words.

In *Ethan Frome* our supper party was meat stew made out of bananas and prune juice to look like gravy. Raymond Massey demanded a change. We had cut-up bread and chocolate sauce, both he and I and Jotham, the hired man, strangled through the scene. Do they teach what won't strangle you at the Academy?

Have you learned to take a snub? Is it part of anything? Is it important? I got snubbed first when I was eight years old, I was a caller who called too often. I rang pretty Mrs. Andrews' doorbell. No answer. Maybe it was out of order. I walked round to the back door. I could see pretty Mrs. Andrews scooting up the back stairs. I rang and rang, but pretty Mrs. Andrews didn't come down. Along the way to civilization did I learn not to give a damn? Only one person has cut me dead. It surprised me and then I thought it seemed dated like a novel by Ouida, but this snub was at the Mark Hellinger Theatre.

I think being snubbed is nothing more than a startle. If that isn't a word, let it be.

If you snub somebody, look into that. It's not the snubee, it's the snubber end that matters. In the last year of his life Thornton Wilder said he was "building bridges, making reconciliations."

God knows who he had to reconcile with, but maybe look around and think are there any you would like to?

When you read a book you love, do you have to stop?

Is it the excessive pleasure? Is it you can't take any more for a minute? *The Mill on the Floss* I put down midway in Chapter II, page 16, and it's a 558-page book.

I'm into reading. *The Mayor of Casterbridge,* next came *Far from the Madding Crowd,* a reread of *Pilgrim's Progress, Tess of the D'Urbervilles.* I had to recover. Now *The Mill on the Floss* page 16 I have to stop. 1979 is turning into my reading year. Or is it only Hardy? There's one who can hold your attention.

Would you believe it? *Mill on the Floss* grabbed me, then somewhere I put it down and haven't picked it up again.

A career is hard to get going and hard to keep going. Help it by choosing a good name. I chose Fentress Serene Kerlin but my mother said if I was going to be that foolish I better stay home. I had a lot to contend with so I compromised on Ruth Gordon. Serviceable, but in the phone book of any city there'll be a "Ruth Gordon," in New York they've shrunk to two. "Mrs. Ruth Gordon," and "Ruth Gordon Enterprises." From Philadelphia came a letter, the letterhead read: THE RUTH GORDON BUILDING AND LOAN SOCIETY. Ever hear of a BUILDING AND LOAN SOCIETY called FENTRESS SERENE KERLIN? Did you ever see Fentress Serene Kerlin in a phone book? If you've got a way insist on it, don't falter.

"Do you spell it O.N. or E.N.?" some people ask. Where do they get E.N.? Gordon Highlanders. Gordon gin. With new inventions everything becomes harder. Until a few years ago no one ever brought up en.

In the third grade I chose some different spelling of my own. I passed in my paper signed "Rythe Gordon Jones Third Grade."

Miss Glavin gave me a bad mark.

"My mother *wants* me to spell it Rythe."

"Don't be silly, write Ruth twenty-five times after school."

When did I get over hating her? Was it when I saw RUTH GORDON up in lights?

RYTHE GORDON
IN
THE MATCHMAKER

Thank you, Miss Glavin.

FENTRESS SERENE KERLIN
AND
BUD CORT
IN
HAROLD AND MAUDE

Thank you, Mama.

How great when you learn something! A letter came post-marked Cambridge, Massachusetts. The single page was headed Y.M.C.A., it was from someone who had seen *Harold and Maude*. He wrote, "Everyone has to have someone to tell it to." In the movie Harold had Maude.

Everyone has to have someone to tell it to. It's the definition, I suppose, of love and living and a reason to stay alive.

Long passages in my life I didn't have someone to tell it to. Some of those years were creative years. In place of having someone to tell it to I told it to my work. The telling was in the performance.

"I'm all right," said Artur Rubinstein. "I have a sense of humor and the love of the public."

Well, I have a sense of humor and the love of the public, but the years when I've had Garson to tell it to are years of love and living and the goodbye will come hard.

Thoughts are lying around inside you and maybe a letter from the Cambridge Y.M.C.A. searches them out.

I don't like everything to be new in a show. About a bride
they say:

> Something old
> Something new
> Something borrowed
> And something blue.

And that's like a show, a little something to remind me and
give me courage comes from something I wore before.

Facing the two days we were to make the six tests for *Harold
and Maude*, I decided to wear my treasure of a costume from
The Loves of Cass McGuire. For that show I had two sets of
costumes. One I hated and one was right. Today's was the right
one that Freddy Wittop designed because of Garson. No wonder
our marriage is in its thirty-seventh year! If it hadn't been for
him there would have been only the horrible costumes all wrong
for Cass, all wrong for me, all wrong for anybody in the world
except David Merrick and Hilton Edwards directing dress rehearsal at Boston's Colonial Theatre where I had heard my
voices. Tonight my voices didn't need to tell me, "You've got
some ghastly junk to wear." Shapeless, dark calico dresses for
Cass, who was loud and tough and loved fellers, why shapeless?
Why calico? Why dark? She'd lived a roaring Bowery life, didn't
save her money, sent it back to her brother and his family in Ireland even though he'd written he was doing well and didn't
need it.

"That's like the Irish," said Cass, "they don't know the truth
if there's a *lie* about," and kept sending the money. Then the
day came her feller was gone. "That's me, I'm off to a life of
ease with my brother and his young, they'll be glad to see me."
And they were, but Cass's coarseness didn't fit in with a
dignified Dublin household and her ways weren't their ways and
she certainly didn't cover up her shape with a shapeless non-
come-hither dark printed calico, high collar, long sleeves, not in
1966. Those calico threads could only come out of a costumer's

head. Director Hilton Edwards said, "Wear them. Mind you, I don't think they're exactly right."

For "exactly right" read "exactly wrong" and in the wrong costume how can you play your part? If you've got the *right* costume, maybe you can't but you can play it better than when it's wrong.

My cue came, I stepped out of the stage-right shadows onto the platform that was Cass's bedroom, a cot, chest of drawers, a chair. I wore an electric blue jersey skirt to a suit Mainbocher had made fourteen years before and an untalented dry cleaner plus the Ogunquit, Maine, sunshine had faded and stretched. Like Cass, it had seen better days. Clothes for the stage that aren't supposed to be stylish ought to be from the back of someone's closet, ought to be contrived out of bargain remnants, ought to have *once* been good. Poor people don't *try* to look like poor people. Crooks don't *try* to look like crooks. Unpopular girls don't try to look unpopular. Mary of Scotland, in her cell, did *not* bring a black high-necked, untrimmed dress.

When Helen Hayes played *Mary of Scotland* I asked, "Wouldn't it be more moving, if, in the cell, we saw Mary wearing an impractical, elegant dress, shabby from age with no maid to take care of it, but enough beauty left to remind of happier days?"

Clothes should remind us of what has been, of what might be. With my faded bright blue jersey skirt I wore an old blouse, a black and white checked jacket, once good, now gone.

"I got good legs," said Cass in the play. My high-heeled shoes were split across the toes, but were still flattering.

"Mr. Merrick says he won't let the rehearsal go on if you wear that," said Hilton Edwards when the Act I curtain fell.

That's a startling remark. In a dress rehearsal you try to get through, move past anything in the way. If furniture isn't in the right place, you walk around it, sit where it is, then *later* give the stage manager hell, but *not* while rehearsal's going on. If a letter isn't there to read, read it anyway. Read the spare that you keep in your pocket, or shoe, or bra or have by coincidence planted on the set. Raise hell once you get the thing over, but while the curtain's up, make do.

"What *does* he want me to wear?"

"Well, of course, dear, I know how you feel about the clothes given you, but that's what Mr. Merrick wants to see."

I came on in my shapeless, dark calico. A skimpy round collar under my chin, the skirt hit me halfway between knee and ankle. I couldn't believe a voice out front wouldn't shout, "Hold it. Go back to the other till we get something that's right."

Any voices?

Tonight, no voices at the Colonial.

How did the author feel? Was this the way *he* saw Cass? Who Brian Friel saw was a Marie Dressler, but David told him I was the one.

> Life is real
> Life is earnest.

In show business, life is *not* real, only the trouble.

That night, when Garson phoned from Philadelphia where he was directing another Merrick show, what could I tell him? He had his troubles there. The only good news I could remember was, "Thornton's coming from Edgartown for the second performance."

"It's got a lot wrong with it," said Thornton. "He could fix it, but I'm not sure he will."

"Talk to him. I think he'd listen to *you*."

"Dear, why do you wear dresses like that?"

I told him.

"So *wrong*. You must wear different clothes."

"I don't think it should come to New York, do you?"

"Oh, if they leave it in this shape, no."

He talked to the author, who listened, but thought he'd stick to his own way. That's an author's right, backed up by Dramatists Guild contract. We're for that.

Garson flew to Boston on Friday. By Friday he knew all the worries via the phone. He *always* has a solution. "Freddy Wittop is out front. I told David to get him to design you something. He's brilliant and he's working for David, doing the clothes for *Breakfast at Tiffany's*," one of the eleven productions David had announced for the season.

After the play, Garson brought Freddy Wittop backstage. Small, shy, Viennese, dripping with talent, he shrugged, "I don't know." He shrugged. "I am up to my eyes, but you can *not* wear those."

"Please help me."

"Will you forgive me? Wear these if you can bear it for here and Philadelphia, and I do it for New York." We kissed, I wept and remembered *how,* so I could do it in Act I. Freddy Wittop rode back to New York on the all-night Greyhound bus, the last plane and train had gone. If you have to design how many clothes for a musical, you can't sleep at the Ritz in Boston.

Philadelphia reaction was as deadly as Boston's. As deadly as my clothes. *I* didn't go, the *play* didn't.

"I don't get it," was the comment that filled the Forrest Theatre dressing room. "Do *you* know what it's about?" My friends couldn't even practice what Thornton called "greenroom perjury."

In Philadelphia, the play and the costumes weren't the only trial, at the Forrest Theatre they forgot the dressing rooms. Someone had brought it to the management's attention and they bought the building behind it and across the alley. If it's not raining you can walk across, but in winter you have to go down cellar, go under the alley, pass the boiler room and crew lavatory, walk up a flight to get onstage. If *you* need a lavatory, forget it. When I played there in *A Doll's House*, those long skirts with a train, those taffeta petticoats! How would an architect like to drag those up and down his long flights of iron and concrete stairs wearing high high heels? Mama said life on the stage was hard and she said it in Quincy when they hadn't even broken *ground* for the Forrest in Philly.

After the Saturday night performance, Jack Schlissel, David Merrick's general manager, came back to my dressing room.

"What do you make of us?" I asked.

"They're counting on Walter Kerr. Catholic. David figures if Kerr goes for it, it can make it."

Garson and I kept track of our life by long-distance telephone and Sunday morning I took the train to Washington.

Chaos! *We Have Always Lived in the Castle* was the play Gar was directing at the National Theatre on Pennsylvania Avenue and the sound effects didn't work, the sound man was no good and something was wrong with the kid's performance, plus more of the same. Get past the moment, but it wasn't easy for me and Garrie Kanin in Washington, which we *enjoy!* All I could think of was, "It's better than when you were in uniform."

Would that comfort *you?* Comfort has to be of the moment, it ages quicker than we do.

Back at the Forrest. "Please tell Mr. Merrick I'd like to see him." After the show he came in. "I wish you wouldn't bring this in."

"I'm going to."

"Everybody that comes back says, 'I don't follow it.'"

"Yes, I admit it's not clear."

"Even if we *get* Walter Kerr, I don't think it'll go. People don't know if it's *happening* or if I'm *telling* it or if I'm *imagining* or if I'm *there.*"

"Yes, it certainly is obscure."

"You've announced eleven productions, do you want the first one to be a flop?"

"No, I don't *want* it to be."

Never ad-lib with an ex-lawyer.

Live through it, get past the moment, kick it under the rug. In my fine bedroom at the Barclay Hotel, I heard voices. "If everybody comes back and says, 'I don't follow it,' maybe straighten it out?"

On a pad of paper I wrote "Act I, Scene I," and worked out the play in chronological order. Instead of skipping back and forth, the scenes went forward, no rewriting, just reshuffling. I rang up David and read the pieces to him.

"It sounds worth a try."

"Could we do it for the matinee?"

"Okay."

"But you have to say it's your idea, he won't like another playwright redoing his play. He wouldn't listen to Thornton."

"All right."

Dennis King, Brenda Forbes, Liam Redmond and the others from Dublin and New York relearned it. We played the matinee.

"I don't see why people say they don't follow it. I followed it perfectly," said the lady from the Harbor View Hotel, Edgartown, who came over from Reading to the matinee.

I thought it was good.

"I'm not sure we don't lose something," said Dennis.

That night, Brian Friel and his agent, Audrey Wood and David arrived.

"I like it," said David, "but they don't go for it and I don't think it's worth a fight."

Back in New York, I took a suite at the Algonquin. Our home was staffed, but who knows when to order dinner? *Or* lunch? Or breakfast? For previews and a New York opening, there's comfort in room service.

"Monday morning at nine, your suite," said the note from Freddy Wittop.

"Mr. Wittop downstairs."

"Send him up."

In came my savior with his fitter. "I *hope* you'll like it."

"I will."

"*We* think it's all right, but you may not."

"I will."

He looked the other way. Saint Barbara Matera put a skirt over my head. "It'll open so you can step in, but for this fitting."

"Go ahead."

It was cheap-looking and soft and clinging. It hung onto the shape of a hip, then flared when it hit the knee. The color was cheap attention-getting garnet.

"Wear the highest heels you've got," said Freddy.

Over my head went another masterpiece, ecru georgette crepe chiffon with a crinkle. Loose, but not really, it hit me about two inches below the top of the satin skirt. Around the neck, a band of ecru, faced back with a sugar-pink cowboy scarf knotted over the left tit.

"It's the greatest! It's a masterpiece!"

"I thought this sweater?"

Saint Barbara eased me into a black loose-crochet cardigan appliquéd with pink sequin flowers set among green sequin leaves, the whole thing edged with black cat fur.

Freddy Wittop, dear, wherever you are, I love you! Why did you have to choose to retire? Freddy, come back, you are an inspiration plus irreplaceable. The show closed, Walter Kerr *didn't* go for it, but your dress was like you, inspiring! Six years later, Bob Balaban, trying out for Harold, walked along with me past our director Hal Ashby's house on the Appian Way, camera truck leading, and to give me courage I wore *your* garnet satin skirt, ecru blouse with the sugar-pink cowboy scarf and Barbara's black cat-fur-trimmed flowered sweater.

As I said so beautifully in my play *Over Twenty-One*, "Once in a while things come out right."

BEGIN-NINGS

"Beginnings, always have beginnings," advised André Previn.

Why not give a lecture? I heard Alexander Woollcott give one and thought *I* could do that. I did. The audience was a thousand English teachers from all over New York State. Not knowing how good I'd be as a speaker, I bought a stylish dress.

Bernard Shaw told Edith Evans, "When you're in an intellectual play, dress beautifully."

This wasn't a play, but with W. H. Auden and Allardyce Nicoll as the other speakers it had to be intellectual. With my hundred-dollar fee I bought a hundred-dollar biscuit color satin dress at Hattie Carnegie's.

Yale's Professor Allardyce Nicoll talked about the theatre. Most of what he said was outside my range, but it was soothing for my first speaking engagement nerves. I followed him at the podium.

My subject was the English language and why use the same stale words over and over? Why not work words into the conversation like words in poems.

"Earth's diurnal course of
rocks and fields and trees,"

why not work diurnal in?

That made the audience laugh. It takes time to get a new thing going.

I did all right, but then came the question-and-answer part of the evening. A lot of questions that should have been asked Professor Nicoll they asked me. "You have practical experience in the theatre, Miss Gordon, do you agree with Professor Nicoll that . . . ?" "You being on the stage understand what Professor Nicholl meant, Miss Gordon, but would you please . . . ?"

What I was saying was clear, nobody asked questions about that, but to explain what Allardyce Nicoll was saying I would have to be Allardyce Nicoll.

At four years old I started off one afternoon and Mama called out the window, "Where are you going, Ruth?"

"B.U.V." and started off some more.

"Ruth, *where* are you going?"

"B.U.V., Mama, that spells up to Marian West's."

Confidence came early. At four I had conviction, also my own spelling.

More places I ate my twenty-nine thousand breakfasts. Newark, Mountain Lakes, Convent, New Jersey, at Hollow Hill Farm, where Fanny Moore's hackney pony Seton Pippin was. Best horse in the show for how many years? And never saw any of the three hundred a month fan letters that Seton's own secretary took care of. Atlantic City, hot salt water faucet let you take a hot salt water bath in your tub and before 9 A.M. you could bicycle on the boardwalk all the way to Ventnor. Shows tried out in Asbury Park, Long Branch, breakfast tasted good or bad according to how last night's performance went. Elberon, where darling Martin Beck had his summer estate. Did I say Trenton? I know I didn't say Princeton, where the audience tried not to laugh in the sad places but had to when I said, "My husband is paralyzed from the waist down." That rocked them. After that I had in my contract, "Must have footlights, won't play Princeton." Summit, where we felt like swells just riding by the Baltusrol Country Club. Grandness itself and I was riding by it with Lily Werner from Quincy, who married rich Frank Parssons and lived in Summit, where they had a Japanese spaniel and a butler. The first breakfast on my first road tour was Mrs. Green's Boarding House, Philadelphia. Breakfast in the dining room, where around the table sat the acrobat act appearing at B. F. Keith's Vaudeville Theatre and the Wendy in our *Peter Pan* company and one of Captain Hook's most high-salaried pirates, David Torrence. After Mrs. Green's my first one-nighter breakfast was in a Greek restaurant. In Quincy we'd never heard of one. Spanish omelet for breakfast. Never heard of that either. Reading, Pa., Lancaster, Allentown, Harrisburg, Pittsburgh, New Castle, where *Fair and Warmer* closed and I'd saved four hundred dollars that I kept pinned in my corset, Coshocton, Hazelton, where the miners came up from the mine black-faced and next morning went down black-faced. Hagerstown, Maryland, Baltimore, Frederick or Fredericksburg, Easton, Wilmington, Delaware, Washington, D.C., Richmond, Virginia, where the Jefferson Hotel had an alligator in a tank in the lobby. A sign said "Do not poke the alligator with your umbrella." Roanoke, Norfolk, Lynchburg we checked out *before* breakfast, the early train stopped at Gordonsville fifteen minutes for everybody to buy a quarter of a fried chicken in a piece of wax paper. It was next best to Vance's chicken dinner near the auto race-track in Indianapolis. Maybe as good. I went back for another wax paper's worth. I liked it the best thing I ate in Virginia.

Bad habits, do they wear off or do they disappear when you don't need them anymore? Jealousy still lurks around, but stealing I've got rid of.

"Money's for those that need it," said the legendary Mrs. Pat Campbell. I don't need it. If I did, would I steal?

The last I stole were dimes off girls' bureaus at the Three Arts Club, where I was trying to get to be an actress. Papa had staked me with fifty dollars. Pinned to my corset it made a bulge. Pretty soon the bulge was smaller. No job, a smaller bulge, then no bulge.

Owe the board bill, but to be an actress you need carfare so when the early girls had gone, a look in their rooms and if there was a dime on a bureau I took it for carfare or a ten-cent dinner at Child's, vegetable soup with a pat of butter, two pieces of graham bread.

I needed the dime and stole it, but did I need Miss Gorham's jewelry? Did I have the instincts of a thief?

Miss Gorham ran a small dry goods store on Newport Avenue in Quincy, sold jabots, collar and cuff sets, Butterick patterns, lace, buttons, yards of this and that including penny-a-yard ribbon. If you're a spender you have to spend. Seven years old and one penny to spend, the choices were a frosted bun with raisins, a frosted cupcake.

"Ruth, don't buy from that bakeshop, he has consumption. Do you want to get consumption?" I wiped my mouth off before I came home. Not only instincts to steal, but to lie.

Choose penny candy? Choose a lovely color? When you're poor, choice is limited, but for the same price at Miss Gorham's I could choose yellow, red, baby blue, light green, a sheet of any color tissue paper, a yard of any color ribbon. She got mad having to cut off one yard, peel off one sheet. "Wait till I get around to it," she snapped.

At May basket time I reached back of the curtain where were empty thread boxes and empty ribbon rolls. Paste the tissue paper on for a May basket and a ribbon roll cut in half and covered with fringed pink tissue paper could look like a carnation. Red tissue paper petals curled around Mama's china-headed hatpin could look like a rose, slide in a fringed yellow tissue square around three pieces of fudge, slip it in the rose and leave on the doorstep, ring the bell and go.

I came up with two empty ribbon rolls, reached further for a thread box. The lid slipped off, what pricked my finger? A gold crescent brooch with a green stone, I sauntered out of the store.

"Ruth, did you steal that?" asked Mama. "Ruth, they'll send detectives out from Boston." Why wasn't Mama a playwright!

I began to cry. "It's Miss Gorham's."

Mama led me back there.

"It's not worth anything," snapped Miss Gorham, and was impatient to be rid of us.

"Did you learn something from all that," asked Zarathustra, "or hasn't anything else appealed to you since?"

"What do you think of all this dreadful pornography?" they ask me as though I had just come across it. I've been dealing with it since I was seven. Mama and I were in the kitchen and Papa's daughter, my half-sister Clare, came home from high school. She said she and Alice Dow were walking along Newport Avenue and when they got to Cousin Gertrude Alden's orchard a man was leaning against Cousin Gertrude's stone wall with his pants open and everything hanging out.

It didn't seem very interesting, but Mama started hollering, "Oh you poor child, Oh my poor Clare, Oh how terrible, we'll have to call the policeman."

That caught my interest. Call the policeman! I knew we had a policeman in Quincy but I *never* heard of anybody *calling* him. And then I heard Mama. "My poor Clare, maybe not, maybe it would be bad if everybody knew you'd seen a man expose himself, maybe we won't even tell Papa, we'll just *forget* it."

Forget it! The things grown-ups expect of you. Forget it, as though it was perfectly sensible. That was when I was seven years old and I haven't forgotten it yet.

Did it do me any harm? I don't think so, unless you count disappointment at not calling the policeman.

Pornography didn't show up again for a year, Mildred Murray said to come down to her house Saturday morning and bring a penny. What was the penny for? Mildred didn't live near a store, but before I even got to her house she called out, "Did you bring the penny?"

I held it up.

She headed across Fayette Street past the dump.

"Where are we going?" I asked.

"Green's Pond," and turned the corner onto Arlington Street.

Green's Pond was at the foot of Arlington, a small marshy pond where we learned to skate, but when we learned we never went back there, the ice was full of frozen reeds and cinders from the nearby trains that dulled skates. But why go to the pond late spring? "Why Green's Pond?"

"To see Albert take off his pants."

Do you ever know you shouldn't do something, don't want to, but do it just the same? Is it you're embarrassed not to? Is it you're afraid of what someone will think? Why didn't I turn around and go home? I just kept tagging along after Mildred's dirty white sneakers.

"Hello, Mrs. Blaikie," she called as though nothing horrible was happening.

Mrs. Blaikie was out on her piazza shaking a long-handled mop. "Hello Mildred, hello Ruth."

We crossed North Central Avenue, no more pavement, our feet felt the soft earth, Mildred parted some elderberry bushes and we stepped onto a damp path through more bushes that opened up and there was Green's Pond. In a circle stood Franklin Jameson, Everet Sayward and Albert Carr, the smallest.

"Show him your penny," said Mildred.

I held it up. Was it too late to go back?

"Hurry up," commanded Mildred, and handed him our pennies.

Albert dropped them in his pants pocket, then tested the ground.

"It's wet, I don't think I'll lie down."

"That's the only way you look any good." Her voice was an order.

He undid his pants, looked at the ground. "I won't do it."

"Here," Mildred unbuttoned her petticoat, spread it out for him like a bed. He lay down. It was the first time I ever saw a boy show everything.

He got up, got his pants on.

"Want to show us you, Ruth?" asked Franklin.

I didn't see the opening in the bushes, but dashed in and

struggled. Behind me I heard Mildred, "She's no fun, want to see me?"

"We saw you."

Ahead I could see North Central Avenue. Shocked, startled, but not damaged except that my first impression of a boy was no good.

Nothing more till I was just going to be eighteen. In New York to study to be an actress, the rich brother of one of the other students invited me to Ziegfeld's Midnight Frolic than which! It was on top of New York's grandest musical comedy theatre, the New Amsterdam. Ziegfeld Midnight Frolic artist Ben Ali Haggin arranged some war tableau posed by Ziegfeld's show girls. Red-haired Jessie Reed portrayed Belgium in skeeky black, Olive Thomas was the beauty chosen to be France. Next Alsace-Lorraine. Curtains parted and there stood blond, fragile beauty Kay Laurell, her Alsatian costume designed by Ben Ali and executed by Follies costumers Schneider and Anderson without regard to the bill.

Alsace-Lorraine's troubles we all knew about, but Kay Laurell had trouble of her own. Schneider and Anderson's work had let go, one breast had come uncovered and pointed right out at Times Square.

"Oh poor thing!" I thought. "Oh *how* could such a thing happen? Oh what will she *do?*"

The audience was sympathetic and applauded to show it was all right, the curtain closed and after time for backstage to bawl out Schneider and Anderson and repair the disgrace, the curtains reopened and Kay Laurell's pink-tipped breast still aimed toward what used to be the Times Building. In Quincy they think of calling the police for indecent exposure, in New York they applaud. I had thought I left home when I took the train from our old Colony depot, but it was the Ziegfeld Frolic took me further on the way to civilization.

1928 took me further. I don't mean the foolish Antibes gendarme arresting Woollcott for wearing an insufficient jockstrap while we were bathing at Elsie Mendl's Château de la Garoupe. I mean sunning on the terrasse at Eden Roc and Steve Wiman, christened Dorothea, but known only as Steve, or Mrs. Dwight Wiman beckoned me down beside her. "My *dear,* you can chase around New York and nothing happens, but in Nice it's autre chose!"

"My *dear!*" I said. That was the summer of "My dear!"

"My dear, they do it absoluement starkers!"

"Do what?"

"What d'you *think,* dear? We went last night."

"Went where?"

"Movies, you *have* to go. I mean you *don't* want to come home without seeing it! Grace Moore and the Countess Valombrosa went with us and, my dear, Grace was so shocked she sat on the floor back-to the movie and held her pocketbook over her eyes!"

"My *dear!*"

"The Countess just sneered at the screen. " 'How does she get *away* with old stuff?' "

"What were they doing?"

"It! Au naturel, naturellement and the leading man, my dear, was waving it around in a close-up!"

"My *dear!*"

"And the subtitle read, *'le sien est le plus grand du monde.'* 'It's not big,' snarled the Countess, 'it just looks big because his hands are so small.' "

I suggested to Woollcott we go at once.

"You don't know what you're talking about."

I was Woollcott's and Harpo's guest at their Villa Ganelon.

"Alec, I'm all alone in the world. If *you* won't take me, who will?"

"Nobody."

"Harpo wants to learn, he and I'll go. You sent us to the Colombe d'Or for dinner that got us stewed on the *omelette au rhum* and we had to walk each other around to sober us before driving back here, but Harpo said, 'What the hell, we're *learn-ing.*'"

He and I made plans to go that night. We shoved past Wooll-cott and got into Harpo's Renault. As Harpo did whatever you do to start a Renault, Woollcott shouted, "Wait for baby!" and squeezed into the back seat.

Dinner at the Hôtel de Paris, Monte Carlo. Do I need to say what that was like? Harpo looked sadly toward the Casino, where he'd lost twenty thousand dollars. "Where do you throw yourself off the rocks?" he asked our waiter.

Back we drove along the Middle Corniche to Nice. Steve had given me the address and Guy, our butler, told us how to get there, it seems everybody was learning. Harpo turned off the Promenade des Anglais and went up a dark street and down one darker. "Stop," said Woollcott.

How did *he* know?

We were in front of a *hôtel particulier* on a tree-lined street of *hôtels particuliers*. Woollcott rang the bell, eyes peered through the slit in the door.

"Monsieur Wooll*cott*," said Alec.

No recognition.

"Monsieur *Alexander* Wooll*cott*."

"*Ne connais pas.*"

"*Mais oui! Monsieur double vay, double oh, double ell, say, oh, double tay!*"

"*Connais pas.*" The eyes shifted back of Woollcott to Harpo. "*Eh voilà, Monsieur Marx!*" The bolt slipped back, a chain clanked, slid out of place, the Madame flung her arms around Harpo.

"Hiya, cutie," he said, and beckoned Woollcott and me to follow him into a Chinese red and black lacquer hall. Abruptly Madame showed us into a small room.

"What happened?" I asked.

"*Quand un client part, personne ne doit pas le voir.*"

"What's she say?" asked Harpo.

"Nobody's allowed to see a customer on his way out," said Woollcott.

Harpo smiled at Madame. "Have you got a lady does it with a dog?"

"Tch, tch, tch." She shook her finger from side to side at Harpo as if to erase what he said.

A cohort gave the signal the way was clear, Madame led us up stairs that had a red velvet handrail, down a hall lined with doors, one open. There were chairs placed in front of a small movie screen, Madame beckoned us to sit down, took a seat behind us. "Champagne?"

"I'll buy *you* some," said Harpo politely, "but I rather see a lady do it with a dog."

Madame got up and left. An iron-faced woman came in with a catalogue of the movies. "Thanks," said Harpo, politely, "do you do it with a dog?"

"*Ne parlez anglais, monsieur.*"

"*Cincinnati tout droit?*" leered Harpo.

Woollcott was glancing over the titles. "*La Veuve et Sa Misère?*"

"What's a verve?" Harpo asked.

"A widow. It's about her trouble. Here's one about a priest."

Harpo brightened. "I like a religious movie."

The screen lit up. A priest was paying a call on a lady, they had their clothes on, then this and that came off. Pretty soon the lady was down to herself, the priest got bashful and wouldn't take off his underdrawers. We sipped champagne and after the priest picture, saw the widow in her misery. To cheer us up, we chose "Behaviour in a Bath Chair à l'Anglaise," followed by a horror picture, "The Young Ladies Seminary," a young lady having a nightmare that they graduated naked, with one girl doing it with the headmistress and the school cutup doing it with her diploma.

Were Harpo and Alec and I any the worse? I never noticed it.
If you're going to get hurt by stuff, learn not to. Take a look but
keep going, it's a long way to civilization and when stuff hurts
you the way is longer.

I wrote Thornton, "I've taken up vindictiveness. Maybe you don't need it in St. Moritz or New Haven or Edgartown, but Hollywood and New York it's a must.

Bella"

Before you're really into it, it may need more work than you've got time for. Like Gertrude Stein said about being a miser. "It is so absorbing."

Is out house one word or two and did you ever go to one?

At 41 Winthrop Avenue, 41 Marion Street, and 14 Elmwood Avenue we had one bathroom for Mama and Papa and me, down cellar was a crude one for Mrs. Carlson, our washwoman, but at French's Boarding House, where we vacationed, they had an out house, a two-holer. I never shared it with anyone.

At Aunt Emma and Uncle George's Camp Nestledown their out house had real toilet paper, at French's Boarding House, they had neatly torn up Portland newspapers.

Who invented bathrooms? Did they know what comfort they were? Why not a bathroom stamp? Write your congressman or woman or senator, mine is handsome, brilliant Edward Kennedy. I guess with a Dad like his and a Ma like the remarkable Rose he never knew what an out house was.

Maybe his grandpa, Honey Fitz, did. Certainly shy Harriet Martineau, a houseguest of Henry James Senior in Cambridge. She was walking down the path to it, while walking from it came Nathaniel Bowditch. As the two passed, shy Harriet murmured, "One cometh and another goeth."

No reply from Bowditch remains, only his Almanach.

The dictionary spells it outhouse. Why is a dictionary right?

Ever since that meeting with André Previn in front of the Beverly Hills Seed Store I have more and more beginnings. I had an overwhelming one when honors, awards, achievement led me onto the Joey Bishop TV show to accept the gold medal that *Photoplay* bestowed on *Rosemary's Baby*.

"Shouldn't Mia accept it?" I asked Bill Castle, the picture's producer.

"It would be embarrassing, they're giving the gold medal for acting to somebody else. You have to."

I did.

Never accept anything from strangers, Mama told me when I was six. I knew she wasn't with it and accepted the gold medal for *Rosemary's Baby* from a charming stranger, head of *Photoplay* magazine. The one who deserved it was our unsung producer, William Castle. In a machine-made world he saw to it that *Rosemary's Baby* was a handmade picture. One morning he rushed onto the set just as the camera was going to roll. "Roman, I saw the dailies and I don't care if we *are* twenty-nine days behind schedule, just keep on directing this picture *great!*"

"*Photoplay*'s gold medal really should belong to William Castle, and to Paramount's top executive Bob Evans, who backed up our man."

When it was going, everybody tuned in on the "Joey Bishop Show" and that included my English teacher, Mrs. Molly Brown Shepherd in Braintree, Mass., my girl friend Mrs. Katherine Follett LeBeau in St. Pete, Mia Farrow on the shore of Lake Tashmoo, Vineyard Haven. Wherever I went I heard, "I loved you on the 'Joey Bishop Show.'" If I didn't hear it, I went out and came in again.

When Rosalind Russell and I took a trip together to bring home a dying friend from the Mayo Clinic in Rochester, Minnesota, Roz loved to say, "What would you have to talk about if you didn't keep saying, 'I come from Boston'?"

"You're just sore because you come from Waterbury and can't use that for a conversation opener."

Not too bright, but we enjoyed it. Only after Joey Bishop, I didn't need an opener, I just needed to say, "Thanks."

"Saw you on the 'Joey Bishop Show,' terrific!"

"Thanks."

Joey asked me to come on again. Happy to. He leaned toward the microphone. "I guess you get a lot of praise for your performance in your new movie, *Whatever Happened to Aunt Alice?*"

"Don't turn me on about *Aunt Alice*! I'm just back from four days in Boston where they had the New England premier of *Whatever Happened to Aunt Alice?* I've come back talking like movie producer Joe Levine. Is that bad, by the way, to talk like the producer of *The Graduate, The Lion in Winter?* Also going to produce *Hetty Green* with me playing 'The Witch of Wall Street.' When I say I talk like Joe Levine I talk like somebody who knows what to say. Mention *Whatever Happened to Aunt Alice?* and I say, 'In New York City alone it played in forty-two showcase theatres and did one million two in *Baltimore,* in a house that averages eleven hundred all the week, *Whatever Happened to Aunt Alice?* did forty-two hundred in *three* days, and in Boston, over the weekend we did a smasharoo of over nineteen thou, and we *also* played last Tuesday in Edgartown, where I haven't got the figure yet, will have it next time I come on the show."

Talk about beginnings! A whole new chapter to life.

"Ruth, would you mind telling them your age?" asked Joey.

"Last time I was on the show I told them how old I was and I don't want to be known just for that. It first happened to me when I married Garson Kanin. Both of us were known for a lot. Even before he wrote *Born Yesterday,* he'd directed Ginger Rogers and David Niven in *Bachelor Mother,* Ginger and Senator Murphy in *Tom, Dick and Harry* and fabulous Carole Lombard and Charles Laughton in *They Knew What They Wanted,* John Barrymore in *The Great Man Votes*! I'd been in Ibsen's *A Doll's House* and Edith Wharton's *Ethan Frome* and at the time we got married I was starring with Katharine Cornell, Judith Anderson, Dennis King, Edmund Gwenn in Chekov's *The Three Sisters,* but the newspaper the day after our wedding ran 'Actress forty-six marries film director thirty.' The best they could come up with was 'Actress forty-six'?

"Garson said he liked it. If it said 'Actress forty-five' a lot of people would say 'She's fifty if she's a day,' but when an actress says she's forty-six, you have to believe her."

Age is ridiculous, sometimes I feel a hundred and sometimes I feel like a chippie, so why is that interesting?

"A chain is as strong as its weakest link," taught beautiful Miss Elizabeth O'Neill, and would you believe that the gift of speaking ad lib came to me because I had to tell Bill Castle I would do it whether I could or couldn't? Where does learning come from? What day are you likely to learn some? Papa's four hundred dollars to send me where I could learn acting bought me fear and shyness and insecurity, rocked my confidence, then all at once, the light shines, the wand waves and I can do it, I know how. I ask to have the lights kept on the studio audience so I can see everybody and away we go.

It took me thirty years to talk to an audience. A long way from my first speech. Was it 1938? It was in Stockbridge, Mass., up in the Berkshires. "Financially, the times were out of joint" and I was playing a week of summer stock, the playhouse windows wide open so the audience wouldn't suffocate. Even open, people sweltered, in the dim light they waved their fans. Their endurance gave me courage to make the first speech I ever made. The final curtain came down on Shaw's *The Million-airess,* applause was meant, but the applauders were too warm. I stepped forward to where footlights should be and were at the Berkshire Playhouse. "Thank you, I don't know about you but I'm so hot my stockings are bagging at the knees."

Not much of a speech, but I never heard that stockings bag from the heat and mine did. It seemed appropriate to mention the suffering was mutual.

"Where are the snows of yesteryear? And where is the brass 14 of 14 Elmwood Avenue and the fluted brass doorknob, the front door, the front porch, the front steps I walked down on my way to become an actress? What became of them and does anyone care but me? Last year at 14 Elmwood Avenue the brass 14 beside the door was the same curly 14 as when I set out in 1914, the fluted brass doorknob the same I turned when I came home from my interview with Mr. John Craig, star, director, producer of the Castle Square Theatre, where his leading lady Miss Doris Olssen *said* he'd engage me and I got so scared meeting him that when he asked, "What experience have you had?" and I *knew* Miss Olssen told him I hadn't any, that I was still a senior at Quincy High, I said, "No amateur experience, just professional," and had to start all over again and say, "I mean no professional, just amateur," and right after that I was walking along the street from Castle Square where Mama said was the *worst* section of Boston and what did I care? I just wanted to die. My first time to meet a manager and failed. When I got home and turned the doorknob that was still there last year my courage was about gone, but it didn't go and has lasted.

"Where the hell have you been?" roared Papa.

Mama knew, but hadn't told.

I burst into tears, sat down, put my head on our dining room table that got sold to the secondhand man, and cried and cried, but I didn't care, I just wanted to go on crying the rest of my life.

After I don't know *how* long, I heard, "Well, he don't sound like much. What did you want to go see *him* for? You go to that acting school like I told you. Write a letter, ask what you have to do in the way of preliminary arrangements."

"Clinton, you're a good man," said Mama.

They were both good. Forget the 14 and the fluted doorknob, the door, the front porch, the front steps, what's real are the memories. They can't renovate them.

God bless beautiful Miss Elizabeth Irene O'Neill, who paved the way for each day of my life to learn an acting lesson. So must it be if you learn how to learn.

Philip Barry didn't always write hits, but what he wrote was always his. He was his own man.

"This one *would* be his best," said Jed, "but he won't wait to get it right."

"Why?"

"He says he has to have a play on every season and it's December. He doesn't think this one is, but thinks he can get it right in rehearsal. It's not that kind of play. I let it go and the Theatre Guild bought it. Five hundred dollars a week you get, no one featured in a Guild play, Philip Moeller will direct. He won't know what it's about, but you have to do it."

This one was called *Hotel Universe,* member of the Theatre Guild Board Lee Simonson did the scenery, a terrace in the South of France. Did I play Dorothy Parker? That's what they said. Phil Barry called the part Lily Malone, changed to "Idli Malone" in treasured *Who's Who,* but the program read, "Lily Malone." She was an actress who cut her wrists a lot and wore diamond bracelets to cover the scars.

A lesson in how to handle yourself or how not to: the first rehearsal of anything is terrifying, it's terrifying to hear yourself doing it all wrong, *not* doing it, *over*doing it. The first rehearsal of *Hotel Universe* was to be Sunday, they hadn't signed my contract. The Guild wasn't businesslike, a contract got signed sometime or other, but I felt insecure since four years before Guth had fired me and that's even more terrifying than a first rehearsal.

"I won't rehearse," I told the Guild.

"You have to," they said.

"My run-of-the-play contract isn't signed, you could fire me."

"We won't."

Would I take a chance on myself? What about Guthrie firing me and he loved me and these people I don't even know. Guthrie who loved me, who knew I was good, who believed he had a wonderful part for me in this new play, *Glory Hallelujah,* had to fire me. The authors, actor Thomas Mitchell and co-author some name I can't remember, didn't want me, they wanted June Walker, lovely actress and a beauty. Guthrie wanted *me*. We went into rehearsal, all the company sat around a table, Guthrie read the play. It was a serious play and the authors thought I wasn't up to it. The only actor I remember in the company was Lee Tracy, not yet a star.

After Guthrie read, he talked to us, then he said he'd like to hear *us*. I surprised myself, for once I sounded as though I'd be good.

That day's rehearsal ended, I felt encouraged. Next day, still reading around the table, the press agent came up to Guthrie, showed him the press announcement he was sending out.

Guthrie read it, then rather flustered ordered press agent not to name any of the cast.

How did I know I was going to be fired? My voices?

Rehearsal over, I came home to Gregory's and my apartment on Central Park South where the Park Lane Hotel is now, we had a cook named Edna, Harpo was coming to dinner with us. Harpo was our best friend. "I'm going to be fired," I told them.

"Guthrie loves you," said Gregory.

Harpo just laughed. He thought I was a wonderful actress and knew how Guthrie felt.

"I *am*, I know it."

"How could you?" asked Gregory. "Did Guthrie say anything?"

"No, but he told the press agent not to announce any names."

"Well, maybe replace someone, but why you?" Gregory knew I was mistaken.

"It's me. I know it is."

The phone rang. Edna answered. "It's Mister McClintic to speak to you."

"He wants to fire me." I got up, answered the phone.

"Can I come over to see you tonight?"

"Sure."

"About eight?"

"Yes."

Gregory rushed off to his play, and Harpo to his.

Guthrie talked about everything under the sun, about how he used to steal when he was a little boy. Nothing he wanted, "Just wanted to see if I could."

"Are you going to fire me?"

"Yes," he said, and burst into tears.

We hung onto each other and wept. He hadn't signed the contract for the play with author Tommy Mitchell and the co-author, but he had ordered the scenery to be built and now Mitchell and his partner said they'd take *Glory Hallelujah* away if he didn't fire me and engage June Walker.

Gregory called up after the theatre. "I'll be right home."

Harpo called up after, "I'll be right there." He stopped at a Broadway nut and fudge store and brought me a wicker sewing basket full of five pounds of salted nuts.

The next day I had an offer from producer Charles Wagner to play the lead in a new play with Sidney Blackmer. It was good, but I didn't dare take it for fear I would be fired.

The next day is hard to handle, thinking of the actors sitting around the table, only today June would sit in *my* chair, read *my* lines.

When trouble happens, your friend is your courage.

I had never been fired, but what if it happened again?

"I won't rehearse without my contract," I told the Theatre Guild manager.

"It's the weekend. Terry Helburn's in Westport, Lawrence Langner in God knows where—"

"I'll take a chance."

Sunday afternoon at the Guild Theatre rehearsal room, the theatre now the ANTA, should I take a chance, *really* take a chance? Go looking awful? A part that's supposed to look chic look awful and see if I'll be wonderful? Put it to a test, do it! I could knock them dead with my new Place Vendôme, Cheruit velvet dress in the closet, instead I wore a dead-ass dress my theatre maid, Margaret Bellinger, had copied from a dress Grande Maison de Blanc made me out of Ralph Barton's map of Paris gray silk print and you didn't have to be Pearl Swope to know the copy was *not* Grande Maison de Blanc. It started as *bois de rose* silk I got sick of and had dyed black. Anybody see a dyed dress come out right? No jewelry. Dyed black, no jewelry and what would look more terrible than a brown hat? Brown hat, dyed black dress, no jewelry, brown shoes wtih black stockings, I showed up looking like a freak. All wasted, the Guild never knew what anybody had on. Lawrence Langner noticed if you were a pretty girl, but if I looked like Gaby Deslys, Phil Moeller wouldn't know it, nor Helen Westley, who normally dressed the way I looked. Wouldn't banker Maurice Wertheim notice? Nor Bryn Mawr graduate Terry Helburn? Lee Simonson? His admiration was only for the very advanced scenery of Appia.

Theresa Helburn, Lawrence Langner, Lee Simonson, Maurice Wertheim, Helen Westley sat back-to the big windows behind Phil Moeller's table and chair. They were the Theatre Guild Board. Assistant director Herbert Biberman sat next to Phil and facing them in a semicircle Glenn Anders, Phyllis Povah, Ruthelma Stevens, Franchot Tone, Earle Larimore, Katherine Alexander, Morris Carnovsky, Gustave Roland and I. Wandering in back of us was elegantly dressed, handsome Phil Barry, doubtful plus terrified.

"We'll read," said Phil Moeller.

That's all I remember.

Next day, my contract was signed, I wasn't fired and I was late for rehearsal for the only time in my life. I walked straight up to Phil Moeller. "Will you marry me? It made me late trying to get the courage to ask you."

"Yes," he said, we hugged and kissed and loved each other forever after. Not sex, just admiration.

Rehearsing a scene, Phil would sidle up to me. "Are you all right?" he'd whisper.

I'd whisper back, "Yes."

"Y'know what you're doing?"

"Yes."

"Good."

He didn't, but trusted me. He and Guth, though Guth knew what I was doing.

All day, terrible fights. The Guild, full of prestige and fights?

"When you say that, dear, you're crying," said Phil Moeller. I started to think about tears.

"When she says that, she's laughing," said Phil Barry. If the rehearsal room split in two and a white horse drove through, Phil Moeller couldn't have looked more astonished. He shrugged. "Well, you wrote it, you ought to know."

Lesson in acting: Now what do *I* do?

"My dear Phil . . ."

"My dear Phil."

The first place we played was Newark, a routine place to open, or Brooklyn, at the Shubert Montauk or the theatre in Stamford. Our week in Newark went well enough.

"Changes needed," said famous director Rouben Mamoulian, who often directed for the Guild and came over to take a look.

What changes? Nobody quite knew and we went to Buffalo.

Franchot Tone invited the company to his home right by Niagara Falls. Would you pick that for an address? Pretty distracting, I liked the Buffalo Statler better.

Midweek Terry Helburn and Lawrence Langner took the sleeper and came to see where Phil's rewriting had gotten us. After the afternoon rehearsal, Terry stopped me. "Oh, Ruth, I'm going back on the midnight, so tonight when you start to do the dance and turn your ankle, really do a dance, then break down. Let me see it tonight."

How'd you like to be up in Buffalo at five o'clock in the afternoon with the New York opening next week and "really do a dance"?

Phil's Lily Malone had started as a ballerina who hated her father he drove her so hard, nothing but lessons, lessons, "up on your *points!*" Going back into Lily's memories, the *Naila* ballet record came on and instead of doing a step and an ankle twist, I'd have to go back into *my* memories and do a dance. Who says don't live in the past? Nobody in show business. If not out of my past where would I get a dance routine at the Buffalo Statler 5 P.M. to do onstage four hours later?

The box by my bed squalled out some music. I'd taken ballet from Kosloff to help fill the time when Gregory opened in New York with *Dulcy*, but the only dance Kosloff had taught us was the dagger dance that I did with him at a convention in the Commodore Hotel and the diners laughed so hard Kosloff had to shake his finger at them.

Try my Dorothy Quincy dance from Mrs. Frost's pageant at the Unitarian Church?

My "To a Wild Rose" dance by Edward MacDowell I did at the charity affair in Quincy on Mrs. Faxon's lawn?

For Lily Malone, never mind was she Dotty Parker, she was written as someone entertaining. What dance would *she* do to-night? Would she do a version of the Charleston that Harpo taught Myra Hampton, Gregory and me to do at Woollcott's birthday party and Woollcott forgot to ask for it? I turned off the radio, tried the Charleston routine to the *Naila* ballet in my head and did my Kosloff gestures.

"That dance is good," said Terry. "Keep it in, I didn't know you were a ballet dancer."

Only one slipup. I forgot Harpo was coming opening night. Harpo on the aisle, Row C, said he thought he'd piss himself!

If you're acting and don't know what you're doing, act as though you did.

And if it's stuff from out of the past tell a friend who's a first-nighter.

That night Papa was in the audience. *Hotel Universe* was my only first night he ever got to. Back in the star dressing room of the Martin Beck Theatre I was surrounded by a glittery bunch of New York first-nighters when through them came Papa, not looking to the right or left, nor saying excuse me, he just parted the crowd ahead of him the way the bow of his schooner must have parted waves in the Indian Ocean. "Daughter, you were *great!*" he pronounced in a voice that had the ring of talking over storms and wind blowing the sails, "Daughter, you were *fine!* Yessir, you were all right."

I've been my country's guest four times. Hospitality has to spread over a lot of people and four times seems fair. My country hasn't been *my* guest once.

The first invite was when Curtis Guild pronounced Guy, with an "ld" on the end, was our Governor in Massachusetts. To celebrate New Year's Day the Commonwealth of Massachusetts invited all residents to shake hands with its governor at Boston's gold-domed State House. Papa accepted for him and me. I wore my garnet-colored wool dress, pleated skirt, yoke bordered with garnet velvet, high velvet collar. On the front of it Mama pinned my gold cherub pin Aunt Alice had brought from Venice. Mama braided my hair, looped it across in back behind my ears with soft taffeta old-rose bows, black-buttoned boots and rubbers, black stockings. My winter coat was a red that clashed with garnet, but my black beaver hat went well with my boots.

On a holiday the Old Colony railroad didn't make many trips from Quincy to Boston but Papa found one that got us to the Governor's reception sometime between the hours in the invite. It was freezing cold on our depot platform, but the waiting room heat was smelly. We stamped our feet and walked up and down till white smoke showed under the Adams Street bridge, the noise got louder, louder, the engineer added a clang clang and stopped the train at just the place I'd seen Philadelphia's Liberty Bell pass by.

"All aboard," warned the conductor, and meant it. Anyone dawdling he gave a boost up the train steps. Fifteen minutes of heat then the South Station. Only a few of us out on New Year's Day, we crossed Atlantic Avenue, no wagons or drays, up Summer Street, up Winter Street cross Tremont, past the Park Street church with the tall white spire, up Park Street to Beacon Street and into Massachusetts' gold-domed State House.

A long line ready to shake Governor Guild's hand inched slowly along a stone corridor as cold as our depot platform. Old dark paintings of soldiers and statesmen dressed warmly stared down. My garnet dress was warm but wasted, no one knew I had it on.

Slowly the line moved, my feet were lumps of ice. Next but one, then next, then the Governor shook my hand and said I was little. I was. He shook Papa's hand without comment, we moved on, the next cold feet had their chance. On the way back to South Station, Papa found a place open that served hot chocolate. I liked that better than being the guest of Massachusetts. Still it was something to talk about.

"What did the Governor say to you, dear?"

"He said I was little."

It distinguished me from children not singled out by the Governor.

No invitation for thirty-seven years when my country invited me again. This time it was to that dinner at the White House for the showing to President and Mrs. Franklin Delano Roosevelt of *Abe Lincoln in Illinois*.

The third time I was my country's guest was luncheon at the White House in honor of Alexander Woollcott, who was visiting there. Mrs. Roosevelt did the honors. Guests were Mrs. Alice Duer Miller, Mrs. George S. Kaufman and Joseph Alsop. Mrs. Roosevelt loved Woollcott and vice versa. What I wore is of no consequence, it was in a lean financial period.

The fourth invitation was written up in the *Congressional Record*. The House of Representatives asked me to appear before Congressman Claude Pepper's Select Committee on Aging. My country would pay my plane fare from New York. "First Class," the letter read, "because congressmen and congresswomen are entitled to travel first class."

A limo to meet me at National Airport, wait for me, return me after the hearing. Twenty-five dollars for a per diem if I chose to stay the night. In Washington that's not a realistic number, but Congress has a lot to think of.

Terrible rain, Garson came with me, limo took us to the

wrong entrance, up a flight we went, down two flights, through
an endless corridor, jog left, take the blue elevator, get off and
after a few wrong turns go right and you're there.

Averell Harriman had just finished being questioned. Handsome as a painting, he gave me a kiss and went on his stylish
way.

Colonel Sanders was being introduced, looking like his ad in
his white suit. His written speech was read for him, then came
the questions. Hard of hearing, he had to have what came over
the loudspeaker repeated.

Up on the dais sat two rows of congressmen, congresswomen,
Claude Pepper direct center. Speakers sat at a table in front of
the dais and well below it. The audience, maybe four hundred,
were in rows back of the speakers. As an actress *I'm* up on the
platform, the audience in front of me. Don't expect everything
to be the way *you* want it, new ways are challenging.

"Beginnings," said André.

Colonel Sanders finished, I'd be next. I had watched and listened from back of the last row of the audience, Garson and I
standing together. They had told me when I was announced, to
walk down the center aisle through the audience.

"Our next witness," began Congressman Pepper—I'm quot-
ing from the *Congressional Record*—"Ruth Gordon, who is
eighty years of age. She has had an incredible career as an actress, playwright and author. In 1915, she made her first appearance on stage as Nibs in 'Peter Pan.' Later, she achieved the
distinction of being the first American actress to appear at the
Old Vic Theatre in London in 'The Country Wife.'

"Her other important roles have included being the original
Dolly in 'The Matchmaker' and Nora in Ibsen's 'A Doll's
House.'

"She has written such plays as 'Over Twenty-One,' 'Years
Ago,' and 'The Leading Lady,' as well as a book, 'Myself
Among Others.'

"Since her 65th birthday, Miss Gordon's career has continued. She received an Academy Award for her role as the witch in 'Rosemary's Baby,' and wide acclaim when she starred in 'Harold and Maude.'

"Her active schedule includes numerous appearances on television, most recently in 'Kojak,' 'Rhoda,' and 'Medical Center,' and early next fall on 'Columbo.'

"In the last year alone, she has starred in a pre-Broadway tour of a play she wrote, 'Ho! Ho! Ho! A Miracle Play' and appeared in a movie for television, to be shown on CBS on June 17, called 'The Prince of Central Park.'

"We are very much honored to have another great American and another example of what one can do in what we call the elderly age.

"Miss Ruth Gordon, would you please come forward.

(Applause)

"Miss Gordon (looking at the program): Miss *R.* Gordon. I usually get better billing, anyway, thank you so much. It is getting late, and I only wish Colonel Sanders had brought along some of his Kentucky Fried Chicken because I could use some.

"There are lots of reasons, of course, why anyone should not retire. I really cannot think of any why you should be forced to.

"I am a legal resident of Martha's Vineyard and we're thinking of seceding so I'm not sure what state I belong to, but I know I was born in the Commonwealth of Massachusetts in 1896. Congressman Pepper, you were a sneak to say I was eighty, that was my punch-line, I was going to save that to surprise everybody. It's a remarkable thing to be eighty and today is the first day my country ever bought me an airline ticket. They bought it for me to come here and they bought me one to go home. And don't tell me they would have done that if I were sixty-five years old because I hadn't yet got this famous. Eighty years old and your country pays your plane fare is a real reward!

(Applause)

"You know, I am writing a new book called 'Ten Lessons.' Doubleday bought it and they haven't seen a scrap of anything on paper, but they have confidence in me, they believe that not only am I *talented* at eighty, but that I am going to live till I finish the book.

"And they're not alone. In New York the guy who runs the obit department of The New York Times saw me and said, 'I would like to have an engagement with you.' Well, I did not know him, but Garson said he probably wants to talk about your obituary. My husband is a witty man but I thought that was a silly thing to say. Then the obit writer called up and said, 'When could we make a date?'

" 'What for?'

" 'Well, I think we have a lot to talk over.'

"I got the message. 'Well, I am going to be going on a speaking tour in September, and then I am going to be in a play. How about around Christmas time?'

"He believed I was going to hold on till Christmas and I did.

"I began working when I was nineteen. I come from hardworking people, it never occurred to me not to work. My father was a foreman of a food factory, he got thirty-seven dollars a week. Out of that he supported me, supported my mother, sent me to school, gave me four hundred dollars to be taught drama so I could go on the stage. *He* wanted me to be a physical-cultural instructress, but I didn't want to do that, I did not care for bloomers, dumb bells, and indian clubs, I wanted something more jazzy and went on the stage.

"Now, my father and I never saw four hundred before, but he got it together and took me to New York. I said, 'Papa, why are you doing this? You don't think I'm going to be an actress.'

" 'Everybody has a right to his chance,' he said.

"I subscribe to that. If we *want* to work, we have a right to.

"At the end of the year the drama school said I was the only one who did not show any promise, 'Don't come back.'

"Forget that, later I *did* show promise.

"Work is life, and life is work. I don't know what people do who are born rich. Do they enjoy life as much as I do? Yesterday I went out speaking, today I'm speaking, Sunday Canada wants me. June 2nd Southborough Academy of Girls voted I give the graduating address. Well, that is a lovely set of engagements and where would I be without them? I would be dead.

"But I will not be without them, because I have to work, and if I was in a profession that would fire me, then I'd have to find another profession. I am smart, but I would not know how to fill in my time if I did not work.

"They said I could take ten minutes. Is that ten minutes?

(Laughter)

"You are a good audience. I wish you were over at the National Theatre when I do a play there, over there they don't laugh as easily as that.

"But anyway, if it isn't ten minutes, I can go on. I could go on indefinitely and then let anybody ask me some questions.

(Laughter and applause)

"I am a believer, and that has to do with retirement, too. My new book is about what it is that keeps you going. The answer is 'Stay up-to-date.' I was up-to-date when I was four years old. I will be up-to-date a hundred years from now. Be up-to-date, because if you're up-to-date you know enough to hang in with *people,* and people will want to hang in with *you.*

"The other day Garson and I were walking down Fifth Avenue, it was a cold, cold day. I said, 'I've got to have a cup of tea.'

"He said, 'Let's go in there.' It was a place called Cafe. A tough looking place. We went in, it *was* a tough place, tough customers, tough waitresses, tough bathroom, the wind chill factor must have been four below.

(Laughter)

"When I came back Garson said, 'They recognized you. Our waitress said to the other one, "You recognize her?" The other one said, "Sure. I saw her on Johnny Carson." The other one said, "*And* 'Rosemary's Baby,' *and* 'Where's Poppa?' She's 80 years old."

" ' "Who says?"

" ' "*She* says."

" ' "Bullshit."

(Laughter and applause)

" ' "What?" said the other waitress.

" ' "Bullshit. She's no more 80 than I am. She *says* she's 80, so she can get her name in the *paper.*" '

"But, you see, that was her compliment to me, and I took it as a compliment. It's not how *I* talk, it's probably not how *you* talk, but I hung in with her, and she hung in with me, because she knew there was nothing old about me, and if I wanted to say that for publicity, that was my business."

"Mr. Pepper: You are wonderful, Miss Gordon.

(Laughter and applause)

"Miss Gordon: I love it. I love it.

"Mr. Pepper: Are there any questions?

"Father Drinan:

"Miss Gordon: Yes, Father?

"Father Drinan: I am Congressman Drinan from Massachusetts, and you say quite rightly, ma'am, that you are up-to-date, but why are you not leading the rebellion of Martha's Vineyard?

"Miss Gordon: I am going to, dear. I *will,* but you see, I'm earning my living. Thornton Wilder said, 'There's nothing more dignified than earning a living.' I'm booked on the ferry boat going to Martha's Vineyard June 12th, and I will be there doing my part.

"Father Drinan: If you put your back to this, Martha's Vineyard will become another nation.

"Miss Gordon: I'm going to put my back *and* my front.

"Father Drinan: Thank you.

"Mr. Pepper: Thank you, Father Drinan. Are there any other questions?

"Ms. Meyner:

"Ms. Meyner: Thank you, Mr. Chairman. Miss Gordon, I am Congresswoman Meyner from New Jersey, and I just want to say that one time Oliver Wendell Holmes made a classic statement when he said, 'To be 80 years young is sometimes far more cheerful and hopeful than to be 40 years old,' and I would think that you are classic example of that.

"Miss Gordon: Listen dear, my first money I ever earned was in the State of New Jersey. I came to New York to go on the stage but I could not get a job. Oh, boy, could I not get a job! But in New Jersey they made movies, over in Fort Lee and Coytesville and someone said, 'If you take the ferry over to New Jersey, you will get $5 a day.'

"$5 a day! This was 1914! My board and room were only $8 a week. $5 a day, did I hop over to New Jersey! They engaged me. $5 a day for a girl who belonged to a hard-working family.

"What I did for that $5 was ride in an automobile along the Palisades with the great movie star, William Farnham, get out of the automobile, say, 'Goodby, goodby, goodby,' and he kissed me, I got $5 and never heard of anything so easy as that.

"When I got the Oscar, and that was in 1968 I said, 'I have been working since 1914, and I don't know why it took me so long to get here.'

"I got a letter on beautiful stationery, turquoise blue border, beautiful, and I opened it and it said, 'Dear Ruth, why *did* it take you so long? Mary Pickford.'

"Mr. Pepper: Well, Miss Gordon, you are the embodiment of Browning's words, 'Come along with me, the best is yet to be,' and we congratulate you on your great future. Thank you so much.

"Miss Gordon: Thank *you* so much.

"(Applause)"

End of *Congressional Record*.

All through everything the TV cameras were going, news

photographers kneeling, circling to get a photo. And next night on ABC, CBS, there I was, guest of the Government, wearing a raincoat and a rain hat and looking okay, speaking for a cause I believed. A pleasant way of spending the day is making a hit. Every so often you have to. If it's not playing a part you love or writing a book you believe in, make a hit on a smaller scale. Bake a cake, take a longer walk than anyone, buy a pumpkin and make a jack-o'-lantern. Is *that* ever hard! Give yourself a different colored manicure, send a present to a friend. Built in confidence can use an outside boost once in a while. It's nice if it comes from anywhere, but from Congress who have now pushed retirement off till seventy years old it's a step on the way to civilization.

Most every moment along the way takes courage. Courage is like a strain of yoghurt culture, if you have some you can have some more.

At 14 Elmwood Avenue I looked out our kitchen window, the train to Boston whizzed by, in Boston, I could take the New York, New Haven and Hartford to New York, the ten-o'clock, the one-o'clock, the four-o'clock, the five-o'clock is the Merchants Limited, extra fare. I watched the trains go and grappled with my courage. I had to get some more.

"Did the school give you what you needed?" asked Papa.

"They thought I and one other girl were the best in the class."

Why not lie to Papa? He had staked so much.

"That's good news. Your letters sounded hopeful, but I didn't know was that for the benefit of your mother."

"No."

"Mama and I talked about floating you for the second year, but her having the stroke, the doctor bill and the nurse—I'm sorry."

In New York, managers were casting and I was shelved, back at 14 Elmwood Avenue. I couldn't even afford to go to a play.

The ad in the Boston *Globe* said:

HOLLIS STREET THEATRE
ETHEL BARRYMORE
IN
TANTE

Fifteen cents for the train, fifty cents for the gallery seat. Then the Plymouth announced Marguerite Clark in *Prunella*.

How could I get carfare and another fifty cents?

"Yoo-hoo," called our neighbor, Mrs. Litchfield, from her piazza, and strolled across the street. "If you spend the night with Sylvia on Thursday, I'll pay you a dollar. Jesse and I are going to the Cochato Club Ball."

Was it pride that I'd never done odd jobs? Was it fear I'd get sidetracked? "I will," I said. I had to see Marguerite Clark.

"Do you like lobster salad?"

Lobster salad *and* a dollar! If I'd made a wrong move it was the right wrong move. "Please hold one gallery seat," I wrote to the Plymouth Theatre. Could I have bought something for Mama with that dollar? She would have for me.

Nurse Parssons and I ate lunch, then she went to massage Mama's helpless arm. In the kitchen I washed the dishes. It was warm, the front door was open, ten-year-old Sylvia Litchfield walked in. "Mama's sick. She was going to Boston on the two-ten to get pink slippers to go with her pink messaline dress for the Cochato Club Ball Thursday night and went up to put her hat on and got sick. She lay right down on the floor, but I got Mrs. Trabert to come over."

Mrs. Trabert was housekeeper for Eaton Pierce who lived in the other side of their house.

"It's great you're going to stay with me Thursday."

"Want to help?" I tossed her a dish towel.

The doorbell rang. It was Mrs. Trabert. "Sylvia with you?"

"Yes."

"Keep her." Always stern, today her face looked hewn out of Quincy granite.

"How's Mrs. Litchfield?"

"She's dead." She cut across the lawn back to the Litchfield house.

I went out to the kitchen. "Mrs. Trabert says stay here."

"Does Mama feel better?"

"Mrs. Trabert said all right to stay." I took the clean dishes into the dining room. Mr. Fay's buggy was turning the corner. His undertaking parlor was up Newport Avenue, next to Flood's fish store where the lobster would not be ordered. "Too hot to put the dishes away," I told Sylvia. "Want to play checkers?"

From the kitchen we couldn't see Mr. Fay's buggy.

"Sure."

"Wipe the table off." Getting the checkerboard from the china closet, I saw Mrs. Gurney hurry up the Litchfields' steps. She was Mrs. Litchfield's best friend, how did she come so fast from up on Warren Avenue? Mr. Fay's black horse tied to the maple tree reached for the leaves.

"We're going to have lobster Thursday," called Sylvia.

I came back with the checkerboard.

"And Mama's going to make us a pan of Parker House rolls to warm up. Don't you *adore* Parker House rolls? I copy how you talk."

"Let's have a tea party while we play."

"Didn't you just have lunch?"

"Not dessert. We'll have orange marmalade sandwiches and peanut butter ones and ice tea."

"I love peanut butter, but I detest marmalade. Do you still say detest?"

The doorbell rang. Mrs. Gurney, white as paper, said, "I'll take her home." She called out, "Sylvia."

Sylvia came through the dining room, looking pleased. "Hello, Auntie Claire, is Mama all right?" She stepped out on our porch and saw Mr. Fay's black undertaker's wagon, fell screaming on our grass.

Mrs. Gurney held her close. "Think of Mrs. Jones, dear. Don't frighten Mrs. Jones."

Tears flooded Sylvia's cheeks, no more screams. In the midst of tragedy she could remember not to scare Mama.

Arms around each other they crossed back of Mr. Fay's black wagon, went through the door Mrs. Trabert held open.

The afternoon of the Cochato Club Ball, Reverend Horst stood at the foot of the stairs Mrs. Litchfield had gone up to put on her hat. People sat in the Litchfield parlor and on the porch shared with Eaton Pierce. Jennie Litchfield had a host of friends. So had Jesse. Mr. Fay's chairs filled every vacant space. Out on the porch steps I looked across at our house. Terrible trouble both sides of the street.

"We are gathered here . . ." Mr. Horst's deep, kind voice eased the burden of wearing Sunday clothes on Thursday. My navy-blue taffeta suit Mama had made looked too happy, my light blue linen suit cut down from Clare's, looked disrespectful. I wore my white piqué Mama made last summer. It had real Irish lace at the neck, around the waist black velvet ribbon and around my Panama hat like rich Jo Smith's at Quincy Point.

"I will read the twenty-eighth Psalm. 'Unto Thee will I cry, O Lord, my rock, be not silent to me.'"

Tonight at the Cochato Club people would be going to the ball.

"'Lest if Thou be silent, I become like them that go down into the pit.'"

Would I give up, go down, sink? I *have* to get to New York! Should I take money from Mr. Wilson? Let him get in bed with me? He was rich. He would give me money for New York.

Mr. Litchfield and Sylvia and Mrs. Gurney passed, went down the steps into the first automobile. Poor Sylvia. Poor Mr. Litchfield. Poor everybody. Upstairs hung the pink messaline dress, in the bureau drawer the elbow-length white kid gloves, and instead of Mr. Litchfield taking her to the ball, Mr. Fay was taking her to Mount Wollaston Cemetery. Poor everybody. Would I get to New York?

"Think of Mrs. Jones, dear."

Was *I* thinking of her? It takes courage to think of yourself.

At Minneapolis' grand department store, Dayton's, fourteen
hundred chairs were filled in their auditorium, out in the hall
people pleading for tickets. I was going to be the speaker, introduced by beautiful redheaded Barbara Flanagan, the city's number one newspaper woman.

Before an afternoon where I talk I like to look at the place,
the people with the lights on. On the stage as I've said I don't
like the lights to dim, I like the audience to be as lighted as I
am.

"Enjoyment in the theatre demands shoulder to shoulder contact," said Thornton Wilder, master in many things and head-
master in knowing how to connect audience and performer.

Out in the lobby, ladies showing their tickets, ladies looking
for the ladies' room, a lady looking for me. "Miss Gordon, I
have the program of your first matinee in Boston." She held it
out.

I was sure it wouldn't be, but interesting to see what she had.
Tears flooded my eyes, it was.

Maude Adams

in

Peter Pan

by

J. M. Barrie

Hollis Street Theatre

April ? 1916

"I was there," she said, "and this is my own program." 1916
to 1978 two meet who in that long ago April had been under
the same roof. "Would you please sign it for me?"

In the order of their appearances:
Eliza   Ruth Gordon

Then somewhere mid-way

Nibs   Ruth Gordon

Did I think somebody in Minneapolis sixty-two years later would ask me to write my name on the program of our first matinee in Boston where I'd bought a gallery seat for so many matinees?

At this first matinee was my father who'd give me four hundred dollars for dramatic school, then ten dollars a week for board and room, plus fifty dollars to tide me over till I got a job, plus some more till I got engaged for *Peter Pan*. For the first matinee Papa took the afternoon off from the Mellin's Food Company, he had bought his balcony ticket. A physical culture instructress he'd hoped but had staked me to be an actress. I never knew he was proud of me, till a lady wrote, "I sat next to your father at the matinee, I dropped my programme. He picked it up and said, 'Nib's father hands you this programme.'"

THE END FOR NOW
THINK IT OVER!

WHO'S WHO
IN THE
CAST

Wesley Addy. Good actor, good looker, good person to be connected with in a pinch.

Adrianne Allen. Raymond Massey's second wife, terribly pretty, stylish, a spiffy actress. Always did what she set out to do.

Maxwell Anderson. He wrote a lot of plays that brought him and actors success. He wrote *Saturday's Children* which brought me success in a serious part. Guthrie McClintic helped me make the changeover from the kind of acting for which I wouldn't be fired, to acting that becomes a memory.

Antoine. A big name hairdresser from Paris, had a salon at Saks Fifth Avenue.

Mr. Edward Atkins. He had his wholesale china business on Atlantic Avenue, Boston. Mama worked as his secretary and when she gave him word she was leaving to marry Papa, Mrs. Edward Atkins came in all the way from Belmont to tell Mama how Mr. Atkins would miss her and presented Mama with a silver cream pitcher and sugar bowl from Shreve, Crump and Low than which! Every night Mama put the silver in a box to go under her bed and in New York every night I look at them on our sideboard.

Jim Barker. Second under Mel Burns in RKO Studio's Makeup Room.

Lilian Baylis. She owned and ran the Old Vic Theatre and the Sadler's Wells Ballet in London. There was no obstacle she could not conquer and running those two theatres along with glory came obstacles. Lilian loved me and I loved her. "I refused it when they wanted to make me a Dame, dear," she confided. "It would double the price of hotel bills."

A replacement went on in a leading role, Lilian watched the performances from her stage box. "You had your chance and you missed it," she told actress Margaretta Scott. She worshipped good acting, tolerated a lot of bad, but never pretended it wasn't.

When Charles Laughton played Macbeth, she went backstage at the finish. "You were a nice little Macbeth."

Sam Behrman. To the public S. N. Behrman, responsible for successful plays. Our professional association was his adaptation into a play of *Serena Blandish, or The Difficulty of Getting Married,* by Enid Bagnold whose father was county folk and commanded his daughter not to draw attention to herself by signing a novel.

Enid was Lady Jones, wife of Sir Roderick, head of Reuter's, who when I asked if he came often to New York replied, "No more. Half of my friends there are dead and the other half are gaga."

Bob Benchley. Drama critic on *The New Yorker.* Said funny funny funny things, was pleasant under all conditions. His wife was named Gertrude and that's about all any of us at the Algonquin knew about her. Bob went home every night and home was somewhere at the end of a train ride. He had a son Nathaniel. Bob thought up something to do in a show called *No Sirree,* which the Algonquin wits and friends got up to play for one night. The thing Bob Benchley thought up was so funny it was added to the New York Music Box Revue. It was called *The Treasurer's Report.*

Main (Rousseau) Bocher. A boy from Chicago who with Dior, Chanel, Balenciaga were the greats in the world of couturiers. As Dior said at a dinner honoring Main, "And Mainbocher does it in America."

His mother and father were folks like anybody's. Main told us, in Chicago he was known in his early days as "George's boy." George was Mr. Bocher, senior. No one ever turned out lovelier clothes. The handwork! It was Mr. Foss sewed on all the beads. Bridget fitted like no one did or has since, tall, red-haired gawky Florence from New Jersey showed the clothes with a newfangled elegance not seen heretofore. A darling man, a theatre buff, he saw every play and saw it again when an understudy went on. He dressed Jean Arthur in the original cast of Garson's *Born Yesterday*. He said, "When you send out the road company have Judy Holliday." She'd acted in one Broadway play that didn't last long. Garson had seen her some years before in a night club act with Betty Comden and Adolph Green.

At a dress rehearsal of *Born Yesterday* in New Haven, we sat behind Main and his partner Douglas Pollard. Jean Arthur was doing the star part written for her, Billy Dawn.

"Do you think Judy Holliday could really play this part?" asked Gar of the back of Main's head.

"I wish I were watching her right now," replied Mainbocher, not even turning around.

Mrs. Ada Boshell. Popular old character actress, who had her own ideas. On the sleeper she didn't know where to hide her diamond earrings for safekeeping and chose her hot water bottle, forgot and next morning emptied them out with the water. Earrings retrieved by the porter. As a treat she ordered oyster stew and where she treated herself was the Hotel Lorraine's dining room, Madison, Wisconsin, summer of 1916, a long way from oyster beds.

Lilian Braithwaite. Stylish English actress, co-starred with Noel Coward in his first triumph, *The Vortex*. We liked each other on first sight.

Richard Bray. My son Jones' friend who lived in Eleventh Street back of our Twelfth Street house. Jones and he were in the same class at Friends Seminary.

Harry Collins. He designed clothes. I never got into money while he was in business, but if I had I'd have gone to him. For Anna Wheaton's appearance at the Palace, he designed a periwinkle blue taffeta embroidered by hand with white cotton flowers and stems and leaves à la Japanese, a full skirt with an organdy bertha and trim. When I go I go, I haven't seen that dress in how much is 1916 from 1979. And then I saw it once.

Marc Connelly. I've known him since he and George S. Kaufman wrote *Dulcy,* Lynn Fontanne's first leading part. She and Gregory Kelly, my husband, were featured in it. They opened in Indianapolis. Was it 1921 or 1922? I was in the Presbyterian Hospital, Chicago, having had my legs broken so I wouldn't be bowlegged anymore. When Gregory left me to go east for rehearsal that was the first time we had slept apart.

Someone interviewed Marc recently and asked did he think conversation was as brilliant as it used to be?

"Mine is," said Marc.

Aaron Copland. Celebrated American composer. He started to do a score for the opera to be made from *Our Town,* but Thornton said he didn't want it to be an opera, he had gotten it right as a play.

Noel Coward. Anyone doesn't know who Noel Coward was should drop this book and read the bio written about him by friend Cole Leslie called *Something Laughter.* The title doesn't matter, it's that Cole got Noel down between book covers.

Frank Craven. His mother was actress Ella Mayer, his father was actor John Craven, two fine supporting players, not stars like son Frank. Frank paid homage to them by naming his own son John and naming the leading role Ella Mayer in his first play, *Too Many Cooks.*

Maisie Craven. Frank's wife. First married Arnold Daly who brought the works of G. B. Shaw to this country where in the beginning they weren't much wanted.

John Cromwell. An actor. In later years he got to be a director, married to pretty actress Kay Johnson.

George Cukor. A stage manager for Gilbert Miller, in the summer he directed summer stock in Rochester. I didn't like him, because he said shit. That didn't hold him back, in California he directed more wonderful pictures than I have space to mention. One was Philip Barry's *The Philadelphia Story,* I sent him a rave telegram and he told Billy Grady, MGM casting director, to hire me for the Greta Garbo film *Two Faced Woman.* Love budded between George and me. Sometimes he'll drive you crazy and sometimes he's the best there is.

Hazel Dawn. A beauty. She sat at tea with her father, mother, little boy Charlie and little Hazel. "Little Hazel can dance like Allyn McClerie, she has a perfect lyric soprano, but she hasn't got my spectacular beauty."

Little Hazel nodded, so did Big Hazel's Mom and Dad. None of us questioned Hazel Dawn's right to describe herself so; if anything it was an understatement. No understatement that seeing her made me go on the stage.

Agnes de Mille. A choreographer like no one else. Her name for one of her dancers in *Oklahoma!* was "The one who fell down," and she did. Agnes wrote an autobiography that got better notices than most anybody's.

Fulco di Verdura made beautiful, original, wildly expensive jewelry. Once Garson sent me a seventy-five-karat emerald from London. From Moscow, Averell Harriman sent his wife Marie a pink diamond. We took our gifts up in the same elevator at Verdura's.

Time passed, my emerald was set in a rope of gold to make a ring. "How did you set Marie's pink diamond?" I asked.

"I didn't." It was a phony.

How about the Kanins get emeralds and Harrimans get pink glass for their money?

Lawrence D'Orsay. A stage star. His most famous role was "The Earl of Pawtucket" or was it? It sounds implausible.

Gretchen Doty. An actress in *Fair and Warmer*. A darling girl, who could have had a career, but chose marriage.

Lady Juliet Duff. A peeress in her own right, but when she came to visit New York the phone operator at the Ambassador Hotel always called her "Lady Duffy."

Dame Edith. The greatest actress I ever saw. She didn't always make it but when she did she joined Mrs. Siddons, Rachel, Peg Woffington, the ones one wishes one had seen. Comedy, tragedy, she was at home with both. Her Queen Catherine, her Rosalind, her Lady Fidget! No one has seen them surpassed.

Abe Einhorn. He was the assistant property man for *The Matchmaker.* I wrote a play called *A Few of the Boys,* the leading role is modeled on Abe. Among unusual things he did was join Miss Esmé Church's Shakespeare study class for any of *The Matchmaker* company who cared to join. Esmé had acted and directed at London's Old Vic. Abe signed for her class and attended its twice weekly sessions on the stage of Forty-fifth Street's Royale Theatre.

Aunt Emma. Mama's younger sister. She got on Papa's nerves, though she had been the one Papa paid some attention to at Boston's Y.W.C.A. Through her he met Mama.

Ruth and Raoul Fleischmann. They fell in love at Ruth's wedding to Allie Botsford who drew the joker when he asked Raoul to be his best man. Raoul was publisher of *The New Yorker.*

Ralph Forbes. An English actor made his New York debut in *Havoc,* a war play. I think financially the management wasn't lavish because he stayed at the Algonquin Hotel in a hall bedroom looking out on a shaft, the door was across the hall from Gregory's and my suite looking out on the Hippodrome. We were having a bathtub gin cocktail party and I said "There's a fellow across the hall, who probably doesn't know anyone, I'll ask him in," and did. It was 1925 when people were making gin.

Forbes said, "I should like to," and probably that was an understatement, the show was on the blink, "and may I ask my costars staying here, Joyce Barbour and Dickie Bird?"

Galeries Lafayette. A department store in Paris where you can find everything and looks like a store in a picture book.

Greta Garbo. The top movie actress that ever was. Looks, talent, everything. She could not make a wrong move, then did: she left the movies.

Reginald Gardiner. Witty actor in musical comedy and revues.

Stanley Gilkey. Guthrie's general manager. Quiet in the midst of McClintic furies, could get a clean glass at a moment's notice in an unoccupied theatre, never forgot a story he ever heard or lived through and heard and lived through plenty, retired to San Francisco's Nob Hill and now is no more.

Sacha Guitry. He married Yvonne Printemps for a time. A triumph as a playwright and actor. When he and Printemps were acting together try to get in.

Nancy Hamilton. She always seems to have a good time. She can write fetching lyrics and poems, but doesn't do many. Do they get in the way of a good time?

Sir Cedric Hardwicke. When he acted a play in London it was a success before he went into rehearsal. He had an idea for us to act Sir Peter and Lady Teazle. Where do ideas get lost to? Cedric Hardwicke and Ruth Gordon in *The School for Scandal* would have been good.

Picsie Hardwicke. Lady Hardwicke, mother of little Edward Hardwicke, who grew up to be an admired actor at London's National Theatre, especially in *Gildencrantz and Rosenstern* or is it the other way? The Picsie came from her maiden name, Helena Piccard. "Mecca Coffee" some mentioned to show she was not only a lady with a title, but an heiress.

Jack Gwynne Emmet Harris. He was born to Heidi Vanderbilt Harris and my son Jones Harris on St. Patrick's Day. Growing up in an apartment on Fifth Avenue he accepted the parade along with his birthday party and the green trimmings.

His beautiful name is Jack for his Great-Grandfather Clinton Jones who early followed the sea, Gwynne for his Grandfather Alfred Gwynne Vanderbilt who lost his father at sea when the *Titanic* went down, Emmet for his father's friend Robert Emmet Sherwood.

Last winter Jack, his father and I were walking in snowy Central Park. It was slippery, my son said, "I'll hold onto you, Mother," and took my arm.

Six-year-old Jack reached up and took my other arm. "Let me help you, dear," he said.

Jed Harris. Former lover.

Jones Harris. My son.

Moss Hart. He wrote shows to remember, also he thought his own thoughts. Woollcott was criticizing him for his reading matter and held up Thornton Wilder as an example. "When he travels on the sleeper he studies the music of Palestrina. Lies there studying Palestrina."

Moss looked dubious. "If he's such a studier of scores how come he knows so much about a whorehouse?"

(In Thornton's *Heaven's My Destination* a highlight was when the hero, do-gooder George Brush, took Sunday dinner at Mrs. Crofut's whorehouse and asked her permission to invite the girls to come with him to a movie theatre afterwards.)

Grace Hayle. The second lead in *Fair and Warmer*. In *My Side* I tell about her.

Ben Hecht. A real writer. Novels, plays, biographies, movies.

Henry. This Henry is English actor Henry Irving. Was he the first actor to be knighted? If you know don't tell me. I wish I could have seen him act. He staged his plays at the Lyceum Theatre in London. Why let it get run down after his death? I tried to find Irving's theatre. The whole dress circle had been ripped out and a dance floor put in.

Pauline Holmes. A little girl who came to dancing school in a memorable dress.

Leslie Howard. English and equally popular in his own country and ours. Equally successful on stage and in films.

Captain Humphrey. Papa sailed with him as first mate. He seemed a very old man, but across the garden from his house in Hingham, Mass., lived his mother who looked the same as he did.

Mabel Humphrey. An old maid. There's a difference between an old maid and a single person and Mabel was an old maid. And nice.

Mrs. Humphrey. Looked pleasant and was. If the captain spilled anything on the tablecloth she made him cover it with change.

Aunt Fanny May Jackson. Mama's playmate in Bainbridge, Georgia, they kept in touch all through the years. Aunt Fanny May got consumption and moved to Asheville, North or South Carolina, and sent us Southern moss which Papa said could bring him back his old malaria. She sent *me* the fine dress I keep in blue tissue paper in the drawer of a Vuitton trunk.

Kay Johnson. She was in an out of-town play, the producer asked me to see it to replace Kay Johnson. I reported, "Nobody could play it better than she does." A lovely actress.

Garson Kanin. My husband.

George S. Kaufman. If you want to read up on a terrific playwright, an original wit than whom, a married man, a lady's man, a friend, read my book *Myself Among Others,* also *My Side*.

Jerome Kern. Composer of lovely music. Nothing bop, bop, just the prettiest hit tunes you will ever hear.

Sidney Kingsley. A fine playwright who wrote the first play presented by the Group Theatre, *Men in White*.

Elsa Lanchester. In London she had her own night club, married Charles Laughton, acted with him in some of the plays and films, a book could be written about her. Why doesn't she?

Talk about talent, talk about original.

Vivien Leigh. Actress, beauty, loving friend, not a day goes by I don't think of her and to think of her is to miss her.

Pauline Lord. A great American actress. We acted together in Edith Wharton's *Ethan Frome*. I loved and admired her and set her down perfectly in *Myself Among Others*. In tragedy or comedy she was not to be surpassed. I was in the audience opening night of Eugene O'Neill's *Anna Christie,* starring Pauline Lord. The audience knew history was happening that night on West Forty-eighth Street at the Vanderbilt Theatre, now torn down and rebuilt as a parking lot.

Don't live in the past some say, but if it's the past or a parking lot which do you choose?

Gertrude Macy. General Manager for Cornell-McClintic Productions. A Pasadena society girl, money, class, two dazzling sisters, a brother, how she knew what to do as general manager she must have picked up after Pasadena.

Dorothy and Raymond Massey. Mr. and Mrs. She was the Butterick pattern for the Katharine Hepburn part in Garson's and my screenplay of *Adam's Rib*. Ray Massey and I acted together in *Ethan Frome, Abe Lincoln in Illinois, Action in the North Atlantic.* Loved each other on and off and for the last forty years; on meeting, Dorothy, he, and I say, "Still shaking hands."

I'd forgotten the rest of the joke, but he and Dorothy hadn't: "A just-married couple are posing for the photographer. 'Would you like this mounted?'

" 'No. Just shaking hands.' "

Barbara Matera. Makes all the most beautiful costumes in all the Broadway shows. She has her own atelier down on West Forty-third or if it's 40 something else does it matter? She's wherever she is, making every designer's design come out. English, tall, gentle, understanding, how did she remain so collected dealing with hit or miss show business?

Mr. Louis B. Mayer. He ran Metro-Goldwyn-Mayer. He was

the first person to get insured for a million dollars. How I know is my beloved Latin teacher, Miss Elizabeth Irene O'Neill's father, Mr. M. C. O'Neill, wrote the insurance. He had scraped up an acquaintance with L. B. Mayer or vice versa sitting on a train and Mr. Mayer said he was opening up a nickelodeon movie theatre that would make a fortune and Mr. M. C. O'Neill invested.

Gilbert Miller. A theatrical producer in New York and London, never a producer like his father Henry, but made lots more money and no one could tell a story better.

Henry Miller. The way I describe him, only more so.

Jack Miller. Draw the veil. No one I knew ever saw him except beautiful actress Ruth Chatterton who said Jack was the best looking of the Miller family and if you want to know about Ruth, and you should, read my book *Myself Among Others*.

Marilyn Miller. Beautiful star of *Ziegfeld Follies, Sally, Sunny, Rosalie,* and other Ziegfeld shows. Could sing, could dance, toe and tap and any kind. Made her debut at two years old in her family's vaudeville act, *The Five Columbians,* in the role of Mlle. Sugarplum. I went to see her in *Sally* twelve times. Once at the Apollo in Atlantic City, eleven times at the New Amsterdam in New York, and once on my first trip abroad only she wasn't in it at the Winter Garden in London, it was adorable Dorothy Dickson.

Milo. In charge of wardrobe at Warner Brothers Studio. He rigged me out to perfection and I mean perfection!

Ferenc Molnár. He wrote the most plays of any playwright except Robert E. Sherwood that were exactly the plays you wanted to see. Toward the end of his life he left his home in Budapest and settled at our Plaza Hotel with his secretary. He said in the olden days he referred to his mistress as his secretary, these days he referred to his secretary as his mistress.

If you don't admire that, skip a Molnár play. Also don't go on with this book.

The Motleys. Three English girls who designed scenery and costumes. Guthrie McClintic put them in charge of *The Three Sisters.* Triumph!

Paul Muni. Fine actor on stage and screen, big star.

Mr. N. G. Nickerson. In the real estate business in Quincy, owned the house I was born in and the cheaper house we moved to when Papa didn't get a raise.

Tarquin Olivier. The son of Laurence and his first wife, actress Jill Esmond.

Maureen O'Sullivan. *Tarzan,* was the movie that made her famous. She married John Farrow, famous screen director and famous Mia Farrow is one of her children and Maureen is pretty famous herself.

Dorothy Parker. The only American G. B. Shaw asked me about. I said Dotty was pretty, small, dark-haired, loved fellers, fellers loved her, said memorable things, said cruel things, drank a lot, went to parties. He was amazed. "I imagined she looked like a schoolteacher."

Walter Plunkett. He designed beautiful costumes for movies. And add one more beautiful when you give him credit for the clothes in *Gone With The Wind.* One beautiful is not enough.

Tyrone Power. Movie star right up at the top, handsomer than anybody and one adorable feller!

Yvonne Printemps. She was in the Folies Bergères, then married Sacha Guitry. They were the rage of Paris in musical comedy, comedy without music, everything you hoped to see when the curtain went up.

Leo Proust. The chauffeur who came with my rented car in Hollywood. How did I lose track of him? He drove for the Tanner Car Co. and when I came out to do *Two Faced Woman* Tanner said he'd left. He was just what I needed and where was he?

Billy Rose. A tycoon who made money at everything. He put on a show in a tank—a fortune. A nightclub, the same. Wrote the words to song hits, "Cheerful Little Earful," "Barney Google with the Goo Goo Googly Eyes" and "I Found a Million Dollar Baby in a Five and Ten Cent Store."

When he gave a dinner party at his New York mansion that had been Mrs. Vanderbilt's, an orchestra played between courses at one end of the room, when it finished, next course was served.

Thomas Ross. A star in a racehorse play called *Checkers.* When he acted in summer stock in Ogunquit those name-in-lights days were over, but he remained sought after and a darling feller.

Mr. Ryder. Company manager of *Fair and Warmer,* he had to see that the show got on whether there was a blizzard, no trains running, or no rooms at the hotel. I wore chamois gloves sometimes; they had seams that looked hand-stitched. "Did you make those?" asked Mr. Ryder. Imagine his noticing gloves when to get to our next stand he had to book us to ride in the caboose!

Alan: Alan's other name is Searle. He was Maugham's secretary and friend. An adorable fellow who can tell a story to hold your attention, but does not write it down.

Robert E. Sherwood. He lived through his first wife and the divorce, married beautiful Madeline Hurlock who after several years of blissful marriage surprised him as a cook.

Everyone knows Sherwood, the playwright, the writer of many of F.D.R.'s Fireside Speeches, I know him as the only person about whom nobody ever said a mean word.

Mrs. Robert E. Sherwood. My best friend since 1930. A beauty, a former leading lady for Ben Turpin in Mack Sennett movies. In one she co-starred with a lion. Madeline driving along in a flivver, lion standing by the road thumbed a ride. She opened the door, lion got in, sat down on seat next to driver. At rehearsal Madeline's not-so-beautiful stand-in drove the car, lion thumbed a ride, stand-in opened door, lion got in sat down beside her, off they drove.

"This'll be a take," shouted director. Madeline took her place at the wheel, got going, lion thumbed a ride, beautiful Madeline stopped the flivver, opened the door, lion took a look and jumped right into the lap of the future Mrs. Robert E. Sherwood.

How many people do you know whose best friend had a lion sit on her?

Lee Shubert. Mr. Lee, who was head of the Shubert Organization, and his wife, the beautiful Marcella, were our dear friends. Read the whole story in *Myself Among Others*. Mr. Lee didn't get where he got by just being a pretty face.

Sir Aubrey Smith. Distinguished character actor. He appeared in films and theatre.

Mr. Sparrow. Our grammar school janitor who also moved furniture and delivered trunks to and from the Old Colony Railroad depot.

Donald Ogden Stewart. He wrote plays, movies, books and knew how to make people laugh.

Jessica Tandy. English actress I first saw at the Old Vic play the French princess opposite Laurence Olivier in Tyrone Guthrie's master production of *Henry V*. I bought tickets to see it five times and was only able to because I had pull with the Old Vic box office.

Laurette Taylor. Stage star I heard about from my friend Anna Witham who went to New York with her grandmother and back in Quincy all she could talk about was an actress named Laurette Taylor in *Peg o' My Heart*.

Olive Templeton. An actress, daughter of a Brookline lady, Mrs. McMackin, who had a son Carl that I met at Miss Corlew's dancing school. Mrs. McMackin told her daughter to look me up when I left home to come to New York. She did and took me to the Algonquin Hotel.

Ellen Terry. England's great stage star who played opposite Henry Irving in many of his productions. Beautiful and beloved.

Cousin Sally and Cousin Ed Thomas. She is my cousin on my mother's side. My great Aunt Rachel of Quincy, Florida, was her great-great aunt or great-grandmother. Anyway we're cousins and love each other and she went deep into our roots and looked up everything there was to know and if she wasn't so pretty I wouldn't thank her for finding all those facts. Never face the facts unless you know how to forget them.

Freddie Vachon. An adorable fellow with his gallery on the port of St. Tropez. He painted St. Tropez with a loving eye, four of which we bought. No five.

Madame Vachon. Freddie's mother. Madame Vachon had her shop a few doors further along the port. She set the St. Tropez flair or is it flare? (Spelling goes in the fussbudget department like a run in your stocking or not quite clean fingernails. In New York what else? Coat them over with solid red and spell so a reader knows what you mean.) The first time I heard of St. Tropez was when Saks Fifth Avenue sold me a broad-brimmed natural straw hat, light green ribbon around the crown holding on a pink silk rose and little white and brown seashells. I have a photo of me wearing it, taken by grand MGM photographer Clarence Bull who asked, "Why are you self-conscious being photographed? Garbo never is."

Kurt Weill. His music I wish I were hearing. Also a dear man. In summer stock I wanted to bolster up a second act scene that needed something. No money to offer by the management, but I took a chance, called up Kurt Weill, went into a long, rambling talk on "September Song" and after mystifying him long enough Kurt Weill suggested would it be something I wanted to use?

"Yes, but the management can't pay you."

"Use it," he said, and I did.

Mrs. Wheaton. She didn't need a writer to write her, she wrote her own character. Mother of stage star Anna Wheaton she was a stage mother ranking with the best. She filled up lonely hours of my time with close-ups of what a successful actress' life is like.

Dame May Whitty. Fine character actress. Made a big hit with Emlyn Williams in his play *Night Must Fall.*

Isabel Wilder. Thornton's adorable sister who likes me. Thornton said, "She doesn't like a lot of women and really *does* like you." When she finishes her saga of the Wilder family, drop everything and buy it!

Thornton Wilder. Friend from 1930 to 1975. Every actress needs a guide and mentor, mine was Thornton who knew all about everything except to spare himself.

Freddy Wittop. He designed costumes for Broadway musical comedies. No one more in demand. Why retire? Freddy, shows miss you.

P(elham) G(renville) Wodehouse. Author of successful novels and the best lyrics to musical comedies.

Haidee Wright. An English stage star, one of a family of stage stars. She gave memorable performances, one as Queen Elizabeth in Clemence Dane's play *Will Shakespeare,* one more recent as Fanny Cavendish in the original *Royal Family.* Her speech was like no one else's in the same way Dame Edith Evans' was.

"**Ruth Gordon,** born Ruth Gordon Jones, daughter to Clinton and Annie Jones, October 30, 1896, Quincy in the Commonwealth of Massachusetts," so reads my birth certificate. Even in my birth certificate I got star billing, no wonder I became one. Mama treated me as if I was a star from before I was born, my christening dress was for someone whose name eventually would be in lights. I have it and my first booties, my first rubbers, my first short dress, my dress for my fourth birthday party where Dr. Adams took little Marcia Adams out on our front porch and gave her a couple of spanks. My first memory was a birthday cake with pink candles and whack, whack.

Quincy was where I was trying to get out of; now it seems like a place in a storybook. The people, the beach, Third Hill, the meadow, the peat bog. The only bad memory is there was not enough money and might be less if Papa got fired from being foreman at the Mellin's Food Factory if President Doliber cut out his Christmas bonus.

Life was happy clambakes at the beach, the dancing school ball, birthday parties, sleigh rides to East Milton, collecting flowers for the Boston Floating Hospital then snap snap came autumn when Mama and I took the trolley to Frost's Coal Company in Neponset to order a ton of egg and a ton of nut. Loved the trolley ride over, coming home worry set in.

Graduation from grammar school, from high school—in *My Side* read the whole story as John Bunyan says in *Pilgrim's Progress* when he didn't want to bother to write the rest of it.

Studied at the American Academy of Dramatic Arts. At the end of the junior year they said I showed no promise. And I didn't. They had scared the pants off me and in 1915 I wore them. The Academy made acting seem hard and it *is* hard, a director must see to it that we're not afraid. Guthrie McClintic set himself to calm down the actors before he held one minute of rehearsal. We all sat around a table to read for one week before we rehearsed it walking around. During that first week, Guth would start with long irrelevent but interesting anecdotes and reach in his pocket for a flask, pour down some straight liquor, cough hard and say, "Where was I?" Sometimes he'd start to climb up the proscenium arch. We thought the director is pie-eyed and won't know if we're doing it right or wrong so no one fired till he gets sober. When I asked him, years later, he said he didn't booze up, just looked like it because, "How can you rehearse a bunch of scared actors?"

If I took a course at the Academy today I'd still be scared. Acting is fragile until it isn't. I don't know what would scare me out of a performance now, but look how long I've been growing confidence.

Before every performance I imagine some person I admire is in front, Brooks Atkinson, Neil Simon, Liv Ullmann, Hal Ashby,

Marlon Brando. And never once has that person been there for the performance I selected them for.

After my term at dramatic school, Mama's paralytic stroke brought me back to Quincy. Terrible for Mama, terrible for me, would I ever get away?

Papa gave me fifty dollars and I left for New York August 1, 1915. I got only movie extra work till December 21 when the curtain went up on Maude Adams as Peter Pan and me as Nibs, one of the Lost Boys who had flown to the Never-Never Land with Peter.

"Ruth Gordon was ever so gay as Nibs," wrote Woollcott in the New York *Times*. Why wouldn't I love him?

The end of my first week as an actress Mama died. I took the sleeper and that afternoon was the funeral, next night back in *Peter Pan*. The New York engagement ended and we toured in Miss Adams' private railroad car. The tour finished in Springfield, Illinois, and I had two hundred dollars pinned to my corset in a boodle bag.

A long hot Broadway summer of running out of money from July 7, 1916, to mid-November when I signed a contract to be a leading lady in a road company of the big Broadway hit *Fair and Warmer,* farce by Avery Hopwood. No one wrote funnier hits, why kill himself at Juan-les-Pins?

Our company was the sixth worst, but I was the leading lady. Letters flew back to Quincy, "My second season I am the leading lady!"

One-night stands every night except one two-nighter when our adorable leading man got arrested for making a pass at the banker's son and had to skip out of Eau Claire, Wisconsin. Police traveled with us till we crossed into Michigan where in Ishpeming a bunch of roses fell through the transom over my door and leading man and I went out to dinner.

Our closing notice was posted on the call-board in Alpena, Mich. Grace Hayle, our second lead, went out and bought herself an eighteen-dollar hat! Courage! Alpena is a long way from

Broadway and mid-April is a bum time to look for a job. I didn't find one until a week before Labor Day, money scarcer and scarcer even with handouts from Papa, then willpower got me to force Miss Austina Mason, casting agent, to send me for the part of blond Babytalk Lady in *Seventeen*. I was not blond, but Gregory Kelly, who played Willie Baxter, the lead, hired me. That began *Seventeen*, in Chicago, New York, Boston, then after a year and four months marrying Gregory Kelly. He taught me to act. How good could I get? "You used to just want to get into, *'And others in the cast,'*" said Gregory, "now you want to be great."

After *Seventeen* came P. G. Wodehouse's and Guy Bolton's *Piccadilly Jim*. No good, but I was the leading lady who wore three dreamy dresses, one made to order and really made to order at Henri Bendel's and really at Henri Bendel's. Read this book and see why the repeat.

In three weeks *Piccadilly Jim,* went out of business and Gregory and I went into the Chicago company of Booth Tarkington's *Clarence*. I played the part Helen Hayes made a big hit in in the New York company. In Chicago I made a hit and so did Gregory. We played that until we gave our notice to leave and I went into the Chicago Presbyterian Hospital to have my legs straightened. After two weeks of sharing my hospital room Gregory left to rehearse *Dulcy* in New York. Was it 1921 or 1922? Midsummer he left *Dulcy* and we opened the Gregory Kelly Stock Company at English's Opera House, Indianapolis, where Gregory had become a big favorite in the local stock company. This was to teach me to act and all our money went into it.

A new play every week, one week the balcony scene from *Romeo and Juliet* as a curtain-raiser for *Fair and Warmer*. About the latter Gregory advised, "Never let anyone see you in it." About the curtain raiser, draw the veil.

After that came tryout in Cleveland of the new play Tarkington and Harry Leon Wilson wrote for us to get me back to New

York and retrieve myself from the knocks I got as the Babytalk Lady. The new play was called *Bristol Glass*. To get the money to put it on, with our new partner Bob McLaughlin at whose Cleveland Opera House we had tried it out, Gregory and I toured in *The First Year*.

When we'd earned enough, we gave our notice, rehearsed *Bristol Glass* in Cleveland with a new company, played a two-week tryout in Chicago at the Blackstone where I had played for two weeks with Maude Adams in 1916. In 1924 we played *Bristol Glass* for two weeks and closed.

We thought the company wasn't as good as we'd had before. Gregory and I spent the summer in Christmas Cove, Maine, where it didn't cost much, left to do *Seventeen* for a week in Cleveland Stock where this time I played Willie Baxter's ten-year-old sister Jane, the best part next to Willie. Early September Bob McLaughlin had scraped up enough money to reopen *Bristol Glass*, renamed *Tweedles* at the Frazee Theatre, the last theatre between Seventh and Eighth Avenues on the downtown side of Forty-second Street. It ran three months and I got notices I treasured. Mr. Tarkington, thank you.

Then came *Mrs. Partridge Presents*, starring famous Blanche Bates, and I made a smash hit. I left at the end of the season to try out Anita Loos's and her husband John Emerson's play *The Fall of Eve*. My name went up in lights at the Booth Theatre opposite Martin's Theatrical Boarding House where I'd boarded through lean days. Now I had a big part, four hundred dollars a week salary, clothes made by Madame Lanvin in Paris and a failure for all concerned except Madame.

A long wait, then Guthrie McClintic cast me in *Saturday's Children*. Success. Me and it. Fell in love with producer Jed Harris. He produced *Serena Blandish* with me as Serena.

Our son Jones Harris was born in Paris.

Back in New York I played in *Hotel Universe, The Violet, Three-Cornered Moon, They Shall Not Die, A Church Mouse, Here Today, The Wiser They Are, Ethan Frome, The Sleeping*

Clergyman, The Country Wife, A Doll's House, The Three Sisters, The Matchmaker.

In 1939 I did my first movie, *Abe Lincoln in Illinois,* followed by *Dr. Ehrlich's Magic Bullet, Two Faced Woman, Edge of Darkness, Action in the North Atlantic.*

In the first week of *The Three Sisters* in Washington, I married Garson Kanin, who was in a captain's uniform. He was working with the O.S.S.

In Washington I wrote *Over Twenty-One* and acted in it for two seasons, a success. I retired, then returned to write and act *The Leading Lady,* not a success. Someday I'll get it so it will go. *The Smile of the World,* it didn't go. *The Matchmaker* in London at the Theatre Royal, the Haymarket, in New York the Royale Theatre. Two weeks before it closed its transcontinental tour I got an offer to act Tante Alicia in *Gigi,* musical movie. I didn't have a number to sing and Gar said no good being in a musical movie without a number. London's brilliant star Isabel Jeans played it. She should have had a number. Maurice Chevalier had a number, Hermione Gingold had a number, but Tante Alicia just sat and described how to eat a partridge. One of *the* pieces of writing in the original *Gigi,* but in the musical it got lost between So and So and So's numbers.

Next, after a vacation abroad, I did *The Good Soup.* Evil befell Felicien Marceau's violent, remarkable play. It ran four years in Paris with Paris star Marie Bell, in New York it didn't, the blow dealt by George Marton now dead. Draw the veil.

In California Natalie Wood nodded her pretty head and I played her mother, the Dealer, in *Inside Daisy Clover,* won a Golden Globe Award, the prize given by foreign critics. Was nominated for an Oscar and didn't win. Nicer said by my beloved friend Mrs. William Goetz. At her California mansion a newspaperwoman interviewing her about her collection of Renoir, Picasso, Van Gogh, Cézanne, Degas, Manet saw a photo of me. "Wasn't she nominated for the Oscar?" asked news lady.

"Yes," replied friend.

"She didn't get it, did she?"

"She didn't *happen* to win."

Definition of a friend.

Acted in *Lord Love a Duck,* acted in *Rosemary's Baby.* Did *happen* to win.

Acted in *Whatever Happened to Aunt Alice?*

Somewhere in there, played in Brian Friel's play, *The Loves of Cass McGuire.*

Pity it didn't get right.

Acted in *Where's Poppa?*

Acted in *Harold and Maude.*

Acted in TV play *Isn't It Shocking* with Alan Alda.

Acted in *Kojak* directed by Telly Savalas, who was also acting his part.

Acted in *Rhoda,* directed by Robert Moore.

Acted in *Medical Story,* TV series. *The Great Houdini,* a TV movie, *Columbo* with Peter Falk, *Boardwalk,* a film, starring Lee Strasberg, Janet Leigh and me, acted in *Every Which Way But Loose,* starring Clint Eastwood. In TV series *Taxi.* In the movie *Scavenger Hunt,* and *My Bodyguard,* and on many shows with Johnny Carson, Mike Douglas, Merv Griffin, Phil Donahue, Dick Cavett, Tom Snyder, *Good Morning America,* with David Hartman, the *Today Show,* wrote *My Side,* attended a ball and banquet, a two day celebration of my eightieth birthday given by my native city. Mayor La Raia and I led the ball, me in my pink satin Givenchy I had bought to receive the Oscar. For the Mayor to lead me into the ballroom I asked for "Darktown Strutters' Ball," and did that orchestra ever play a jumping up and down rendition!

I have done an afternoon or evening with only myself on stage at Town Hall, New York, in colleges from New Jersey to California with stops in between. I speak for an hour and a half without notes, then take an hour of questions. It is exhausting. Too bad. I love it best of all or do I love talk shows better?

"I didn't know where to look," reprimanded Thornton Wilder when I said the play I loved to act most was *Here Today*. I loved it because it was no strain.

I wanted to be an actress in 1912, I want to be an actress today. That walk from the darkness backstage through the door or opening in the scenery where I make an entrance into the bright lights with that big dim mass out beyond, which bursts into applause, then the first terrifying sound that comes out of my throat, which they describe as a voice, but that first instant it is the siren of terror and intention and faith and hope and trust and vanity and security and insecurity and blood-curdling courage which is acting.

INDEX

Castle Cave (restaurant), 153
Castle Square Stock Company,
    36–37, 326
Cats, 124, 210
Cavett, Dick, 117, 372
Central Park, 40, 153
Chamberlain, George, 89
Chamfort, Sébastien, 40
Chapman, 223, 260
Charles of the Ritz, 132
Chasen's restaurant, 159
Château de la Garoupe, 317
Chateau de Ville, Randolph,
    Massachusetts, 232, 233
Chateau Elysee, 156, 157, 158,
    164, 167
Chatterton, Ruth, 361
Chesterton, G. K., 135
Chevalier, Maurice, 371
Chicago *Examiner,* 178
Child's, 153–54, 312
Church Mouse, A, 370
Cilento, Diane, 79–80
Clair, René, 31, 252
Claire, Ina, 129
Clarence, 58, 142, 369
Clarens, Miss Elise, 198–99,
    202–7
Clark, Dick, 117
Clark, John, 117
Clark, Kelly and Benjy, 117
Clark, Marguerite, 344
Clark, Nathan Gibson, 153,
    239
Cleveland Opera House, 370
Clifford, Mr., 248
Coates Opera House, 118
Cochato Club, Braintree,

Massachusetts, 240, 344,
    346
Coco, 294
Cody, Mr., 100–1
Cohan, George M., 243
Cohn, Harry, 225–26
Cohn, Mrs. Harry, 226
Collier, Constance, 129, 131,
    132, 134, 135, 136, 137
Collier, John, 132
Collinge, Patricia, 127
Collins, Harry, 354
Colonial Theatre (Boston),
    22–23, 132, 300
Columbia Pictures, 225
Columbo (TV show), 338,
    372
Comden, Betty, 353
Come What May, 246
Congressional Record, 336,
    337–42
Congressman Claude Pepper's
    Select Committee on
    Aging, 336–42
Connelly, Marc, 129, 148, 160,
    354
Cook, Madge Carr, 211
Cooke (Boston caterer), 201,
    202
Copland, Aaron, 132, 354
Copley Theatre (Boston), 241
Coquelin, 154
Corlew, Miss, 240, 364
Cornell, Katharine, 28, 120,
    128–37, 179, 192, 325
Cornhill (Boston), 271
Coronation, 85, 88, 89, 90
Cort, Bud, 276, 298

Roosevelt, Ted, 277–78
Rosalie, 361
Roscius, 79, 80
Rose, Billy, 135, 277, 362–63
Rose Descat, 239
Roseland, 23
Rosemary's Baby, 76, 266, 323,
    338, 341, 372
Ross, Harold, 148
Ross, Thomas W., 74, 363
Rosse, Michael, 257
Rousseau, Henri, 82
Rowland, Marila, 277
Royale Theatre, 371
Royal Family, 366
Royall, Virginia Portia, 274
Rubinstein, Artur, 21–22, 299
Rugged Path, The, 83
Rules, 106
Russell, Hal, 57
Russell, Rosalind, 323
Ruth Gordon Theatre, 17, 63
Ryan, Miss, 157, 159
Ryder, Mr., 141, 363
Ryerson, Dr., 94, 110

Sadler's Wells Ballet
    (London), 352
St. Gaudens, Homer, 154
St. Martin's Theatre
    (London), 161
St. Nicholas Magazine, 273
St. Patrick's Cathedral (New
    York), 153
Saks Fifth Avenue, 157–58,
    285, 351, 365
Sally, 361

Sanders, Colonel, 337, 338
Sardi, Vincent, 192–93
Sardi's, 191, 192–93, 261
    Belasco Room, 192
Sargent, John Singer, 257
Saturday's Children, 71–75,
    98, 295, 351, 370
Savalas, Telly, 372
Savoy, Bert, 114
Sayward, Everet, 315
Scars, 110–11
Scavenger Hunt, 372
Schiaparelli, 285, 286, 287
Scheftel, Stuart, 155, 173
Schlissel, Jack, 304
Schloss, Dr., 275
Schneider and Anderson, 316
School for Scandal, The, 129,
    357
'Sconset (Siasconset,
    Nantucket), 127
Scott, Margaretta, 352
Screen Actors Guild, 122
Selwyn, Archie, 205
Selwyn, Ruthie, 155–56, 173
Selznick, David, 130, 135, 137
Selznick, Irene, 252
Serena Blandish, 165, 352, 370
Seven Lively Arts, The, 135
Seventeen, 14, 94, 98, 175,
    241, 369, 370
Shakespeare, 111, 112, 114,
    137, 167
Shanghai Gesture, The, 133
Shapiro, Mel, 276
Sharpe, Henry, 101
Shaw, Bernard, 307, 325, 355,
    362